Palgrave Studies in Race, Ethnicity, Indigeneity and Criminal Justice

Series Editors
Chris Cunneen
University of Technology Sydney
Sydney, NSW, Australia

Katheryn Russell-Brown
University of Florida
Gainesville, FL, USA

Shaun L. Gabbidon
Penn State Harrisburg
Middletown, PA, USA

Steve Garner
School of Social Sciences
Birmingham City University
Birmingham, UK

This pioneering series brings much-needed attention to minority, excluded, and marginalised perspectives in criminology, centred on the topic of 'race' and the racialization of crime and criminal justice systems. It draws on a range of theoretical approaches including critical race theory, critical criminology, postcolonial theory, intersectional approaches and Indigenous theory. The series seeks to challenge and broaden the current discourse, debates and discussions within contemporary criminology as a whole, including drawing on the voices of Indigenous people and those from the Global South which are often silenced in favour of dominant white discourses in Criminology.

More information about this series at
http://www.palgrave.com/gp/series/15777

Lisa J. Long

Perpetual Suspects

A Critical Race Theory of Black and Mixed-Race Experiences of Policing

Lisa J. Long
Leeds Beckett University
Leeds, UK

Palgrave Studies in Race, Ethnicity, Indigeneity and Criminal Justice
ISBN 978-3-319-98239-7 ISBN 978-3-319-98240-3 (eBook)
https://doi.org/10.1007/978-3-319-98240-3

Library of Congress Control Number: 2018950560

Cover credit: jpa1999/Getty Images

This Palgrave Macmillan imprint is published by the registered company Springer Nature Switzerland AG
The registered company address is: Gewerbestrasse 11, 6330 Cham, Switzerland

Dedicated to
Janet Alder,
fearless in the face of multiple injustices, an inspiration
and to my small but perfect family,
Zachary Long, Jasmine Long and Rose-Lily Brown.

Preface

My journey to writing this book began in 2001 when, as an undergraduate Criminology student at University of Teesside, I attended the local Crown Court for an observation of court processes. By chance I selected the public gallery in the court which was hearing the prosecution evidence against five police officers, from Humberside Police, charged with the manslaughter of Christopher Alder. It was during this visit that I met Christopher's sister, Janet Alder. Janet approached me and asked me about my interest in the case. I did not have a particular interest at that point, I was merely observing proceedings and the different roles of court staff as required by my assignment. Also, from the proceedings, I was unable to establish the nature of the case before the court. Janet took the time to explain to me the circumstances surrounding Christopher's death in police custody (see, Chapter 3). I was shocked. Until that point I had never had a reason to doubt that the police would do everything in their power to protect citizens. Why would I? I am a White woman. The worst I had experienced was in my teenage years when a police officer confiscated my cigarettes outside of the school gates. I have never been pulled over by the police whilst driving, I have never been arrested, and on the occasions when I have had to call upon them for help, they have offered their services and treated me with care and respect.

At the end of the prosecution's case, the presiding Judge ruled that the five police officers had no case to answer. An inquest jury had previously found that Christopher had been unlawfully killed. Christopher's death had been captured on CCTV. I had fully expected the five police officers to be found guilty. My faith in the British justice system, shaped by my White privilege, had led me to this expectation. After the collapse of the trial I began to research deaths in police custody in more detail and found the disproportionate number of Black and ethnic minority deaths in custody of concern, particularly in relation to Black men. I went on to write my undergraduate dissertation, entitled *A Licence to Kill?*, on Black deaths in police custody and the lack of accountability in these cases. A career within the Criminal Justice System no longer seemed like a desirable option. Instead, I went in the direction of the third sector. I worked for a number of years in various roles in the advice and support sector with refugees and people seeking asylum. In my meetings with service users, in particular Black men, they told me stories about their encounters with the police—often hostile and occasionally cruel. One example of this hostility was brought to my attention by a Black African man who was physically attacked whilst watching a football match in a pub. When the police arrived at the scene, rather than offering him support, they told him that he should not have been wearing an England football shirt. Anecdotal evidence like this kept the issue of police racism on my radar. I later worked for a non-departmental government body with responsibility for police training and development, in an equality and diversity role. I naively hoped that I could change something from the inside. I was sorely disappointed at the tokenistic nature of the post and the efforts to eliminate racism from the police service, mostly through ensuring that documentation complied with legislation. My stay was short lived.

The response to the police shooting of Mark Duggan in 2011, and the political and media response to the riots that followed, piqued my interest in understanding how Black communities experience policing after the *Stephen Lawrence Inquiry Report* and whether anything had changed for them. I developed a proposal for a Ph.D. project looking at Black and Black mixed-race people's experiences of policing. I completed my doctoral thesis in 2016—the thesis forms the basis of this book.

Most importantly, I hope that some of the research participants will have the opportunity to read this book and that they feel it does justice to their experiences—both individually and the experiences of Black communities.

I also hope that students across a range of disciplines will find the book helpful in their studies and that they will pause to reflect on the operation of race within institutions. I also hope that it will inform their professional reflexivity as they move into their chosen career.

Finally, I hope serving police officers will read this book and that it will encourage them to engage in an honest, reflexive appraisal of their own practice and the operational practices in their locality.

Leeds, UK

Lisa J. Long

Acknowledgements

I owe a huge debt of gratitude to my research participants. It was an honour and a privilege that they agreed to share their stories with me and I hope I have done them justice here.

I acknowledge with thanks the University of Leeds for the Teaching and Research Scholarship which enabled me to complete this project. Also, I would like to thank Dr. Paul Bagguley and Dr. Yasmin Hussain for their supervision and feedback on the Ph.D. research.

I am hugely grateful for the support of colleagues and friends. Special thanks to Lynley Aldridge, Linzi Ladlow, Remi Joseph-Salisbury, Claudia Paraschivescu and my son Zachary Long for their honest and constructive feedback on my draft chapters.

Contents

Part I

Contextualising the Race-Crime Nexus

1
Introduction

Stop and search has long been a source of contention for Black communities in the UK. Disproportionality in stop and search is eight times higher for those who are Black and more than two times higher for those who are 'mixed' (this includes ethnicities other than Black-mixed-race) (Home Office 2017). Ethnic profiling is a common police practice in several countries within the EU; Ethnicity, religion, race, or national origin are the criteria for police decision making around identity checks and stop and search (Open Society Justice Initiative 2009). Similar patterns are evident in the US where stop and search, or 'stop and frisk' has become a key part of Zero Tolerance Policing (see Fagan and Davies 2000; Camp and Heatherton 2016), and car stops are disproportionately experienced by Black drivers, for the offence of 'driving while Black' (Lundman and Kaufman 2003). This draws ethnic minority populations, in particular Black people, into the criminal justice system in disproportionate numbers. Kelley, argues that broken windows policing and its zero tolerance for minor infringements, such as walking in the middle of the street, serves to punish black communities, transforming them 'from citizens to thugs' (Kelley 2016). This is acutely evident in

L. J. Long, *Perpetual Suspects*, Palgrave Studies in Race, Ethnicity, Indigeneity and Criminal Justice, https://doi.org/10.1007/978-3-319-98240-3_1

mass incarceration in the US context. African Americans are more than five times more likely to be incarcerated than their White peers (Nellis 2016). Comparably, there is increasing disproportionality in the UK prison population; 13.1% of UK prison population is Black compared with 2.7% of the general population. This is particularly pronounced in the UK's youth justice estate, where 41% of young people (under 18 years of age) in custody are from an ethnic minority background (Lammy 2017).

The disproportionate use of force by police officers when dealing with Black 'suspects' and deaths in custody (or otherwise at the hands of the police) are a significant concern for Black communities, impacting upon trust and confidence in the police (see Chapters 3 and 4). Black people are more likely to be subject to police use of force during detention and custody (Dearden 2017; Gayle 2015) and are more likely to die in restraint related circumstances (Angiolini 2017). The Institute of Race Relations (2015) shows that between 1991 and 2014 there were 509 'BME' deaths in custody, 348 in prison 137 in police custody and 24 in immigration detention (p. 4). In the US context, in 2017 alone, 1129 people died at the hands of the police, 27% were black (two times their representation in the general population and of the 1129 who were not armed when they were killed, 37% were Black. Only 12 police officers were charged with an offence following these deaths (Harriot 2018). Whilst police powers for the use of force and the routine nature of arming police officers varies between national jurisdictions, the UK and the US have in common that Black people are disproportionately represented amongst those who die at the hands of the police. Further, neither individual police officers, or the police as an institution, are held accountable for their use of lethal force.

In Australia, a similar picture emerges in the context of the police treatment of ethnic minorities, in particular the indigenous Aboriginal population. The aboriginal population are over-represented at all stages of the Australian criminal justice system and are incarcerated at 12 times the rate of the non-Aboriginal Australian population, despite making up less than 3% of the Australian population (Australian Institute of Criminology 2015). Further, there are ongoing concerns pertaining to Aboriginal deaths in police custody, similar to those of Black communities in the US and the UK and across Europe. The history of settler colonisation and the Australian police services role in the enforcement of legislation permitting the dispossession of land, and suppressing Aboriginal resistance to European settlement, paves the way for their ongoing marginalisation (Bowling et al. 2004). The impact of colonial histories upon Aboriginal communities was acknowledged by the *Royal Commission in to Aboriginal Deaths in Custody*, the Commission concluded that, in the 99 cases examined, Aboriginal ethnicity played an instrumental part in the victim's death (Johnston 1991). Recommendation 60, that the police work towards eliminating racist and degrading treatment of Aboriginal communities, led to a programme of reform, however its effectiveness at eliminating racist treatment of Aboriginal populations has been limited. Aboriginal populations still face economic and social marginalisation, high rates of victimisation and have a disproportionate presence in the Australian criminal justice system (Cunneen and Tauri 2016).

Similarly to the Australian context, widescale reform to policing in the UK, in the wake of the publication of the *Stephen Lawrence Inquiry Report* (Macpherson 1999), has not been successful in eliminating racism from the police (see Rollock 2009). This is borne out in the disproportionate representation of Black and Black mixed-race people in all areas of policing, as discussed above. This book will address the question, how do Black and Black mixed-race people experience policing contemporarily? A Critical Race Theory (CRT) framework informs the lens through which the enduring presence of racism within policing is analysed. As argued by Mills (1997: 1) 'White supremacy is the unnamed political system that has made the modern world what it is today'. Within this system of racial categorisation, premised on 'White supremacy', Blackness is a marker for a particular form of Otherness that symbolises threat. This book will consider how, through processes of racialisation, race has become meaningful (Garner 2010) in the context of crime. This has particular significance for the contact between Black communities and the police who are tasked with monitoring and controlling the Black other. From the perspective of racialised subjects of policing, the book develops a counter story to dominant racialised narratives. It chooses to draw upon the specificities of being racialised as Black, as opposed to the broader experiences of ethnic minority communities which are oftentimes homogenised in relation to issues of race and policing. Whilst the data is UK specific, the findings have some relevance in the international contexts discussed above because of the legacy of their imperial histories, and the endurance of 'White supremacy' as a system of global ordering.

This chapter will go on to discuss the CRT framework and method, and its utility in criminological research. It will then outline the chapters to follow.

The Research

Critical Race Theory as Framework

Developed in North America through the work of black scholars—notably Derrick Bell (1991, 1992), Marie Matsuda (1987, 1989), Kimberle Crenshaw (1989, 1995), and Richard Delgado (1994, 1996)—the origins of CRT can be found in Critical Legal Studies. Its core principles were developed through challenges to the US legal system and in particular racial inequalities in jurisprudence. The foundational standpoint of CRT is one of 'racial realism' (Bell 1991). This proposes that racism is an 'endemic' and 'deeply ingrained' (Tate 1997) system of inequality which directly shapes systems of power. Whilst essentialist notions of race, premised on biological categorisation, are broadly discredited in scholarly works (Warmington 2009: 282), the salience of race as a key organising principle within society is the fundamental starting point for Critical Race scholars (Omi and Winant 1993: 5). Within this system of racially predicated social organisation, Whiteness is the norm (Dyer 1997: 10) and the non-White is othered for the purpose of maintaining 'White privilege' (Mills 1997). Therefore, as Fanon (1986) argues, 'not only must the Black man be Black, he must be Black in relation to the White man' (p. 110). By extension, the Black body must also be Black in relation to the White institution for the maintenance of White power. This is a useful approach to understanding the operation of race within the police/citizen encounter and criminal justice processes more broadly.

Criminology has hitherto understood the relationship between police and black communities in dichotomous terms—either as a problem of race or as a problem of class. It is dominated by attempts to explain the over-representation of ethnic minority groups in the Criminal Justice System through an assumption that some groups have a greater propensity for criminality than others—Black people in particular are constructed as being predisposed to criminality (see Chapter 2). Phillips and Bowling's (2003) case for developing 'minority perspectives' in criminology has largely been ignored within the discipline. Further, explanatory frameworks within the discipline take a 'colour-blind 'approach' (Webster 2012: 106), disregarding the structural oppressions which create the conditions for crime, victimisation and disparities in criminal justice responses to racialised groups. These explanations, predominantly written by White men, for White men, emanate from a position of 'White ignorance' (Mills 2007). A CRT approach recognises the ways in which this 'White epistemology of ignorance' (Scheurich and Young 1997; Sullivan and Tuana 2007) operates in the production of scholarly knowledge, to reproduce racist assumptions. CRT research opens up the possibility for ontological resistance to the racialised narrative which attributes particular ways of being to Black bodies through its key tenets.

The CRT framework is broadly premised on five tenets. Firstly, a CRT approach foregrounds race and racism. Secondly, it challenges the dominant narratives which explain the experiences of racialised people through the development of counter-stories/narratives. Third, experiential knowledge is central to developing the counter-story/narrative. Fourth, it engages with multiple disciplines and finally it has a commitment to achieving social justice (see Hylton 2008; Delgado and Stefancic 2001; Solorzano and Yosso 2002). As Ladson-Billings (2000) argues, '*racialised discourses and ethnic epistemologies or the liminal perspective may be deployed [in CRT research] … to reveal the ways that dominant perspectives distort the realities of the other in an effort to maintain power relations…*' (p. 263). The research discussed throughout this book adopts the CRT approach and in doing so privileges the voices of the racialised other; the emerging counter story challenges the dominant, colour-blind explanations for Black and Black mixed-race people's over-policing and under-protection.

Critical Race-Grounded Theory Method

The approach taken utilised CRT as a framework and blended it with a Grounded Theory method. The utility of adopting a Critical Race-Grounded Method in research which seeks to challenge racism within the police institution is evident in the work of Malagon et al. (2009: 264). They argue that a Critical Race-Grounded Theory method facilitates research which builds upon the experiential knowledge of Black communities, to reveal the ways in which race intersects with other oppressions to shape their lived realities Interviewing is one tool that can be employed to create a different narrative about Black people, drawing from their knowledge, which can be used to challenge racist practices (Parker and Lynn 2002: 11). Semi-structured interviews were used in this research because they allow for the exploration of the key research questions with some flexibility and permit the researcher to be responsive to unplanned or unscheduled topics. This approach gives the participant the freedom to share their own stories, whilst allowing the researcher to keep the interview focused on the specific topic. The semi structured interview method proved effective for accessing participant's experiences and perspectives. As argued by Matsuda (1997), 'storytelling creates a tension between a tale of oppression and a tale of innocence leading to only two possible conclusions: someone is lying, or someone is deeply deluded' (p. 51). The counter story that emerged from their experiences, presented throughout this book, challenges the dominant, 'deluded' narrative of denial and reveals the entrenchment of racism within contemporary policing practices.

Twenty participants took part in the research interviews. The sample was purposive, participants were selected on the basis that they self-identified as either Black or Black and White mixed-race, were aged sixteen or above and had experience of police contact. Participants' reflected a diverse range of age, class and national identities. They were as follows[1];

[1]Pseudonyms are used to protect participant's identity.

Eric, 32, Black, African male
Phillip, 45, Black, African male
Alice, 38, mixed-race, British born, female
Robert, 27, mixed-race, British-born, male
Janice, 37, Black, British-born, female
Kenneth, 38, Black, African, male
Levi, 50, Black, British-born, male
Marcus, 44, Black, British-born, male
Charles, 40, Black, African, male
Shawn, 39, Black, British-born, male
Samuel, 45, Black, African, male
Jean, 40, Black, African, male
Thomas, 55, Black, British-born, male
Andrew, 41, mixed-race, British-born, male
Bianca, 25, mixed-race, British-born, female
Lee, 23, mixed-race, British-born, male
Carol, 49, Black, British-born, female
Earl, 54, Black, British-born, male
Derek, 46, Black, British-born, male
Cynthia, 42, Black, British-born, female.

Participants' were not asked to state their class background; however, where this is relevant to the discussion, the term 'professional' is used throughout the book to analyse the intersection of race with professional status, or respectability, in encounters with the police. The type of police contact was not specified in the call for participants', this was important as the researcher was interested in a wider understanding of police relations with citizens and communities rather than a focus on one particular form of police contact such as stop and search or arrest. This approach resulted in a breadth of participant experiences in a range of contexts, the three most significant contexts for police contact were as victim of crime, police-initiated contact and contact with the police as a volunteer or paid professional.

Drawing on the Critical Race-Grounded Theory framework, the research adopted a theoretical sampling strategy. This is the described by Glaser and Strauss (1967: 45) as a process whereby the researcher simultaneously identifies codes and analyses the data and, on this basis, decides what data to collect next. The data collection is complete when it is 'saturated'-there are no new codes emerging from the interviews. Further, purposive sampling can be assumed to garner a sample with some commonalities, in this case where a degree of homogeneity is assumed the data would be expected to reach saturation more quickly (Guest et al. 2006: 76). There was some homogeneity in the sample for this research to the extent that participants were recruited on the basis that they identified as Black or Black mixed-'race' and had some experience of contact with the police. Similarly, to the findings in Guest et al. (2006), there were no significant new codes emerging from the data after analysis of around thirteen interviews. At this point the data was sufficiently saturated to allow for the development of some theoretical claims which are explored throughout this book.

Overcoming Limitations

Research premised on a CRT approach is focused on the story and the counter story, rather than on the generalisability of findings. However, the absence of the perspectives of Black and Black mixed-race youth is acknowledged as a limitation in this research insofar as it is young people who most commonly come into contact with the police. The planning for the research included a proposal to interview at least thirty participants. In order to address the research questions, particularly those pertaining to the intersectionality of race with class and gender in police encounters, a purposive sample was proposed. This would include ten women, ten people who self-identified as Black and White mixed race and five people in the sample who could, on objective indicators, be described as middle class. The recruitment of younger participants proved difficult and the majority of participants interviewed were drawn from those people who were contacted as potential gatekeepers, or through established professional 'BME' staff groups within local authorities and third sector organisations. This resulted in a smaller sample than planned; twenty participants were interviewed in total.

The participants were predominantly over the age of 25 and many have professional jobs. This demographic is not typically associated with police contact. This incidentally proved to be useful in establishing a historical understanding of the ways in which the experiences of policing have or have not changed over time. Comparison between the experiences of younger participants and those of older participants revealed the extent to which the experience of policing remains unchanged, despite police reforms. Further, they revealed that older participants continue to experience over-policing, although frequency declines with increasing age. Additionally, access to Black professionals facilitated an understanding of how race operates at its intersection with class and professional status (see Chapter 7). It is likely that successful recruitment of a younger sample would have simply reproduced the findings of existing (albeit scant) research on the experiences of Black young people (for example, Sharp and Atherton 2007).

Researcher Positionality

There are some challenges inherent in the White researcher drawing on a CRT framework whilst possessing 'White privilege' (Mills 1997). However, as recognised by Matsuda, it is neither possible nor practical to develop a 'random ability to see all points of view'. Instead, she advocates choosing to 'see the world from the standpoint of the oppressed' (Matsuda 1989: 9). Working from a CRT framework, which prioritises racialised voices, aided the researcher in developing this standpoint of 'multiple consciousness'. Seeing the world through the experience of those who had experienced racialised policing, which the researcher had not, allowed for the emergence of a counter story which challenges the dominant White narrative, rather than reproducing racism through scholarly work which is premised on a White 'epistemology of ignorance' (Mills 2007). However, it is possible that perceived racial difference affected the stories that the Black and Black mixed-race participants in this research were prepared to disclose to a White researcher (Edwards 1990; Aitken and Burman 1999). Further, in the context of police research, the interviewer could be assumed to be working for or with the police. Edwards (1990), observed that, as a White researcher interviewing Black women, rapport was easier to establish once the researcher acknowledged the difference in structural position within the interviewer/participant relationship (Edwards 1990: 486). Recognising the multiple identities that all participants in a research relationship occupy, including race, but also recognising gender, class and the professional relationship, are beneficial to the research relationship (see Aitken and Burman 1999; Gunaratnam 2003).

Rather than attempting to subvert the risks that come with researching across race difference with methodological strategies such as interviewer matching, Gunaratnam (2003) advocates 'actively searching out and valuing the complexity and richness that comes with the mess' (p. 104). Building trust and rapport between the researcher and participant was essential to the success of the project, but also to avoid harm to the participants. The researcher sought to build trust through working in a self-revelatory mode (Ladson-Billings 2000; Hunter 2005), which required the researcher to reveal their own background and interest in the area of research. However, an acknowledged limitation of the research is how this may have shaped the participants willingness to talk about some of their experiences or the ways in which they talked about them. For example, the disclosure that the researcher had been drawn to the research from an activist stance, in regards to deaths in police custody, had the potential to lead participants to the assumption that the researcher took a negative standpoint towards the police. Working in a self-revelatory mode necessarily opens up the research relationship to researcher bias. In the interests of balance, participants who recalled wholly negative experiences were asked if they had any experiences that were different or had left them with a positive impression of the police. This approach allowed participants the opportunity to discuss both positive and negative experiences of policing.

Black and Black Mixed-Race

The term Black is used in this research to refer to the experiences of people of African descent. Further, this is the term that participants used to describe their own identity. This term also signifies the ascribed identification based on skin colour which makes race meaningful in the context of the police encounter.

The term Black mixed-race is used to refer to participants of mixed parentage where one parent was of African descent and where participants had used this term to describe their own identity. Whilst there is a burgeoning literature surrounding identity formation of mixed-race Britons (Song and Aspinall 2012; Aspinall and Song 2013; Joseph-Salisbury 2018), there is very little research which seeks to understand their experiences of discrimination within the criminal justice context. Some scholars have suggested that mixed-race people encounter less discrimination because they appear phenotypically closer to Whiteness. Bonilla-Silva argues, that in the US context a tri-racial system is emerging, through which 'multiracials' will become honorary Whites (Bonilla-Silva 2004: 933–394). Similarly, Yancy (2006) predicts that non-Blacks will align with the dominant groups, leaving Black people to stand alone in the fight for racial equality. In the UK context, Aspinall and Song (2013), did not find that there was anything 'inherently distinctive' about the racism suffered by their mixed-race participants'. The racism they encountered from White people was not because they were mixed-race but because they were non-White. On this basis they conclude that for those Whites engaged in racist behaviour, they may not be aware of the person's mixed-race identity and even if they were it would not be of consequence (ibid.: 124). As Tate (2015) argues, 'The one drop rule … emerging from enslavement which insists that African descent makes one Black in perpetuity irrespective of mixing, stops this possibility of extension ['towards Whiteness']' (p. 15). Whilst the language of the 'one drop rule' may have more salience in the US context, UK research finds that Black and White mixed-race participants" can object to being mono-racially identified as Black when they feel unable to identify as White (Aspinall and Song 2013). This was also present in the accounts of participants' in this research. There was an assumption that in the context of police contact Black mixed-race people would be identified as Black and this is borne out in their experiences (see Long and Joseph-Salisbury 2018). As Alice, a Black mixed-race woman said;

> I think that's why I identify myself as Black because my dad…always said to me it doesn't matter that your mums White and your dads Black and you yourself your half and half. People always see you as Black and he was right. I've never been called you half caste this or you White this. It's always been you Black this or you Black that. That's why I identify myself as Black because that is how I'm seen and treated.

Further, when a police officer is unable to establish the individual's self-reported ethnicity they rely upon the 6 + 1 IC classification. The options for recording ethnicity using this system are limited to 'monoracial' categories such as Black. This book does not differentiate between the experiences of Black and Black mixed-race people as the research finds that they are policed as a black monolithic.[2]

Structure of the Book

The following chapter will discuss the processes of racialisation and criminalisation that have produced Black people as the perpetual suspect in the UK context.

Chapter 3 will situate over policing, through the examples of stop and search and police use of force, within the context of the colonial dimension of the emergence of the police. It will consider explanations for the problem of police racism rooted in an occupation police culture and address the failure of the diversity agenda to tackle police racism.

---

[2]As Black mixed-race people are racialised as Black in the specific encounter of police contact, and their experiences of policing are the same (see Long and Joseph-Salisbury 2018), in some places throughout the book where it makes grammatical sense to do so, or for ease of reading, Black is used instead of the full-term Black and Black mixed-race. Unless stated otherwise, Black refers to Black and Black mixed-race people throughout.

In the second part of the book (Chapters 4–7) the experiences of interview participants' will be utilised to develop a counter story to dominant narratives of race, racism and policing. Chapter 4 will focus on how Black and Black mixed-race people experience police-initiated contact. It will consider the impact that this has on their relations with police as individuals and communities. It concludes that Black and Black mixed-race people are the perpetual suspect. Chapter 5 goes on to consider how this suspect position shapes their experiences as victims of crime. It will show that the processes of institutional racialisation in the operation of police decision making and the legitimisation of White fear construct Black victims of crime as the (Un)Victim.

Chapters 6 and 7 adopt an intersectional analysis to consider the relationship between race and other oppressions in police-community encounters. Chapter 6 offers an intersectional analysis of race and gender which addresses Black and Black mixed-race women's experiences of policing. These experiences are compared with male participant's accounts to offer some insight into the operation of subordinate Black masculinities and femininities in police-community contact. Chapter 7 considers the intersection of race with class and citizenship, through the experiences of Black professionals and recent migrants. It highlights the centrality of race in understanding the nature of police encounters and argues against wholly class-based explanations for the over-policing of Black communities.

In the concluding section, Chapter 8 makes the case for a CRT of policing. Drawing on the counter-story which emerges within Chapters 4–7, it argues that a CRT approach to research can interrupt the permanence of racism within the institutions through making it visible. Finally, in the spirit of counter storytelling, it offers some suggestions for improving Black and Black mixed-race peoples encounters with the police based on participants voices. It draws the book to a close with consideration to the possibilities for CRT research to advance criminological understanding.

References

Aitken, G., & Burman, E. (1999). Keeping and Crossing Professional and Racialized Boundaries. *Psychology of Women Quarterly, 23,* 277–297.

Angiolini, E. (2017). *Report of the Independent Review of Deaths and Serious Incidents in Police Custody*. London: Home Office. www.gov.uk/government/publications/deaths-and-serious-incidents-in-police-custody. Accessed 20 January 2018.

Aspinall, P., & Song, M. (2013). *Mixed-Race Identities*. Basingstoke: Palgrave Macmillan.

Australian Institute of Criminology. (2015). *Indigenous Justice in Focus*. http://www.aic.gov.au/crime_types/in_focus/indigenousjustice.html.

Bell, D. (1991). Racial Realism. *Connecticut Law Review, 24,* 363–379.

Bell, D. A. (1992). *Faces at the Bottom of the Well: The Permanence of Racism*. New York: Basic Books.

Bonilla-Silva, E. (2004). From Bi-Racial to Tri-Racial: Towards a New System of Racial Stratification in the USA. *Ethnic and Racial Studies, 27,* 931–950.

Bowling, B., Phillips, C., Campbell, A., & Docking, M. (2004). Policing and Human Rights: Eliminating Discrimination, Xenophobia, Intolerance and the Abuse of Power from Police Work. In Y. Bangura & R. Stavenhagen (Eds.), *Racism and Public Policy.* Durban: United Nations Research Institute for Social Development.

Camp, J. T., & Heatherton, C. (2016). *Policing the Planet: Why the Policing Crisis Led to Black Lives Matter*. New York: Verso.

Crenshaw, K. (1989). Demarginalizing the Intersection of Race and Sex: A Black Feminist Critique of Antidiscrimination Doctrine, Feminist Theory and Antiracist Politics. *University of Chicago Legal Forum,* Issue 1989: 139–167.

Crenshaw, K. (1995). *Critical Race Theory: The Key Writings That Formed the Movement*. New York: The New Press.

Cunneen, C., & Tauri, J. (2016). *Indigenous Criminology*. Bristol: Policy Press.

Dearden, L. (2017, August 1). Metropolitan Police Use Force Disproportionately Against Black People in London, New Statistics Reveal. *The Independent*.

Delgado, R. (1994). Rodrigo's Eighth Chronicle: Black Crime, White Fears—On the Social Construction of Threat. *Virginia Law Review, 80*, 503–548.

Delgado, R. (1996). *The Coming Race War: And Other Apocalyptic Tales of America After Affirmative Action and Welfare*. New York: New York University Press.

Delgado, R., & Stefancic, J. (2001). *Critical Race Theory: An Introduction*. New York: New York University Press.

Dyer, R. (1997). *White: Essays on Race and Culture*. London: Routledge.

Edwards, R. (1990). Connecting Method and Epistemology: A White Women Interviewing Black Women. *Women's Studies International Forum, 13*, 477–490.

Fagan, J., & Davies, G. (2000). Street Stops and Broken Windows: Race, and Disorder in New York City. *Fordham Urban Law Journal, 28*(2), 457–504.

Fanon, F. (1986). *Black Skin, White Masks*. London: Pluto Press.

Garner, S. (2010). *Racisms an Introduction*. London: Sage.

Gayle, D. (2015). Black People 'Three Times More Likely' to Be Tasered. *Guardian*. www.theguardian.com/uk-news/2015/oct/13/black-people-three-times-more-likely-to-have-taser-used-against-them. Accessed 13 October 2017.

Glaser, B. G., & Strauss, A. L. (1967). *The Discovery of Grounded Theory: Strategies for Qualitative Research*. Chicago: Aldine Publishing Company.

Guest, G., Bunce, A., & Johnson, L. (2006). How Many Interviews Are Enough? An Experiment with Data Saturation and Variability. *Field Methods, 18*, 59–82.

Gunaratnam, Y. (2003). *Researching 'Race' and Ethnicity: Methods, Knowledge and Power*. London: Sage.

Harriot, M. (2018, February 1). Heres How Many People Police Killed in 2017. *The Root*. https://www.theroot.com/heres-how-many-people-police-killed-in-2017-1821706614. Accessed 13 April 2018.

Home Office. (2017). *Police Powers and Procedures England and Wales Year Ending 31 March 2017*. London: Home Office. https://www.gov.uk/government/statistics/police-powers-and-procedures-england-and-wales-year-ending-31-march-2017.

Hunter, S. (2005). Negotiating Professional and Social Voices. *Journal of Social Work Practice, 19*, 149–162.

Hylton, K. (2008). *Race and Sport: Critical Race Theory*. London: Routledge.

Johnston, E. (1991). Royal Commission into Aboriginal Deaths in Custody. *National Report* (5 Vols.). Canberra: AGPS.

Joseph-Salisbury, R. (2018). *Black Mixed-Race Men: Transatlanticity, Hybridity and 'Post-racial' Resilience*. Bingley: Emerald.

Kelley, R. D. G. (2016). Thug Nation: On State Violence and Disposability. In J. T. Camp & C. Heatherton (Eds.), *Policing the Planet: Why the Policing Crisis Led to Black Lives Matter*. New York: Verso.

Ladson-Billings, G. (2000). Racialised Discourses and Ethnic Epistemologies. In N. Denzin & Y. S. Lincoln (Eds.), *Handbook of Qualitative Research* (2nd ed.). London: Sage.

Lammy, D. (2017). *The Lammy Review: An Independent Review into the Treatment of, and Outcomes for Black, Asian and Minority Ethnic Individuals in the Criminal Justice System.* https://assets.publishing.service.gov.uk/government/uploads/system/uploads/attachment_data/file/643001/lammy-review-final-report.pdf. Accessed 3 January 2017.

Long, L., & Joseph-Salisbury, R. (2018). Black Mixed-Race Men's Perceptions and Experiences of the Police. *Ethnic and Racial Studies,* https://doi.org/10.1080/01419870.2017.1417618.

Lundman, R. J., & Kaufman, R. L. (2003). Driving While Black: Effects of Race, Ethnicity, and Gender on Citizen Self-Reports of Traffic Stops and Police Actions. *Criminology, 41,* 195.

MacPherson, W. (1999). *The Stephen Lawrence Inquiry: Report of an Inquiry.* London: The Stationary Office. http://webarchive.nationalarchives.gov.uk/20130814142233/, http://www.archive.official-documents.co.uk/document/cm42/4262/4262.htm. Accessed 4 January 2017.

Malagon, M. C., Huber, L. P., & Velez, V. N. (2009). Our Experiences, Our Methods: Using Grounded Theory to Inform a Critical Race Theory Methodology. *Seattle Journal for Social Justice, 8,* 253.

Matsuda, M. J. (1987). Looking to the Bottom: Critical Legal Studies and Reparations. *Harvard Critical Law Review, 22,* 323–400.

Matsuda, M. J. (1989). When the First Quail Calls: Multiple Consciousness as Jurisprudential Method. *Women's Rights Law Reporter, 11,* 7–10.

Matsuda, M. J. (1997). *Where Is Your Body? And Other Essays on Race, Gender and the Law.* Boston: Beacon Press.

Mills, C. W. (1997). *The Racial Contract.* New York: Cornell University Press.

Mills, C. W. (2007). White Ignorance. In S. Sullivan & N. Tuana (Eds.), *Race and Epistemologies of Ignorance.* New York: University of New York Press.

Nellis, A. (2016). *The Colour of Justice: Racial and Ethnic Disparity in State Prisons Washington: Sentencing Project.* www.sentencingproject.org/publications/color-of-justice-racial-and-ethnic-disparity-in-state-prisons/.

Omi, M., & Winant, H. (1993). On the Theoretical Status of the Concept of Race. In C. McCarthy & W. Crichlow (Eds.), *Race, Identity and Representation in Education.* New York: Routledge.

Open Society Justice Initiative. (2009). *Ethnic Profiling in the European Union: Pervasive, Ineffective and Discriminatory.* New York: Open Society Institute.

Parker, L., & Lynn, M. (2002). What's Race Got to Do With It? Critical Race Theory's Conflicts with and Connections to Qualitative Research Methodology and Epistemology. *Qualitative Inquiry, 8*, 7–22.

Phillips, C., & Bowling, B. (2003). Racism, Ethnicity and Criminology: Developing Minority Perspectives. *British Journal of Criminology, 43*, 269–290.

Rollock, N. (2009). *The Stephen Lawrence Inquiry 10 Years On: An Analysis of the Literature*. London: Runnymede Trust.

Scheirich, J. J., & Young, M. D. (1997). Coloring Epistemologies: Are Our Research Epistemologies Racially Biased? *Educational Researcher, 26*, 4–16.

Sharp, D., & Atherton, S. (2007). To Serve and Protect? The Experiences of Policing in the Community of Young People from Black and Other Ethnic Minority Groups. *British Journal of Criminology, 47*, 746–763.

Solorzano, D. G., & Yosso, T. J. (2002). Critical Race Methodology: Counter-Storytelling as an Analytical Framework for Education Research. *Qualitative Inquiry, 8*, 23–44.

Song, M., & Aspinall, P. (2012). Is Racial Mismatch a Problem for Young 'Mixed-Race 'People in Britain? The Findings of Qualitative Research. *Ethnicities, 12*, 730–753.

Sullivan, S., & Tuana, N. (2007). *Race and Epistemologies of Ignorance*. Albany: State University of New York Press.

Tate, S. (2015). *Black Women's Bodies and the Nation: Race, Gender and Culture*. Basingstoke: Palgrave Macmillan.

Tate, W. I. V. (1997). Critical Race Theory and Education: History, Theory, and Implications. *Review of Research in Education, 22*, 195–247.

Warmington, P. (2009). Taking Race Out of Scare Quotes: Race-Conscious Social Analysis in an Ostensibly Post-racial World. *Race Ethnicity and Education, 12*, 281–296.

Webster, C. (2012). The Discourse on 'Race' in Criminological Theory. In S. Hall & S. Winlow (Eds.), *New Directions in Criminological Theory*. London: Routledge.

Yancy, G. (2006). Racial Justice in a Black/Nonblack Society. In D. Brunsma (Ed.), *Mixed Messages: Multiracial Identities in the "Color-Blind" Era*. Colorado: Lynne Reinner Publishers.

2

Racialisation and Criminalisation of 'Blackness'

This chapter reflects upon the construction of Black criminality in Britain. It traces the emergence of the race-crime nexus. In particular, it examines the processes of racialisation and criminalisation in the post-war period. It considers post-war migration and troubles the notion that the problematisation of Black presence in Britain is limited to the post-war, post-Windrush era. Situating belonging in the context of nation, it argues that Britishness is constructed as 'White'-it shows how the racialised Black Other was situated outside of narratives of Britishness through their construction as criminal. Drawing on Hall et al. (1978) this chapter argues that we are still 'policing the crisis'. Black men in particular continue to be cast as the folk devil in multiple fears around crime and criminality. With consideration to policing the 'war on drugs' and the police response to the problem of 'gang' crime, the chapter discusses the ways in which racialised meanings are attributed to particular crime types. This analysis reveals that the persistence of stereotypes of criminality continue to inform police responses to Black and Black mixed-race men. This is reflected in their experiences with the police, as

---

See Fanon (1986) for discussion on the Fact of Blackness.

L. J. Long, *Perpetual Suspects*, Palgrave Studies in Race, Ethnicity, Indigeneity and Criminal Justice, https://doi.org/10.1007/978-3-319-98240-3_2

shown in the limited available research which is discussed in the latter part of the chapter. The chapter concludes that processes of racialisation, which criminalise Blackness, are significant in understanding how Black people experience policing in the contemporary context.

Racialisation: Constructing the 'Colour Problem'

To facilitate an understanding of the race-crime nexus it is necessary to understand the construction of Black people as the cause of the 'colour problem' in the British domestic context. The arrival of the Empire Windrush at Tilbury Docks in 1948 carrying 493 passengers from the Caribbean islands (Phillips and Phillips 1998), two thirds of whom had served in Britain during World War Two (Ward 2004: 124), is viewed as a watershed in British migration history. The 1948 Nationality Act conferred British Citizenship upon Citizens of the British Commonwealth; this granted commonwealth citizens the right of entry and abode in the United Kingdom. This legislation facilitated the movement of a migrant workforce to support in the post-war rebuilding of Britain. Further, it supported the political aim of maintaining a united British Commonwealth throughout the process of de-colonisation (Law et al. 2008: 3). However, scholars have argued for a break in the narrative which positions Black Britain as a post-war phenomenon, with the Empire Windrush as the focus for the White gaze, and as the signifier for the beginning of the 'colour problem' (Perry 2015; Hesse 2000). According to Perry (2015), these narratives present a 'deficient and myopic accounting of the historical genealogy context and implications of post-war Caribbean migration' (p. 14). Consideration to the longer historical trajectory of Black presence in Britain reveals that both settled Black presence, and the notion of a 'race relations' problem attributed to that presence, is observable long before the arrival of the Empire Windrush in 1948. Liverpool is thought to have the longest traceable history of Black settlement which can be traced for ten generations (Bourne 2014: 147). Many ex-servicemen who had served Britain in World War One settled in England, particularly in the port towns. Following the First World War, Cardiff's Black community increased from 700 in 1914 to 3000 by 1919 (ibid.: 139). Whilst thousands of Black servicemen fought and lost their lives in World War One, this history is not broadly acknowledged; Bourne, addresses this in Black Poppies (Bourne 2014). It is the decision of these servicemen to make England their home, particularly seamen, following the war, which explains this increase in the Black population in the port towns and cities of England.

These Black communities, in the ports of Liverpool and Cardiff, came under sustained attack in 1919 following the return of demobilised White soldiers, who were opposed to their employment and relations between Black men and White women (Fryer 1984; Rowe 1998). Black men in the streets of Liverpool were being attacked regularly. One such attack, which resulted in the stabbing of a 'West Indian' migrant, provoked a revenge attack by eight of his friends. Police seeking those involved in the attack raided a boarding house used by Black seamen. Violence ensued and two policemen were shot, one slashed and one had his wrist broken. Charles Wootten ran from the house pursued by two policemen and two to three hundred strong lynch mob, hurling missiles. The mob tore him from the police and threw him into the water at Queens Dock and pelted him with stones, to cries of 'let him drown'. His corpse was later pulled from the water; however, no arrests were made (Fryer 1984: 300; Bourne 2014: 151). The police failure to pursue the perpetrators is an early manifestation of the under-protection of Black people in Britain-this is later manifest in high profile cases including the failure to prosecute following the murders of both Kelso Cochrane in 1958 and Stephen Lawrence in 1993.

Similar lynch mobs were at work in Cardiff and, according to reports in the Western Mail, police efforts were focused on preventing the White mobs from damaging property (Fryer 1984: 307). Indeed, a racialised response to the 'riots' led to accusations of unfair treatment from within established Black communities. Following the attacks in Cardiff, Dr. Rufus Leicester Fennell—a 'leader' of Cardiff's Black community—complained to MPs and the Home Office about the unfair way in which voluntary repatriations were being handled. He accused Cardiff police of prejudice against Black people in their supervision of the departure process (ibid.: 309). The refusal to allow Black troops to take part in

London's victory celebrations in July of the same year added insult to injury. In an editorial response to this Hercules, the General Secretary of the Society for Peoples of African Origin, wrote in the Africa Telegraph, 'the supineness of the Imperial government during the race 'riots' drives home the fact that they approve of them, that they are in line with Imperial policy' (ibid.: 315–316). The failure of the police to respond appropriately to the attacks illustrates that the 'race relations' problem was not seen to be caused by the White racist mobs, but by the presence of the Black Other.

Britain has been described as 'a nation of immigrants and their descendants' (Ward 2004: 116). However, there is evidence that all newcomers have experienced some degree of hostility on their arrival (Panyani 1996). Prior to the arrival of the post-war migrants from the Caribbean, Britishness was already racialised as White. The Pan-African Congress in 1945 opened with a full day addressing the 'colour problem in Britain' (Perry 2015: 51), illustrating how the problems faced by Black Britons were viewed as part of a global Black empowerment agenda. However, in the post-war/post-colonial period there was a shift from the 'politics of race as Empire to the politics of race as Nation' (Hesse 1997: 92–94). The arrival of the Empire Windrush served as both the point at which race-relations became part of the national post-colonial project and as a symbol for 'nationalist fears of the White racist imagination' (ibid.: 98). Nationalist fears came to the fore following the 1958 'riots' in Nottingham and Notting Hill. Similarly, to the 1919 'riots', they were the result of Black migrants being subjected to attacks by Whites. Unlike later 'riots', in which racist policing was a factor (Scarman 1981; Keith 1993), the role of the police in the 1958 'riots' was to protect the Black community from attack (Miles 1984). Miles argues, in stark contrast to accounts of later 'riots', that there is no recorded evidence of hostility between the police and the Black community at this time (ibid.). Fryer's (1984) analysis of newspaper reports of the day reveals that Nottingham's Black community felt that the police were biased in their dealings with them. Further, this account shows that the police-'already hostile to Black people'—had not extended protection to the Black community during the attacks (ibid.: 380). Racialisation was the product of the structures and practices employed by the media and the press at this time (Miles 1984: 255); reference to cultural attributes of welfare, spongers and sexual vice contribute to the formation of the race-crime link (ibid.: 259; also see Gilroy 1987). The 'riots' came to be seen as an inevitable consequence of race difference. The narratives surrounding them reflecting a 'White angst' about Black presence and the erosion of security in the neighbourhood and the home (Perry 2015: 113). However, as demonstrated in the earlier 1919 'riots', the seeds of the 'colour problem' narrative, attributed to the presence of the Black Other, had already been sown.

The construction of a 'race relations' problem paved the way for successive legislation limiting immigration at a time when managing decolonisation sensitively was a key political concern. The 1958 'riots', which were essentially attacks on Black citizens by Whites, were interpreted racially and a link was made between unrestricted commonwealth migration and an emerging race problem (Solomos 1988: 33). Immigration legislation, passed in 1962, introduced controls on Commonwealth immigration through a work voucher scheme. Further controls were imposed in 1968 with the Immigration Act which introduced the concept of 'patrials'; this extended immigration control to those without a parent or grandparent who was a citizen of or born in the United Kingdom. Implicit in the provisions of the legislation was the desire to prevent any further increase in non-White British citizens. This had the effect of creating a 'White Britain policy' (Solomos 1988: 40). The introduction of race relations legislation in the same period created a dichotomy whereby discrimination within Britain was outlawed as the means to manage sensitive international relations, whilst racism was codified within immigration provisions (Gilroy 1987). For Gilroy, this creates an inextricable link between the race and the concept of national belonging and (White) homogeneity. The nation is constructed with reference to both biological and cultural attributes of Britishness through phrases such as the 'Island race' and 'Bulldog breed'. It is the obviousness of difference, and the threat of dilution of the 'national stock', that is presented as a threat to the British way of life. Therefore, banishing the Other was seen as a legitimate response to the threat that is posed to the nation (ibid.: 44–45). This was manifest in Enoch Powell's infamous 'Rivers of Blood' speech in 1968, prompted by the Race Relations Bill (later the 1968 Act). In the speech he called for an end to immigration as the only solution to the 'race relations' problem, created by the presence of Black migrants. He declared of the imminent Race Relations legislation;

> Here is the means of showing that the immigrant communities can organize to consolidate their members, to agitate and campaign against their fellow citizens, and to overawe and dominate the rest with the legal weapons which the ignorant and the ill-informed have provided. As I look ahead, I am filled with foreboding; like the Roman, I seem to see "the River Tiber foaming with much blood. (Telegraph 2007, 6 November)

The Conservative Party distanced the speech from their official party politics; however, the speech had a significant impact on the politics of race relations and immigration discourse. For Gilroy, the speech was indicative of a new form of racism that defined Black communities as a threat to legality, the 'alien wedge', serving to link them inextricably with criminality (Gilroy 1987: 85).

In the context of the increasing fear about 'race relations' and Black peoples cultural proclivities towards criminality, *Policing the Crisis* (Hall et al. 1978) was the first sociological study to include an explicit analysis of the racialisation of policing. It contributes to an understanding of the construction of the race-crime nexus and the process through which young Black men became the 'enemy of the state'. The authors argue that the period in which the 'mugging' panic occurred was characterised by a 'crisis of hegemony', which is manifest in the response to 'mugging' (ibid.: 217). Through an analysis of the media and judiciary response to 'mugging' it is argued that the young Black man became a convenient scapegoat in order to legitimate a law and order response to mugging directly, and also more broadly, to address the fears surrounding social order manifest in strikes. 'riots' and other forms of protest from the late 1960s. The media used the term 'mugging', imported from the US context, to describe street robbery. Positioned as a new strain of crime, an old offence was given a new label with an already established racialised meaning. In the resulting moral panic young Black men were cast as the folk devil. In the wake of the 'crisis' the terms 'mugging' and 'Black crime', became 'virtually synonymous' (ibid.). The racist stereotypes that coalesced around the image of the 'mugger' are a central point in the trajectory of the development of the race-crime nexus. It was through 'mugging' that Black men were constructed as criminal and the resulting race-crime nexus continues to inform and produce contemporary fears surrounding Black men's criminality.

The treatment of Black communities at the hands of the police has been at the heart of resistance. Gilroy claims that is it in fact the police treatment of Black people that made them a political community (Gilroy 1987: 140). Resistance to racist and racialised police responses from Black communities, and the ways in which these responses have served to reinforce the race-crime link, will be considered next.

Resistance and the Racialisation of 'Riots'[1]

The growing African Caribbean community in England following the arrival of the *Empire Windrush* and the subsequent racialisation of relations and representations, occurred in the global context of decolonisation and Black empowerment. The Pan-African movement was gathering momentum with a focus on decolonisation, independence for African nations and the unity of Black people across the globe. Pan-African ideology was represented in global movements in the Caribbean Islands, America, England, France and the movements key protagonists were instrumental in the demands and rise of the American Civil Rights Movement (Angelo 2009). The Black Power movement in Britain took its ideological lead from the United States. The emergence of a specific movement—the British Black Panther Movement (BBPM) -was mobilised following visits from influential Black power activists. This included Martin Luther King, under whose instigation Campaign against Racial Discrimination (CARD) was formed, Malcolm X which

[1]'Riots' is used here as it is the predominant term used in the literature. However, it is used in inverted commas to indicate that the term 'riots' problematically depoliticises the motivation. Further, it a racialised term which locates blame within Black communities. Also, see, Farrar (2002, 2012).

led to the formation of Racial Adjustment Action Society (RAAS) with Michael X at its helm and later the Black Panther, Stokely Carmichael (Angelo 2009; Bunce and Field 2011). However, its 'roots' were, according to (Wild 2015: 42) 'specifically UK' focused, shaped by the context of post-coloniality and the treatment of non-White migrants in the hostile 'mother country'.

One significant event in understanding the politicisation of Black Caribbeans in the UK, is the murder of Kelso Cochrane in Notting Hill in 1958. The murder of an innocent man on his way home from a hospital appointment, was blamed on the police lack of response to White fascist activity in the area which had been evident in the earlier 'riots' (Wild 2015: 35). For some, the 'riots' of 1958 and the murder of Kelso Cochrane, forced their return to the Caribbean. Wild argues that Kelso Cochrane's death 'was to extinguish their belief in a benevolent mother country or that they were British in any meaningful way' (ibid.: 35). For others it was the catalyst for the evolution of solidarity in the face of oppression. 'Kelso Cochrane's death provided Black Britons with an opportunity to retool the injured Black body as a grievable subject and citizen' (Perry 2015: 129). For Black British activism, Cochranes murder, and the police response to it, transformed the immigrant into that of a 'disenfranchised citizen'. It was the catalyst for the assertion of a politics of Black Britishness.

The Labour government was elected in 1964 following a hard-fought election campaign along immigration lines. Peter Griffiths, The Conservative MP for Smethwick, notoriously ran his election campaign under the slogan 'If you want a nigger for your neighbour, vote labour'. He was condemned by the Labour Party; however, under the Labour government further restrictive immigration legislation followed which, according to Sivanandan (1982), institutionalised race and at local and national levels race became a 'site of struggle for power' (p. 18). The Race Relations Act was introduced in 1965 to outlaw racial discrimination in public places, (the provisions of the Act were later extended to include indirect discrimination and discrimination in housing and employment). Ironically, one of the figures associated with the British Black Power Movement (BBPM), Michael X was prosecuted for incitement to racial hatred in the year of its inception (ibid.: 17). The statutory bodies that were established in the wake of the legislation including the Race Relation Board, responsible for investigating complaints under the Act, and National Committee for Commonwealth Immigrants, were responsible for the dissolution of immigrant grass roots organisations as the statutory bodies moved in to their areas of work and enlisted support of the communities and existing groups such as CARD. This led to militants severing links with these organisations (Sivanandan 1982). The anti-immigration lobby was on the rise and 1967 saw National Front candidates stand for the Greater London Council elections. Inspired by the Black Power movement in the USA and Stokely Carmichael's visit to London in 1967, Obi Egbuna formed the Universal Coloured People Association (UCPA). Internationally, revolution was in the air and the following year, 1968, has been named 'The Year of Revolt'. The state's fear that the Black communities of Britain would rise up, as had happened across the Atlantic, was apparent when, following the speech that inspired Egbuna to form the UCPA, Carmichael was advised to leave the country earlier than planned; he was banned from returning (Bunce and Field 2011: 392).

The British Black Panthers were formed in 1968, when, following irreconcilable ideological factions within the UCPA, Egbuna resigned as chairperson and announced that he was forming the British Black Panthers. There were several British groups that associated themselves with the Black Power Movement at this time, which led to several publications which dealt with Black politics both at an academic and a grassroots level. When Egbuna was imprisoned the following year, the Black Panther Movement shifted its focus from ideology to action based in communities (see Bunce and Field 2011). It involved itself in the struggle for community-based action around education, employment and police brutality. A defining moment in the Black Power movement was its support for the Mangrove nine. The Mangrove restaurant in Brixton had become a hub for the Black community and the police had raided it several times. In protest at the perceived aggressive policing, a group of people marched, according to campaigners to 'expose the racist brutality that Black people experience at the hands of the police' (Organised Action in Self Defence flier 1971, cited in Angelo 2009: 24). Police clashed with protesters and charges of assault, incitement to riot and possession of an offensive weapon were brought against nine Black protestors. Throughout the course of the trial British Black Panthers protested outside of the Old Bailey. The Mangrove nine were eventually acquitted in what has been held up as a defining moment in the history of the Black Power Movement in Britain. Whilst the ideology of the British Black Panthers had a transnational focus based around the US citing slavery, class conflict and state oppression its action was based in local communities with a strong focus on police brutality (ibid.). The Black Power Movement in Britain formed an intrinsic part of the wider development of the Pan-African identity globally united through resistance to oppression.

The link to a wider global movement is evident in the adoption of a Rastafari identity amongst second generation African Caribbean in the UK. Undoubtedly some of the earlier immigrants came to the UK with Rastafari beliefs; however, this did not manifest as a UK Rastafarian movement until much later when it emerged amongst second generation Black Britons (Murrell et al. 1998: 179). According to Campbell (1985), 'in order to escape the cultural assault of the racism and ethnocentrism of the society, young Black people searched for avenues of self-expression and development, and one of the most compulsive aspects was that of the Rastafari philosophy, which gave them a sense of pride in being Black' (Campbell 1985, p. 186). Many were attracted to the politicised 'conscious' lyrics of reggae music which, promoted globally by Chris Blackwell, had developed an international appeal. Artists such as Bob Marley, Pete Tosh and Burning Spear sang of global oppression of the Black man, slavery, and colonialism; the message was to fight the powers of 'Babylon'.[2] The adoption of Rastafari by second generation Black Britons is significant to understanding both resistance and policing. Rastafari was viewed as a threat by the establishment. John Brown's government commissioned report, '*Shades of Grey*', focused on the 'Police/West Indian Relations' on the Handsworth estate in Birmingham. Brown claimed that the 'couple of hundred

[2]According to Murrell et al. (1998) Babylon refers to 'Western political and economic domination and cultural imperialism' (p. 1).

'hard-core' Dreadlocks who now form a criminalised subculture in the area live in squats. Almost all are unemployed. And apart from the specific crimes for which they are responsible, they constantly threaten the peace of individual citizens Black, brown and White' (cited in Gilroy 1982: 160). Perhaps Brown meant to say criminal? However, this error resulted in at least one truth in his argument. The report, accompanied by a BBC documentary with the same title, linked the outward expression of Rastafari, 'plaiting their hair in locks and wearing gold, green and red woollen hats' (ibid.), with criminality. Rastafari had indeed become criminalised, compounded by Brown's contribution, the widespread media coverage and the adoption of his findings by the police themselves (Campbell 1985; Gilroy 1982). Further, the link between Rastafari and marijuana use was drawn upon to make link between Black communities and drugs.

On the 2nd of April 1980, St Pauls in Bristol saw the first 'riots' of the decade. The 'riot' occurred when the police targeted a cafe frequented by Black youths, looking for cannabis and alcohol. The raid was perceived to be an 'unjustified and unprovoked police attack' by both Black and White residents of the St Pauls area (Reicher 1984: 8). The St Pauls riot, as it is referred to in popular terms, marked the beginning of a series of 'riots' in this decade, though it is the Brixton 'riots' a year later that are the subject of the *Scarman Report.* The 'riots' of the 1980s took place within the context of fragile relations between the police and Black communities and although the causes of the 'riots' were complex and not attributable only to Black rioters they were reported, analysed and historically located as 'race 'riots''.[3] Lord Scarman's inquiry into the Brixton 'riots' in 1981 concluded that the 'riots' were an outburst of anger by Black youths, attributable to the structural conditions in inner city areas such as poor housing, unemployment and racial prejudice. A climate which created a 'predisposition towards violent protest'. He also found evidence of discriminatory

[3]An analysis of the events and proposed causes of the 'riots' in detail is discussed at length elsewhere J. Benyon and J. Solomos (1984, 1987), P. Gilroy (1987), Keith (1993), Rowe (1998), and Scarman (1981).

stop and search being used against Black people and recommended that the 'sus'[4] law be scrapped. Locating the source of discrimination with individual officers as opposed to an institutional problem. Scarman recommended lengthier training to include diversity courses; making discriminatory behaviour a sackable offence and the recruitment of Black people in to the police service. Further, the Police and Criminal Evidence Act 1984 (PACE) was introduced with the aim of balancing police powers. Ironically it is the power to stop and search conferred by PACE, that continues to be the source of much consternation contemporarily, as will be discussed in the next chapter.

Lord Scarman's report was heavily criticised for its over reliance on police reports of events, a failure to grasp the concept of institutional racism (Keith 1993: 77) and the pathologising of Black deviance through familial stereotypes (Gilroy 1987: 104–106). Nonetheless, the enquiry forced the police to confront their own practice for the first time in their history. The Broadwater Farm 'riots', four years later in October 1985, suggest that Scarman's recommendations did not have a significant impact on improving the experiences of policing for Black people. Tensions in the Broadwater Farm estate, between the police and the community escalated following the death of Cynthia Jarrett. Cynthia died when teh police raided her home looking for her son-during the raid she either collapsed or, as claimed by Cynthia Jarrett's family, was pushed by a police officer. In the 'riots' that followed PC Keith Blakelock was stabbed to death. The then Police Commissioner, Sir Kenneth Newman, vowed to authorise the use of plastic bullets and CS gas in response to future incidences of disorder; this marked a significant turning point in the move towards a law and order policing agenda (Rowe 1998: 135–161). This time the government was not interested in the reasons for the 'riots' and there would not be an enquiry. The media set about drawing its own conclusions, relying upon and reproducing the racialised discourse that 'the cultural proclivities of Black people' were to blame for their conflict with the police (ibid.: 144). Rioting was not

[4]'Sus' law was a commonly used term for the power to stop and search an individual on suspicion of loitering under The Vagrancy Act 1824.

a new phenomenon in Britain. There is evidence of protest, 'riot' and insurrection throughout British history. Whilst the previous 'riots' in 1919 and 1958, had been constructed as evidence of a 'race-relations' problem, the later 'riots' of the 1980s came to define second generation Black Britons as the fundamentally opposed to the values of Britishness-the criminal, alien 'wedge' (Gilroy 1987).

Significantly for understanding the research sites, are the riots which occurred in the West Yorkshire area. One example is the Bonfire Night 'riots' in Chapeltown in 1973, 1974 and crucially in 1975, which culminated in the critical injury of two police officers, the arrest of several 'rioters' and the detention of four young men (Farrar 2002). These events occurred in the aftermath of the 1972 trial of two police officers, Inspector Ellerker and Sergeant Kitchener, who hounded David Oluwale to his death in the River Aire, in a sustained campaign of racist violence (Aspden 2007). Further, evidence submitted by the Leeds United Caribbean Association (UCA) to the Parliamentary Select Committee in 1972 expressed concerns around the 'harrassment' and 'intimidation' of Black youth, wrongful arrest and police brutality. Leading to the conclusion that, 'policemen have every black person under suspicion of some sort and for that reason every Black immigrant here in Leeds mistrusts the police, because we think that their attitudes are to start trouble, not prevent it' (Farrar 2012: 73). Similarly, to the other riots of the 1970s and 1980s, on Bonfire Night 1975 the young Black people of Chapeltown were fighting back against their treatment by the police. As with other areas of the country, Chapeltown saw further 'riots' during the 1980s. The discrete histories of these spaces of resistance and the specificities of the racialisation of the communities that inhabit these spaces, contributes to the localised race-crime nexus, reproduced through the police and local media. Using the example of Chapeltown in Leeds, which has been the site of several 'riots', through its racialisation is has become known as a space of criminality and sexual deviance (Carrington 2009; Farrar 2002). The racialisation of the space here, shaped by the history of 'riots' and migrant presence in the space, results in the over-policing of the area and its inhabitants. The example of Chapeltown illuminates the link between 'riots' and the racialisation of space through which spaces become symbolic of resistance to policing-this compounds the race-crime nexus.

Still 'Policing the Crisis'?

Whilst the moral panic surrounding the 'mugging' phenomenon has left its mark on the ideological imagining of young Black men, there is evidence of new and multiple fears which have fixed the link between young Black men and particular forms of criminality. Similarly, to the 'mugging' label, as argued in 'Policing the Crisis', more contemporary fears have in common that they have been attributed labels imported from a US context, with racially inscribed meanings which shape understandings of risk and legitimise control. One example is the 'war on drugs' originating in the US Nixon administration, a war in which 'the enemy is racially defined' (Alexander 2012: 98). For Chambliss (1995), it is not a war on drugs but a 'war on people of colour' which systematically destroys the lives of both Latino and Black communities (pp. 105–108). It has served to create a 'new racial caste system' which permits the segregationist policies of the Jim Crow era under a new name (Alexander 2012: 180–181).

Similar effects can be seen in the policing and criminal justice response to drug offences in the UK. Eastwood et al. (2013), find that drugs laws are a key driver of disproportionate representation of Black people in the criminal justice system. Studies have shown that White people are more likely to engage in drug use. Further, it is also the case that there is insufficient empirical support for the stereotype that Black people are more likely to be involved in drug dealing offences. (ibid.: 16). However, the rates of drug offending are not reflected in proportionate stop and search, arrest and convictions for Whites. The policing of drugs offences is heavily racialised; searches for drugs are disproportionate for Black, Asian and mixed-race people (ibid.: 12). This is reflected in their disproportionate arrest and charges brought for drug possession. A 'war' against Black people that began in 1970s US has shaped British consciousness on drugs and drug use and sustained the link between Black and mixed-race people and drugs. This image is proliferated in media reproductions of 'drugs, gangs and yardies' (Gabriel 1998, cited in Cushion 2011). These specific racialisations are 'coded through culture' (Murji 1999), serving to Other the migrant body as being in conflict with British values thus strengthening the race-crime link.

The gang concept carries with it racialised connotations which are evident in the media use of the 'gang' label in response to violent crime committed by Black youth. Utilising the word 'gang' in the press and political and policy responses creates the risk of events which are not 'gang-related' being defined as such (Marshall et al. 2005: 7), further contributing to the perception that there is a gang epidemic. Further, informal peer groups are at risk of being labelled as gang members even when they are not involved in criminality (Bullock and Tilley 2002: 23). Williams and Clarke (2016), through an analysis of police 'gang' lists in London, Manchester and Nottingham, found that the 'gang' label is disproportionately applied to Black and Asian minorities when compared with the size of the Black and Ethnic Minority 'BAME' population in the area, and the number of White people listed as 'gang' members. They conclude that 'the gang construct is racialised to Black and Brown men' (Williams and Clarke 2016: 10). This is not reflective of their involvement in violent crime; however, of concern is the shift from myth-making to policy-making (Alexander 2004), which is evident in the law and order response. The law and order response to the 'gang' is evident in the use of joint enterprise principle to secure conviction by association. It is no coincidence that young Black men in particular are significantly over represented in joint enterprise convictions (Crewe et al. 2014). The 'gang' ideology further consolidates the stereotype of violent Black masculinities, which shape police responses to them. Further it constitutes them as a threat; the fear of the potential 'gang' member contributing to an increase in the perception of risk in the police encounter. It can be argued that this perceived risk pre-empts and justifies the use of force, including lethal force (see Chapter 3).

Minority Perspectives on the Police

Minority perspectives are broadly absent from the literature on race and policing in both the US and the UK context, with few exceptions (see US: Anderson 1990; Weitzer 2000; Brunson and Miller 2006; and UK: Yarrow 2005; Sharp and Atherton 2007; Barrett et al. 2014; Keeling 2017). However, these studies all draw similar conclusions in relation to the ways in which Black people (and other ethnic minority groups) experience policing. Black people are shown to be disproportionately targeted for police attention, particularly in relation to routine procedures like stop and search, and that these experiences are characterised by hostile treatment. Further, in both the UK and the US context, Black people report lower levels of trust and confidence in the police, primarily based on their experiences with them. The different policing models in operation in both contexts and the social and historical context of the emergence of the police service in different geographical spaces, does not facilitate a simple comparison between experiences and perceptions in these different contexts. Therefore, this section will focus on the UK evidence base to facilitate analysis of the empirical data upon which this book is based.

Black people constitute a criminalised sub population and race has meaning during encounters between the two groups (Britton 2000: 701–703). This is a consistent finding in Sharp and Atherton (2007), Barrett et al. (2014), and Keeling (2017). Similarly, to the research in this book, Sharp and Atherton (2007) use a qualitative interview method to develop an understanding of the impact of police misconduct on people from Black and other ethnic minority groups. The research focused on respondents age 15–18 with a high level of social exclusion and reported encounters with the police. Overwhelmingly, participants felt that the police racially discriminated against them and that they were harassed on the basis of racialised stereotypes. This is consistent with Keeling's (2017) finding that young Black people feel that they are stopped more frequently because they are stereotyped as 'gang' members (p. 16), and Barrett et al.'s (2014), finding that young Black people perceive the police to be racist. Negative and repeat experiences of stop and search are particularly damaging to young people's perceptions of, and trust and confidence in, the police. This is heightened when they do not feel that there is a legitimate ground for the stop (Sharp and Atherton 2007; Keeling 2017). These encounters make young people feel 'victimised' and 'humiliated' (ibid.).

Young Black men in particular lack trust and confidence in the police (Yarrow 2005; Sharp and Atherton 2007), which is explained, in part, through their perceptions of police racism. Negative police-community relations and the impact of stop and search impacts upon their willingness to trust the police in the context of victimisation (Barrett et al. 2014). Most of the young Black men in Yarrow's (2005) study, who had reported crime, were dissatisfied with the police response. Further, some expressed that they would not contact the police if they were the victim of crime, regardless of the severity. Similarly, to the finding in Sharp and Atherton (2007: 755), it is found that young Black men they have develop strategies for or managing their own experiences as victims of crime and this is one that actively excludes the police (also see Chapter 5). Both Sharp and Atherton (2007) and Britton (2000) find that experience is more important than rumour, in forming perceptions of the police. This is supported in Barrett et al.'s (2014) mixed methods study; they conclude that whilst positive experience can improve perceptions, negative experiences can 'damage views or reinforce negative pre-conceptions' (Barrett et al. 2014). As shown in Britton's (2000) study, views based on personal experiences are the most difficult to change (p. 700). This finding underlines the importance of developing knowledge pertaining to Black and Black mixed-race peoples encounters with the police, in order to challenge racialised and racist policing.

Conclusion

This chapter has analysed the construction of the race-crime nexus, through an analysis of the historical trajectory of black presence and settlement in the UK. Drawing on histories of migration and the politicisation of immigration in the post-colonial period, it finds that the politicisation and racialisation of immigration is evident long before traditional narratives which position the decade following the arrival of the Empire Windrush in 1948 as the point from which the 'colour problem' emerged.

Further, the chapter has shown how the race-crime nexus was constructed through the criminalisation of second generation Black Britons. Drawing on the seminal text, 'Policing the Crisis', it located 'mugging' as the point at which the young black men were inextricably linked with criminality. Through an analysis of contemporary racialized fears, including the 'war on drugs' and recent responses to the 'gang' problem, it argued that we are still 'policing the crisis'. This is reflected in the over-policing of Black and Black mixed-race people. In the UK context there is a paucity of empirical research that addresses Black and Black mixed-race peoples experiences of policing from their perspective. The extant literature focuses on young Black people and shows that they continue be targeted for disproportionate policing, significantly in the context of stop and search. Further, their experiences when they encounter the police are overwhelmingly negative resulting in negative perceptions of the police and a lack of trust which leaves them under protected as victims. It is from the small body of work, identified in this chapter, that this book will develop its analysis of Black and Black mixed-race people's experiences of policing, thus contributing to the limited body of work from this perspective.

The following chapter will focus on policing the racialised Other, from a post-colonial perspective. It will evaluate explanations for police racism with a focus on disproportionality in stop and search, use of force and deaths in police custody.

References

Alexander, C. (2004). Imagining the Asian Gang: Ethnicity, Masculinity and Youth After 'The Riots'. *Critical Social Policy, 24,* 526–549.

Alexander, M. (2012). *The New Jim Crow: Mass Incarceration in the Age of Colorblindness*. New York: The New Press.

Anderson, E. (1990). *Streetwise: Race, Class, and Change in an Urban Community*. Chicago: University of Chicago Press.

Angelo, A. M. (2009). The Black Panthers in London, 1967–1972: A Diasporic Struggle Navigates the Black Atlantic. *Radical History Review, 2009,* 17–35.

Aspden, K. (2007). *Nationality: Wog: The Hounding of David Oluwale*. London: Jonathan Cape.

Barrett, G. A., Fletcher, S. M., & Patel, T. G. (2014). Black Minority Ethnic Communities and Levels of Satisfaction with Policing: Findings from a Study in the North of England. *Criminology and Criminal Justice, 14,* 196–215.

Benyon, J. A. (1984). *Scarman and After: Essays Reflecting on Lord Scarman's Report, the Riots, and Their Aftermath*. Oxford: Pergamon Press.

Benyon, J., & Solomos, J. (1987). *The Roots of Urban Unrest*. Oxford: Pergamon Press.

Bourne, S. (2014). *Black Poppies: Britain's Black Community and the Great War*. Gloucestershire: The History Press.

Britton, N. J. (2000). Examining Police/Black Relations: What's in a Story? *Ethnic and Racial Studies, 23*, 692–711.

Brunson, R. K., & Miller, J. (2006). Young Black Men and Urban Policing in the United States. *British Journal of Criminology, 46*, 613–640.

Bullock, J., & Tilley, N. (2002). *Shootings, Gangs and Violent Incidents in Manchester: Developing a Crime Reduction Strategy*. London: Home Office.

Bunce, R. E. R., & Field, P. (2011). Obi B. Egbuna, C. L. R. James and the Birth of Black Power in Britain: Black Radicalism in Britain 1967–72. *Twentieth Century British History, 22*, 391–414.

Campbell, H. (1985). *Rasta and Resistance: From Marcus Garvey to Walter Rodney*. Antigua: Hansib.

Carrington, B. (2009). Leeds and the Topographies of Race: In Six Scenes. In P. Bramham & S. Wagg (Eds.), *Sport, Leisure and Culture in the Postmodern City*. Surrey: Ashgate.

Chambliss, W. J. (1995). Another Lost War: The Costs and Consequences of Drug Prohibition. *Social Justice, 22*, 101–124.

Crewe, B., Hulley, S., & Wright, S. (2014). *Written Evidence: Submitted to Justice Select Committee*. Cambridge: Cambridge Institute of Criminology.

Cushion, S., Moore. K., & Jewell, J. (2011). *Media Representations of Black Young Men and Boys: Report of the REACH Media Monitoring Project*. London: Department for Communities and Local Government.

Eastwood, N., Shiner, M., & Bear, D. (2013). *The Numbers in Black and White: Ethnic Disparities in the Policing and Prosecution of Drug Offences in England and Wales*. London: Release.

Enoch Powell's 'Rivers of Blood' Speech. (2007, 6 November). *Telegraph* (online). www.telegraph.co.uk/comment/3643823/Enoch-Powells-Rivers-of-Blood-speech.html. Accessed 1 November 2012.

Fanon, F. (1986). *Black Skin, White Masks*. London: Pluto Press.

Farrar, M. (2002). *The Struggle for 'Community' in a British Multi-Ethnic Inner-City Area*. London: Edwin Mellen Press.

Farrar, M. (2012). Rioting or Protesting? Losing It or Finding It? *Parallax, 18*, 72–91.

Fryer, P. (1984). *Staying Power: The History of Black People in Britain*. London: Pluto Press.

Gilroy, P. (1982). Police and Thieves. In CCCS (Ed.), *The Empire Strikes Back: Race and Racism in 70s Britain*. London: Hutchinson.

Gilroy, P. (1987). *There Ain't No Black in the Union Jack*. London: Hutchinson.

Hall, S., Critcher, C., Jefferson, T., Clarke, J., & Roberts, B. (1978). *Policing the Crisis: Mugging, the State, and Law and Order*. London: Macmillan.

Hesse, B. (1997). White Governmentality: Urbanism, Nationalism, Racism. In S. Westwood & J. Williams (Eds.), *Imagining Cities*. London: Routledge.

Hesse, B. (2000). Diasporicity: Black Britain's Post-colonial Formations. In B. Hesse (Ed.), *Unsettled Multiculturalisms: Diasporas, Entanglements, Transruptions*. New York: Zed Books.

Keeling. P. (2017). *No Respect: Young BAME Men, the Police and Stop and Search*. Criminal Justice Alliance. http://criminaljusticealliance.org/wp-content/uploads/2017/06/No-Respect-290617-1.pdf.

Keith, M. (1993). *Race, Riots and Policing: Lore and Disorder in a Multi-Racist Society*. London: UCL.

Law, I., Hunter, S., Osler, A., Swann, S., Tzanelli, R., & Williams, F. (2008). *Ethnic Relations in the UK* (Working Paper No. 3). Leeds: University of Leeds.

Marshall, B., Webb, B., & Tilley, N. (2005). *Rationalisation of Current Research on Guns, Gangs and Other Weapons: Phase 1*. London: Jill Dando Institute of Crime Science, University College London.

Miles, R. (1984). The Riots of 1958: The Ideological Construction of 'Race Relations' as a Political Issue in Britain. *Immigrants and Minorities, 3*, 252–275.

Murji, K. (1999). White Lines: Culture, 'Race' and Drugs. In N. South (Ed.), *Drugs: Culture, Controls and Everyday Life*. London: Sage.

Murrell, N. S., Spencer, W. D., & Macfarlane, A. A. (1998). *Chanting Down Babylon: The Rastafari Reader*. Philadelphia: Temple University Press.

Panyani, P. (1996). *Racial Violence in Britain in the Nineteenth and Twentieth Centuries*. Leicester: Leicester University Press.

Perry, K. H. (2015). *London Is the Place for Me*. New York: Oxford University Press.

Phillips, M., & Phillips, T. (1998). *Windrush: The Irresistible Rise of Multi-racial Britain*. London: HarperCollins.

Reicher, S. D. (1984). The St. Pauls' Riot: An Explanation of the Limits of Crowd Action in Terms of a Social Identity Model. *European Journal of Social Psychology, 14*, 1–21.

Rowe, M. (1998). *The Racialisation of Disorder in Twentieth Century Britain*. Aldershot: Ashgate.

Scarman, L. (1981). *The Scarman Report: The Brixton Disorders 10–12 April 1981*. London: HMSO.

Sharp, D., & Atherton, S. (2007). To Serve and Protect? The Experiences of Policing in the Community of Young People from Black and Other Ethnic Minority Groups. *British Journal of Criminology, 47*, 746–763.

Sivanandan, A. (1982). *A Different Hunger: Writings on Black Resistance*. London: Pluto Press.

Solomos, J. (1988). *Black Youth, Racism and the State*. Cambridge: Cambridge University Press.

Ward, P. (2004). *Britishness Since 1870* (1st ed.). London: Routledge.

Weitzer, R. (2000). Racialised Policing: Residents' Perceptions in Three Neighborhoods. *Law and Society, 34*, 129–155.

Wild, R. (2015). "Black Was the Colour of Our Fight": The Transnational Roots of British Black Power. In R. D. G. Kelley & T. Stephen (Eds.), *The Other Special Relationship: Race, Rights and Riots in Britain and the United States*. New York: Palgrave Macmillan.

Williams, P., & Clarke, B. (2016). *Dangerous Associations: Joint Enterprise, Gangs and Racism. An Analysis of the Processes of Criminalisation of Black, Asian and Minority Ethnic Individuals*. London: Centre for Crime and Justice Studies.

Yarrow, S. (2005). *The Experiences of Young Black Men as Victims of Crime*. London: Criminal Justice Unit and Victims and Confidence Unit.

3

Policing the Racialised Other

This chapter offers a critical analysis of the emergence of the police through imperial linkages (Cole 1999). It reflects upon the impact that this has upon the policing of Black communities contemporarily, significantly with regard to over policing through stop and search. It continues, in this regard, to consider the use and abuse of police force and disproportionate Black deaths in police custody. In order to situate this book within the broader field of literature, police culture as an explanation for the endurance of racism within the police service will be addressed. The evident gaps in knowledge, pertaining to Black and Black mixed-race people's experiences of the police, will be highlighted to illustrate the contribution that this book makes to the field. The chapter will conclude that the role and function of the police service is incongruous with the notion of consensual policing, particularly in regards to the policing of the racialised Other.

L. J. Long, *Perpetual Suspects*, Palgrave Studies in Race, Ethnicity, Indigeneity and Criminal Justice, https://doi.org/10.1007/978-3-319-98240-3_3

The Emergence of the New Police

The first British police force, London's Metropolitan Police Service, was founded in 1829 by the then Home Secretary Sir Robert Peel. Orthodox understandings of the development of the police service in England are premised on the notion that the police were a necessary response to the problems of order brought about by industrial and urban revolution (Reiner 2010: 40). According to Reith (1956), their purpose was to prevent crime and disorder and to provide an alternative to military repression. The British Policing Model is attributed to foundational principles set out by Peel, commonly referred to as 'Peelian principles'. The precise nature and history of the emergence of principles is contested (see Reiner 2010 for fuller analysis). However, the British Policing Model is broadly based on principles of crime prevention rather than prosecution and policing by consent, rather than military repression—'the police are the public and public are the police' (ibid.). The historical integrity of these accounts has been called into question by revisionist accounts of policing history. Revisionist historians argue that the Metropolitan Police Service was created for the purpose of controlling the burgeoning working class (Emsley 2008; Reiner 2010). According to revisionist histories, the working classes, who have always been the focus of social control through policing, were opposed to the new police viewing them as a 'plague of blue locusts' (Storch and Engels 1975). These accounts contest the orthodox notion that the working classes, or those considered 'police property' (Lee 1981), have ever consented to policing. Indeed, there is evidence of opposition to the 'new police' from their inception.

If the notion of policing by consent is in fact an 'invention', as Lentz and Chaires (2007: 73–74) claim, it is a pervasive myth that pervades the political and policing lexicon. Confidence and consent in the police was a central concern of the two most significant inquiries into policing, the Scarman Report and The Stephen Lawrence Inquiry. In the wake of the Stephen Lawrence Inquiry Report finding that the police were institutionally racist, it was recommended that a Ministerial Priority be established for all Police Services 'to increase trust and confidence amongst minority ethnic communities' (Macpherson 1999: 375). The shift that occurred from the language of racism and anti-racism, towards the language of diversity represents a 'subtle renegotiation' of the principle of policing by consent (Rowe 2004: 145). Inherent in policing diversity is the notion that different publics require different responses to deliver equality of outcomes (ibid.). Premised on business speak, diversity is commodified and it is valued in the context of its worth as a human resource (Ahmed 2012: 53). A proliferation of the language of diversity has led to the erasure of race within the institution (the police and institutions more broadly), making racism invisible (Goldberg 2014; Tate 2016).

Neighbourhood Policing emerged in the wake of the *Scarman Report* to improve police-community relations. It has seen a number of iterations, including reassurance-based policing in the 1990s, and was formalised as the Neighbourhood Policing Model (NPM) in 2001 (see Longstaff et al. 2015). It aimed to improve police visibility, get the community involved in identifying local priorities, and engage in collaborative problem-solving with multi-agency partners and the public (Quinton and Morris 2008: 7). Whilst the aims may appear laudable, Crawford suggests that the NPM is simply a concession to pacify the public and the 'unattainable expectations' they place on police performance (Crawford 2007: 144). As Henry (2007) argues, even if the community engagement element of the NPM makes policing more palatable, the principle of policing by consent is fundamentally incompatible with the control and law enforcement function of policing (p. 105).

Despite this demonstrable incompatibility, Peelian principles continue to provide the rationale for contemporary policing policy and practice. In her 2015 speech, announcing a review of deaths in custody, Home Secretary Theresa May said:

> In 1829, when Sir Robert Peel founded the Metropolitan Police, he declared that the police must maintain a relationship with the public 'that gives reality to the historic tradition that the police are the public and that the public are the police'... in this country we believe in policing by consent and it's a principle I know every officer, every chief constable, and every PCSO subscribes to and believes in. (Home Office 2014)

The 'invention' of and insistence upon the myth of consent in policing is problematic for two key reasons. Firstly, because there is little evidence that all sections of British society have ever consented equally to policing (Storch and Engels 1975). Further, it cannot be claimed that the police are the public, when, in an increasingly diverse society the police remain predominantly ethnically homogenous (White).

If the emergence of the police is reframed within a postcolonial perspective, it can be argued that the function of the police is antithetical to policing by consent. Brogden and Ellison (2013) contend that, 'the new police were invented as an 'urban prophylactic' against the normative practices of the Other' (p. 152). Its origins are in the control and oppression of the Other for the purpose of maintaining White power. Therefore, the development and formation of state policing in England cannot be understood without reference to the impact of colonial histories on the policing systems in the 'mother countries'—their 'imperial linkage' (Cole 1999). From this perspective, it is both the target of policing, the Other or the native, and the systems of policing informed by 'imperial linkages', which continue to shape the discriminatory policing experience in the 'domestic colonies' (Sivanandan 1982; also Gabbidon 2010). This is evident in Bowling et al.'s (2004) analysis of discrimination and abuse of power in policing across four jurisdictions, Australia, Britain, South Africa and USA. In all jurisdictions they identify a common pattern; the community policing model, which could be aligned with 'Peelian principles' in the British context, is used for 'middle class, wealthy, suburban White populations', whilst paramilitary policing is used in poor, Black and minority ethnic areas (Bowling et al. 2004: 6). The public order function of the contemporary police can therefore be understood through an analysis of 'the centrality of colonial conquest and imperial legitimation to institutional development in Victorian England' (Brogden 1987: 5). This re-telling of the historical narratives that have developed around the birth of the modern police, with the inclusion of previously omitted perspectives, reveals that the notion of a police service developed on the principle of policing by consent is an 'invention'. Instead, the police and the Other are locked in an oppositional relation (Brogden and Ellison 2013: 132). The police function of control over the Other implicates the police service in racist practices shaped through 'imperial linkages' (Cole 1999: 88).

Stop and Search

Research over the past four decades has consistently evidenced that Black people in Britain are more likely to be targeted for stop and search and are more likely to report experiencing rude or aggressive treatment when they are stopped (Bowling and Phillips 2007; Barrett et al. 2014; Equality and Human Rights Commission 2013; also see Chapter 1 for international context). This discriminatory treatment is seen to be one of the most damaging factors in the relationship between Black people and their communities and the police (Bowling and Phillips 2002). According to the Home Office (2011), stop and search is an investigative power for the prevention and detection of criminal activity. Its primary purpose it to enable police officers to 'allay or confirm' police officers suspicions about an individual without relying first upon their powers of arrest. There are a number of legislative provisions for stop and search; however, the majority are carried out under Section 1 of the *Police and Criminal Evidence Act 1984*. The *Police and Criminal Evidence Act* was enacted following the repeal of 'sus' powers after the publication of *Scarman Report*. It was intended to provide a balance of police powers with accountability, increasing trust between police and the communities they serve (Jones 2011: 698).

Discretion is considered a necessary element of operational policing affecting decisions about patrol areas, what incidents to investigate, whether to stop and search a person and also when not to take any action or 'turn a blind eye'. The use of discretion to stop and search under PACE powers relies upon the interpretation the legal test of 'reasonable grounds for suspicion'. Further, it is required that the officer will be able to explain their suspicion on the basis of the grounds specified in the code of practice. According to Bowling et al. (2004), where there is the greatest police autonomy and discretion 'abuse of power is most discriminatory' (p. 8). Further, it is the least senior officers who have the most discretion as they are on the streets making decisions daily (Wilson 1968, cited in Reiner 2010: 85). Stop and search is, by its nature, low visibility and the combination of low visibility with police officer discretion makes it difficult to regulate. Additionally, the concept of reasonable suspicion is ill defined and relies upon subjective judgement which may align with officer bias, or policing priorities (Sanders and Young 2008: 281–312). There is some evidence to suggest that reasonable suspicion is misunderstood by police officers and therefore they fail to establish a legal ground for the stop and search (Quinton et al. 2000; Bowling and Phillips 2007: 939). However, the revision of the *PACE: Codes of Practice* (2014) to include specific guidance on this has not reduced disproportionality in the use of stop and search. In fact, conversely, disproportionality has increased.

A cursory glance at the statistics, discussed in chapter one, suggests that racial profiling informs the use of police stop and search powers. This argument is viewed as simplistic by Waddington et al. (2004). Drawing on the approach adopted in Miller (2000), they test the 'availability' thesis and find that some ethnic groups are more available for stop and search by their presence in public spaces. They conclude that there is insufficient evidence of the existence of racial profiling. Rather, stop and search reflects the 'racial composition' of the available population (p. 910). However, as Bowling and Phillips (2007) suggest, availability is not a neutral criterion. The extent to which a particular ethnic group is available is dependent on structural factors such as unemployment, school exclusion, homelessness, employment in night/shift work patterns (ibid.: 946). Further, this does not consider time spent in public places on a general level but relates to areas where stop and search powers are more extensively used (ibid.). The question of whether stop and search hotspots are also crime hotspots inevitably arises. Miller et al., show that areas with a high resident population from 'BME' communities are targeted for stop and search, even where local crime rates do not warrant the intrusion (Miller 2000). This lends additional weight to Choongh's (1998) claim that the police deliberately operate two sets of processes, the official criminal justice processes and a second tier which begins and ends at the police station. The latter operates within a social disciplinary model; arrests take place without the need to establish factual or legal guilt. Arrests made within a social disciplinary model are not for the purpose of crime detection, but for the purpose of reproducing social control and maintaining police authority. This can intersect with official criminal justice processes but the police have a preference for subjecting its targets to a system outside of crime control and due process models in which the police control the parameters (p. 625).

In an attempt to improve police accountability for stop and search, and trust and confidence in the police, the *Stephen Lawrence Inquiry Report* recommended that police officers record all police stops and searches and record the reason for the stop, the outcome and the self-defined ethnicity of the person subject to the stop and search (Macpherson 1999: R61). This recommendation was piloted in four police force areas, including both urban and rural areas with a range of ethnically mixed populations. Analysis of the schemes found that stop and search was under-recorded and that officers recorded selectively, particularly where a search did not follow a stop. Further, requesting self-defined ethnicity within the context of a police stop proved problematic in some cases where the individual stopped did not understand the reason for being asked and viewed it as further evidence of racism (Bland et al. 2000). Recording stop and search led some officers to think more carefully about stop and search decisions and providing the appropriate information, regarding the decision to stop, to the individual. However, others viewed the attempt to establish accountability for discretion as an 'imposition' (ibid.). Those police officers in the latter group would be unlikely to change their behaviour as a result of the recommendation. Members of the public did see some value in being provided information about the stop, not least of all the provision of the police officers details in case they needed to make a complaint. However, being fairly treated as well as being given a good reason for the stop is an important factor in increasing trust and confidence in the police and their use of stop and search powers (Bland et al. 2000: 92–95). Stone and Pettigrew (2000) find that, whilst recording stop and search may go some way to improving accountability, the most important factor in determining trust and confidence in the police is how the individual is treated by the police officer, including a respectful attitude and legitimate reason for the stop. In March 2010 the requirement to record stop and account incidents was abolished in an attempt to cut police paperwork and bureaucracy.

One way in which the recording of stop and search in this way is helpful is that, for the subject, it establishes the reason for the stop, increasing perceptions of procedural justice. The procedural justice thesis is premised on the notion that fair, respectful treatment that follows established procedures will increase the legitimacy of police authority.

Legitimacy encourages compliance with the law. Further it increases satisfaction with the police, crime reporting and assisting the police in crime investigation (Tyler and Lind 1992[1]). However, procedural justice is considered to be less effective at establishing police legitimacy in 'ethnic minority' communities (Murphy 2013; Murphy and Cherney 2011). Bradford et al. (2014) argue that social identity operates as a 'social-psychological bridge' between perceptions of fairness and legitimacy. When police officers do not treat people fairly, they are forced to question their identity in relation the powerful group and legitimacy is reduced as a result. Improving community perceptions of the legitimate use of stop and search is one of the ways in which the UK Home Secretary, Theresa May, sought to address the issue of disproportionality.

The voluntary *Best Use of Stop and Search* scheme, launched in 2014, re-introduced a recording requirement to assess the use of the test of 'reasonable suspicion'. In compliance with the scheme, participating forces were required to record the outcome of stops (Home Office 2014). Further, community participation in the reform programme was proposed as a measure of improving transparency and accountability. Participating forces allowed members of the public to accompany police officers on patrol. In addition, a community trigger was introduced which, in the event of a large number of stop and search complaints, would place a responsibility on the police to explain how the powers were used. Other measures to improve transparency included the addition of stop and search data to crime maps and the inclusion of stop and search data in HMIC annual inspections (ibid.). All forty-three forces in England and Wales signed up to the scheme; however, thirteen forces were suspended from the programme in February 2016 for failing to adhere to the requirements (Dodd 2016). The programme did result in an overall decline in the use of stop and search and, for the 2014/2015 recording year, a marked decline in disproportionality. The likelihood of being stopped and searched for Black people in 2011

[1]For more nuanced perspectives on procedural justice also see Tyler and Lind (1992). Tyler and Huo (2002), Sunshine and Tyler (2003), Tyler (2003, 2006), Kristina (2009), Murphy (2015), Barkworth and Murphy (2016).

was six times higher than for Whites, by 2015 this was just over four times more likely (Home Office 2015). However, in spite of an overall decline in stop and search, most significantly for Whites (decline of 38% compared with a decline of 8% for Blacks), in the 2016/2017 recording year likelihood of being stopped and searched rose sharply for Black people to more than eight times more likely than Whites (Hargreaves et al. 2017). This is instructive of the difficulties inherent in limiting police discretion or increasing accountability for its use. Bowling and Phillips (2007) argue that the absence of a penalty for unlawful use of stop and search powers allows them to be used without accountability (p. 939). Similar issue of discretion in police officer's interpretation of legal principles, and limited accountability for their use, are evident in relation to police use of force.

Use of Force and Deaths in Police Custody

Black people and Black mixed-race people are more likely to be on the receiving end of police use of force and restraint. This is borne out in analysis of use of force by the Metropolitan Police Service, which reveals that they are more likely to use force in the restraint of Black people (Dearden 2017). Further, there is increasing evidence that Tasers are more likely to be discharged in contact with Black and Black mixed-race people (Gayle 2015; Dearden 2018). The police are empowered to use force in the exercise of their powers by *Section 117* of *Police and Criminal Evidence Act*. However, for the use of force to be lawful, the common law principle of reasonable and necessary applies.[2] As with stop and search decisions, this judgement is reliant upon police officer discretion. One of the concerning factors in the evidence base is the role of racialised stereotypes, pertaining to threat, in the decision to use force. As argued by Long and Joseph-Salisbury (2018) 'racialising and

[2] Test based on what the 'reasonable man' (i.e. jury) would deem reasonable and necessary in the circumstances, see *Palmer v R, [1971] AC 814*; approved in R v McInnes, 55 Cr App R 551.

criminalising narratives' are used to rationalise the use of force directed towards Black suspects (also see Erfani-Ghettani 2015). Further, Angiolini (2017) in her review into *Deaths and Serious Incidents in Police Custody*, concluded that there is a need to confront discriminatory assumptions and stereotypes in police training.

Both Angiolini (2017) and the United Nations (see Dearden 2018) have raised concerns regarding the lack of accountability for the police use of force and restraint which, in the extreme, can result in death. Black people are disproportionately the victims of restraint related deaths in police custody. However, there has never been a successful manslaughter prosecution of a serving police officer in the UK, even when an unlawful verdict has been reached at inquest the cases of Roger Sylvester and Christopher Alder are just two of many that illustrate this point. Roger Sylvester, a thirty-year-old Black man, died as a result of excessive restraint in 1999. The family of Roger Sylvester called the police for help as Roger was in mental distress. Two officers attended initially and found Roger naked in his front garden. They called for backup and within minutes another six officers arrived. Eight police officers, in total, brought Roger Sylvester to the ground, handcuffed and restrained him. He was then taken to a psychiatric unit in a police van, upon arrival up to six officers are said to have continued to restrain him for twenty minutes. Roger collapsed, stopped breathing and never recovered consciousness. He died a week later (IRR 2003). The inquest jury ruled that Sylvester had been 'unlawfully killed'; however, no charges were brought against the police officers in this case.[3]

There was a similar failure to prosecute following the death of Christopher Alder. Christopher died in police custody in Hull in 1998 after being arrested outside of Hull Royal Infirmary. He was captured on CCTV walking to the police van in handcuffs. However, on his

[3]The aim of the inquest is to establish the facts of the death, and not to attribute blame to any individual for the death. Possible verdicts, which can apply to deaths in police custody, include: natural causes, accidental death, suicide, lawful killing, and open verdicts (where insufficient evidence prevents any other verdict). Inquest verdicts are subject to a civil burden of proof which is lower than in criminal cases and it is based on the balance of probability. However, in the case of unlawful killing or suicide verdicts the standard of proof is in line with that in the criminal courts, beyond all reasonable doubt (CPS 2017).

arrival at Queens Gardens Police Station, a short five minutes away, the CCTV footage showed him being dragged unconscious out of the van with his trousers around his ankles. He was dragged into the custody suite where he was dumped on the floor and left to choke on his own blood (audibly on CCTV) whilst police officers stood around chatting and joking. Further, evidence of racist 'monkey noises' could be heard on the CCTV recordings. The noises were made by one of the officers present in the custody suite after Christopher's death, and whilst he was still lying on the floor (Dodd 2002). An inquest jury found that Christopher Alder had been 'unlawfully killed' (Wainwright 2000). Charges of manslaughter and misconduct in public office were brought five Humberside police officers. However, the trial collapsed after the prosecution summing up, when, on the basis of conflicting medical evidence presented by the prosecution, the presiding judge ruled that the police officers had no case to answer[4] (Wainwright 2003). There appears to be a manifest reluctance on the part of the criminal justice system to run a successful prosecution against serving police officers. The loyalty inherent in the 'cop culture' results in a closing of ranks when things go wrong and as stated by Institute for Race Relations (1991) the 'chain of command becomes a chain of cover up' (p. 2). The roll call of deaths in similar circumstances is too long to examine fully.[5] However, the cases of Roger Sylvester and Christopher Alder illustrate the lack of accountability for the use of force inherent in the system.

Following a death in police custody the victim is depicted as deviant or criminal and/or having displayed violent or aggressive behaviour towards police officers, which in many cases is later proven untrue (Pemberton 2008). Victims are often portrayed as being under the influence of alcohol or drugs or displaying signs of mental illness. These stereotypes of deviant behaviour, 'drug addict' and 'schizophrenic',

[4]This was not the end of the trauma exacted upon the family of Christopher Alder. In 2011-a decade after Christopher's body had been buried-his badly decomposing body was found in a mortuary in Hull. It was revealed that instead of burying Christopher, the family had instead buried the body of an elderly Nigerian lady-Grace Kamara. Later, in 2014, it was revealed that the police had ordered surveillance on the family and supporters at the inquest into Christopher's death.

[5]For further discussion of deaths in custody see Athwal and Bourne (2015).

commonly applied to Black people, can have fatal consequences and prevent the recognition and treatment of certain illness by police officers. 'Because 'drug addict', 'drunk' and 'schizophrenic' are the labels police attach to Black people, they can overlook quite serious and potentially fatal diseases. Further, this legitimises the police response and, in the case of Black victims, serves to embed racial stereotypes '…ascribing to Black people stereotypical characteristics of extraordinary strength and dangerousness' (Ward and Coles 1998: 109). 'State talk', the discursive processes which the police use to misrepresent the dangers inherent in their job, including the manipulation of identities of suspects, legitimizes excessive use of force (Pemberton 2008: 238). Framing the victim as dangerous, and the police officer or wider public as in danger, detracts attention from the police and apportions blame to the victim. The disproportionality in restraint related deaths in police custody and the subsequent lack of accountability, gives the police a licence to act with 'impunity' (United Nations, cited in Dearden 2018).

The Persistence of Racism and Police Culture

The stubborn persistence of racism within the police service has been attributed to a deeply ingrained and persistent distinct occupational culture. As argued by Shearing (1981), the values embedded in the police culture act as subterranean processes in the maintenance of power. Cop culture literature is grounded in Skolnick's (1966) work on the police personality, which develops as a response to both danger and authority in the nature of police work and a pressure to get results. Police see crime fighting as their core role and as such police culture is characterised by a sense of mission and an elevated priority on crime fighting and action focused response (Reiner 2010; Loftus 2009; Holdaway 1983). From this perspective, suspicion and cynicism derive from a need to be alert to danger and crime. The police view themselves as the 'thin blue line' that safeguards social order (Reiner 2010: 120). The policing terrain is socially mapped out to establish those who pose the biggest threat to the police. These groups, have low social status and therefore limited power (Reiner 2010: 25); therefore, they are considered to be 'police property' (Lee 1981). Stereotyping is embedded in mapping the terrain and relates not only to Black and other ethnic minority groups but those on the margins of society (Webster 2008; Loftus 2009; Reiner 2010). It is argued that stereotyping is an essential part of operational policing and that 'cop culture' offers a way of coping with the occupational dangers and strengthens group loyalty (Paoline 2003: 203; Waddington 1999). However, this is problematic because stereotyping is expressed through jokes and banter, including the use of derogatory and offensive language (Smith 1985; Holdaway 1983). Waddington claims that racist language and stereotyping by police officers does not have an effect on policing practice (Waddington 1999: 109). This claim is countered by the findings of the *Stephen Lawrence Inquiry* which found that within the police service there is a tendency towards reliance on racialised stereotypes which particularly impacts upon the way that police officers deal with Black people (Macpherson 1999: 6.50). Similarly, HMIC (1997) concluded that 'there is a direct and vital link between internal culture in the way people are treated and external performance'. There is evidence to suggest that, following the reforms arising from the publication of the *Stephen Lawrence Inquiry*, both overt racist language and stereotyping continue in the safety of 'White spaces' (Loftus 2008). Whether racialised stereotypes are expressed overtly or operate covertly through racializing and criminalising narratives, Reiner (2010) views stereotyping as an inescapable fact of policing. However, as he points out, the organisation of policed populations with reference to stereotypes reflects the structure of power within society (p. 121).

There has been a recent shift in the police culture literature, from the conceptualisation of police culture as monolithic, towards a plurality of cop cultures which reflect police roles, geographical spaces and specialism (Chan 1996; Loftus 2009; Cockcroft 2013). This is driven by the diversification of the police (the inclusion of women and ethnic minorities in particular) and the globalised nature of policing. Nevertheless, there are core features of police culture that have remained untouched and continue to be pervasive both in the UK and identified globally. These traits are associated with a masculine police ethos, such as 'suspiciousness, cynicism, pessimism, conservatism and a thirst for action'

(Bowling and Sheptycki 2011: 26). Reiner (2010) proposes that it is reasonable to assume that an increasing number of women entering the police service may contribute to the dilution of the 'masculine ethos' (p. 134); however, Loftus (2009), in her ethnographic study, did not find that this was the case. Instead, she found that the insecurity at the loss of White privilege, in the face of an increasingly diverse police force and a focus on 'recognising and respecting diversity' of the public's (ibid.: 60), led to 'ressentiment'—an 'entrenched sense of resentment which becomes directed against those who possess desired goods or values' (ibid.: 82). This is expressed by one of the participants' in Loftus's research, a White police officer who expressed his dismay that heterosexual White men were becoming a 'dying breed' in the police service (Loftus 2009: 76). The resentment comes from both the expectations placed upon the police from a diverse public, based on a widely publicised reform agenda, and the fear of the erosion of White privilege within the police service itself.

There has historically been a consistent under-representation of Black and other ethnic minorities with the police service, compared to their representation within the national population. Only 1% of police officers currently serving are Black. Between 2007 and 2011, the percentage of police officers from an ethnic minority background rose from 3.9 to 4.8%; however, the rise was accounted for by 1.9% rise in Asian police officers and 1.3% defining ethnicity as mixed. The percentage of Black police officers remained at 1% with no increase during this time (Ministry of Justice 2011: 76). Both Scarman (1981) and Macpherson (1999) recommended positive action strategies to stimulate recruitment from ethnic minority communities. As pointed out by Cashmore (2002), the fact that Macpherson made the same recommendation as Scarman eighteen years previously is indicative of the little progress that had been made in the interim (Cashmore 2002: 328). Stereotyping of Black and mixed-race people has served to racialise the relationship between White police officers and their Black colleagues, as well as the public. Research into the experiences of serving ethnic minority police officers consistently reveals experiences of racism from colleagues in the form of racist banter and stereotyping (Cashmore 2001; Holdaway 1997; Smith 1985). Further, evidence from *The Secret Policeman* documentary aired in 2003 demonstrated that, four years on from *The Stephen Lawrence Inquiry Report*, racism had not been eradicated from the recruitment process.

Endemic and consistent racism is a barrier to recruitment for potential recruits from ethnic minority communities. Stone and Tuffin (2000) research garnered the views of those from an ethnic minority background on police service careers. The research involved 32 focus groups with a total of 290 respondents between the ages of 18 and 30 from a range of ethnic minority backgrounds, age groups and geographical areas. The research found that the expectations of the respondents were similar to the actual experiences reported by serving police officers. There were some positive responses in terms of the type of work carried out by the police and the potential to help and support communities. However, this was overshadowed by the perception that ethnic minority police officers would experience racism from colleagues and members of the public, that they would be isolated in a White dominated environment, and that potentially racist colleagues may not be supportive in threatening environments encountered in the course of police duties (Stone and Tuffin 2000). There remains a clear consensus in the literature that police officers from Black and Ethnic Minority backgrounds experience racism and this prevents recruitment from under represented communities (Holdaway and Barron 1997; Stone and Tuffin 2000; Cashmore 2001; Dodd 2013). The racist elements of police culture remain a significant barrier to reform in the police service. As Skolnick suggests in his seminal work on police culture, legal and formal rules on police behaviour are mediated through the organisational structure and perspective of the police (Skolnick 1966, cited in Dean 1995: 346). Training offers only temporary liberalising effects and racism may increase with prolonged service (Reiner 2010: 131). Rather than eradicating racism, the diversity agenda has created resentment towards diverse publics and towards colleagues who represent the changing face of policing and the erosion of White privilege.

The diversity agenda gained significant momentum in the public sector following the publication of the *Stephen Lawrence Inquiry Report*. The definition of institutional racism that Macpherson sets out, and which has since been adapted into the legal framework of equalities legislation, facilitates the erasure of race in the institutional context. Macpherson defines institutional racism as:

> The collective failure of an organisation to provide an appropriate and professional service to people because of their colour, culture or ethnic origin. It can be seen or detected in processes, attitudes and behaviour which amount to discrimination through unwitting prejudice, ignorance, thoughtlessness and racist stereotyping which disadvantages minority ethnic people. (Macpherson 1999: 6.34)

One of the ways in which it facilitates the erasure of race is through its colour-blind approach, on the basis of post-race logic (Garner 2010: 107). Through an emphasis on the 'unwitting' nature of racism there is an obfuscation of responsibility—'If *all are guilty, then none are guilty*' (Anthias 1999: 2.7). The post-Macpherson period has seen an almost complete erasure of the language of race within the police and institutions more broadly (see Kapoor 2011). The resulting shift towards the language of diversity, as Ahmed (2012) shows, serves as a mechanism for reproducing racism. The utility of Macphersons definition for tackling racism is limited. It is, as Garner (2010) also points out, prescriptive rather than analytical. Therefore, it does not contribute to an understanding of the processes and actions, or lack thereof, through which institutional racism operates (pp. 102–116; also see Phillips 2011). Whilst it may have ushered in a new language, it has not succeeded in ushering out racism, rather it has contributed to the process of making racism 'raceless' within the institution (see Tate 2016; Goldberg 2014). This makes its manifestations impossible to challenge through an agenda which does not use the language of race.

Race and Intersecting Oppressions

Within the criminological literature there is a divide between arguments focused on racism as an explanation for ethnic disproportionality in policing outcomes and those focused on class. Bridges (1983) argues that the structural position of Black people in the UK economy positions them in the 'urban wasteland' and it is this position that brings them into frequent contact with the police and subjects them to harsh policing regimes (Bridges 1983: 31–32). Similarly, Jefferson insists than rather because they are Black it is because they are 'young and male and "rough" working class and Black' (Jefferson 1993: 35). Black people are disproportionately represented in the lower socio-economic groups and remain disproportionately resident in 'deprived' areas (Equality and Human Rights Commission 2011; Barnard and Turner 2011). Black African and Black Caribbean (alongside other ethnic minority groups) children are twice as likely to live in poverty than White children (Platt 2009: 7). Disproportionate unemployment has been a long-term problem for the Black community in Britain. In the period October 2011–September 2012, 44.1% of young Black people (16–24 years old) were unemployed in comparison to 19.9% of their White British peers (Office for National Statistics 2013). Race inequalities persist in the education system, the impact of this on the life-chances of young Black people, in particular boys, is significant (Gillborn and Rollock 2010: 147). Indeed, the evidence suggests that growing social inequality increases the groups considered 'police property' (Loftus 2009: 159; Reiner 2010). The police express 'class contempt' to the visible poor who are both police adversary and evidence of what is wrong with society (Loftus 2009: 183). For Webster (2008), this class contempt results in the criminalisation of both the White working class and the Black the working class,. Further, the criminalisation of the working classes serves to condone middle-class crime, this both reinforces and reproduces the class hierarchy (p. 294). However, race intersects with class in different ways for the Black working classes and the White working classes within these criminalising narratives. Blackness is inextricably linked with criminality (see Chapter 2) regardless of class position. The criminalisation of Blackness places Whiteness at further proximity to crime. Particular forms of criminality are constructed as being just what Black people do. For example, this is evident in David Starkey's claim, following the August 2011 'riots', that the White rioters had taken part in the 'riots' because they had 'become Black' (Quinn 2011).

In recent decades there has been an increased upward mobility across Black and other Ethnic Minority groups (Virdee 2010: 87–89). There has also been a shift in spatial mobility with ethnic minority communities moving up the housing ladder (Harrison and Phillips 2010: 22). With consideration to Bridge's (1983) argument, that it is their position in the urban wastelands that brings Black people into contact with the police (Bridges 1983: 31–32), it can be expected that the middle-class experience of policing will be equal to that middle-class Whites. There is no empirical research to draw on in this regard, in relation to police encounters. However, Chigwada-Bailey supposes that 'a Black person of professional standing will still be treated with the same suspicion as those in the lower classes' (Chigwada-Bailey 2003: 46). Anecdotal evidence regarding stop and search, for example the Archbishop of York's revelation that he had been stopped and searched eight times (Dodd 2000) strengthens Chigwada-Bailey's assertion. This book offers empirical support for this position through the data presented in chapter seven.

There is an absence of literature pertaining to Black women's experience of the police. This is a critical gap in knowledge, particularly as the police are the gateway to the criminal justice system. Black women are increasingly disproportionately represented within the UK prison system (Lammy 2017). The nature of their contact with the police, which is currently under-researched, could have some bearing on their criminalisation. Statistically, pedestrian stop and searches on women are shown to be relatively uncommon (Clancy et al. 2001: 122[6]); gender is currently not published with the UK stop and search data. However, in the case of vehicle stops, Black women, like Black men, are more likely to be

[6]Note age of data here based on British Crime Survey Data. Gender of those stopped and searched is not routinely recorded in police statistics.

stopped than their White peers (Bowling and Phillips 2007: 947). More recently, evidence that emerged after the August 2011 UK riots shows that young women have experienced stop and search. One rioter interviewed after the August 2011 riots stated, 'there's not one police officer I feel like I like, "…" they treat us like we're shit. Do you know how many times I've been stopped and searched? I'm a girl' (Topping et al. 2011). This may indicate that there is an increasing focus on young Black women in urban areas. However, research in this regard is lacking.

In the context of victimisation, racialised stereotypes are shown to impact upon the police response towards Black women. In Britton's (2000) research, one participant recalled an occasion when her daughter was the victim of an attack at a funfair, the victim shouted to a nearby police officer for assistance; the woman's shouting was mistaken for aggression and she was wrongly arrested (Britton 2000: 704). This is consistent with other studies that show that Black women are assumed to be the aggressor when they report their victimisation. For example, research has established a link between the stereotypic view of Black women and partner justification for domestic violence (Gillum 2002: 80). Further, there is some evidence that police do not respond to Black women's reports of domestic violence on the basis that they do not need protecting (Mama 1993-note age of source). Whilst the empirical evidence is limited in regards to suspects, the evidence pertaining to Black female victims of crime suggests that race and gender operate to disadvantage Black women in their contact with the police. This book considers the intersection of race and gender for both suspects and victims of crime in Chapter 6 and contributes some knowledge to the evident gap in understanding Black and Black mixed-race women's experiences of policing.

Conclusion

Initiatives which seek to improve police-community relations have relied upon the notion that the British Policing Model operates on the principle of consent. Therefore, securing the trust of Black and ethnic minority communities has become a key goal of the police service (Macpherson 1999; May 2015). However, as argued in this chapter, the very premise of the police is rooted in the control of the racialised Other (Brogden and Ellison 2013). Further, racialised and racist policing contemporarily cannot be understood without reference to coloniality and the 'imperial linkages' (Cole 1999) which sustain narratives of the dangerous Other and inform policing strategies (e.g. increasing use of force/militarization; see Fekete 2013). The impact of this can be seen through the examples used in this chapter, pertaining to stop and search, use of force and deaths in police custody. When police racism is called out it is silenced through denial. It is either blamed upon deficient individuals or 'unwitting' institutional racism. This colour-blind approach absolves both the individual and the institution from blame. This serves to make racism raceless and perpetuates the myth that the police service is post-race.

This chapter has shown that there are significant gaps in understanding how Black and Black mixed—race people experience policing. The chapters to follow will seek to offer some insight into their experiences and perceptions of the police, drawing on interview data.

References

Ahmed, S. (2012). *On Being Included: Racism and Diversity in Institutional Life*. London: Duke University Press.

Angiolini, E. (2017). *Report of the Independent Review of Deaths and Serious Incidents in Police Custody*. London: Home office. https://www.gov.uk/government/publications/deaths-and-serious-incidents-in-police-custody. Accessed 20 January 2018.

Anthias, F. (1999). Institutional Racism, Power and Accountability. *Sociological Research Online*, 4. Available: www.socresonline.org.uk/4/lawrence/anthias.html. Accessed 13 July 2017.

Athwal, H., & Bourne, J. (2015). *Dying for Justice*. London: Institute of Race Relations.

Barkworth, J., & Murphy, K. (2016). System Contact and Procedural Justice Policing: Improving Quality of Life Outcomes for Victims of Crime. *International Review of Victimology, 22*(2), 105–122.

Barnard, H., & Turner, C. (2011). *Poverty and Ethnicity: A Review of Evidence*. York: Joseph Rowntree Foundation.

Barrett, G. A., Fletcher, S. M., & Patel, T. G. (2014). Black Minority Ethnic Communities and Levels of Satisfaction with Policing: Findings from a Study in the North of England. *Criminology and Criminal Justice, 14,* 196–215.
Bland, N., Miller, J., Quinton, P., & Britain, G. (2000). *Upping the PACE? An Evaluation of the Recommendations of the Stephen Lawrence Inquiry on Stops and Searches*. London: Home Office.
Bowling, B., & Phillips, C. (2002). *Racism, Crime and Justice*. Harlow: Longman.
Bowling, B., & Phillips, C. (2007). Disproportionate and Discriminatory: Reviewing the Evidence on Police Stop and Search. *The Modern Law Review, 70,* 936–961.
Bowling, B., Phillips, C., Campbell, A., & Docking, M. (2004). Policing and Human Rights: Eliminating Discrimination, Xenophobia, Intolerance and the Abuse of Power from Police Work. *Racism and Public Policy*. Durban, South Africa: United Nations Research Institute for Social Development.
Bowling, B., & Sheptycki, J. (2011). *Global Policing*. London: Sage.
Bradford, B., Murphy, K., & Jackson, J. (2014). Officers as Mirrors: Policing, Procedural Justice and the (Re)Production of Social Identity. *British Journal of Criminology, 54,* 527–550.
Bridges, L. (1983). Policing the Urban Wasteland. *Race & Class, 25,* 31–47.
Britton, N. J. (2000). Examining Police/Black Relations: What's in a Story? *Ethnic and Racial Studies, 23,* 692–711.
Brogden, M. (1987). The Emergence of the Police—The Colonial Dimension. *British Journal of Criminology, 27,* 4–14.
Brogden, M., & Ellison, E. (2013). *Policing in an Age of Austerity: A Postcolonial Perspective*. Abingdon: Routledge.
Cashmore, E. (2001). The Experiences of Ethnic Minority Police Officers in Britain: Under-Recruitment and Racial Profiling in a Performance Culture. *Ethnic and Racial Studies, 24,* 642–659.
Cashmore, E. (2002). Behind the Window Dressing: Ethnic Minority Police Perspectives on Cultural Diversity. *Journal of Ethnic and Migration Studies, 28,* 327–341.
Chan, J. (1996). Changing Police Culture: Policing in a Multicultural Society. *British Journal of Criminology, 36,* 109–134.
Chigwada-Bailey, R. (2003). *Black Women's Experiences of Criminal Justice: Race, Gender and Class: A Discourse on Disadvantage*. Winchester: Waterside Press.
Choongh, S. (1998). Policing the Dross: A Social Disciplinary Model of Policing. *British Journal of Criminology, 38,* 623–634.

Clancy, A., Sims, L., & Britain, G. (2001). *Ethnic Minorities' Experience of Crime and Policing: Findings from the 2000 British Crime Survey*. London: Home Office.

Cockcroft, T. (2013). *Police Culture: Themes and Concepts*. Oxon: Routledge.

Cole, B. A. (1999). Postcolonial Systems. In R. I. Mawby (Ed.), *Policing Across the World: Issues for the Twenty-First Century*. Abingdon: Routledge.

CPS. (2017). *Coroners*. (online). Available: https://www.cps.gov.uk/legal-guidance/coroners. Accessed 14 May 2018.

Crawford, A. (2007). Reassurance Policing: Feeling Is Believing. In D. J. Smith & A. Henry (Eds.), *Transformations of Policing*. Hampshire: Ashgate.

Dean, G. (1995). Police Reform: Rethinking Operational Policing. *Journal of Criminal Justice, 23*, 337–347.

Dearden, L. (2017, August 1). Metropolitan Police Use Force Disproportionately Against Black People in London, New Statistics Reveal. *The Independent*.

Dearden, L. (2018, August 27). UN Issues Warning Over Deaths of Disproportionate Number of Black People in Police Custody and 'Structural Racism' in UK. *The Independent*.

Dodd, V. (2000). Black Bishop 'Demeaned' by Police Search. *Guardian*. Available: http://www.guardian.co.uk/uk/2000/jan/24/race.world. Accessed 24 January 2017.

Dodd, V. (2002). Monkey Chants as Black Man Died 'Not Racist'. *Guardian*. Available: www.theguardian.com/uk/2002/jul/23/race.world. Accessed 23 July 2017.

Dodd, V. (2013). Black and Gay Police Officer Hounded Out of Force 'Like Enemy of the State'. *Guardian*. Available: http://www.theguardian.com/uk/2013/may/17/kevin-maxwell-gay-black-police-officer-hounded-out. Accessed 17 May 2013.

Dodd, V. (2016). UK Police Forces 'Still Abusing Stop and Search Powers'. *The Guardian*. Available: www.theguardian.com/law/2016/feb/11/uk-police-forces-still-abusing-stop-and-search-powers. Accessed 11 February 2018.

Emsley, C. (2008). The Birth and Development of the Police. In T. Newburn (Ed.), *Handbook of Policing*. Willan: Abingdon.

Equality and Human Rights Commission. (2011). *How Fair Is Britain: Equality, Human Rights and Good Relations in 2010*. London: Equality and Human Rights Commission.

Equality and Human Rights Commission. (2013). *Stop and Think Again—Towards Race Equality in Police PACE Stop and Search*. London: Equality and Human Rights Commission.

Erfani-Ghettani, R. (2015). The Defamation of Joy Gardner: Press, Police and Black Deaths in Custody. *Race & Class, 56,* 102–112.

Fekete, L. (2013). Total Policing: Reflections from the Frontline. *Race & Class, 54,* 65–76.

Gabbidon, S. (2010). *Race, Ethnicity, Crime, and Justice: An International Dilemma*. Thousand Oaks, CA: Sage.

Garner, S. (2010). *Racisms an Introduction*. London: Sage.

Gayle, D. (2015). Black People 'Three Times More Likely' to Be Tasered. *Guardian*. Available: www.theguardian.com/uk-news/2015/oct/13/black-people-three-times-more-likely-to-have-taser-used-against-them. Accessed 13 October 2017.

Gillborn, D., & Rollock, N. (2010). Education. In A. Bloch & J. Solomos (Eds.), *Race and Ethnicity in the 21st Century*. Hampshire: Palgrave Macmillan.

Gillum, T. L. (2002). Exploring the Link Between Stereotypic Images and Intimate Partner Violence in the African American Community. *Violence Against Women, 8,* 64–86.

Goldberg, D. T. (2014). *Sites of Race: Conversations with Susan Searls Giroux*. Cambridge: Polity.

Hargreaves, J., Husband, H., & Linehan, C. (2017). *Police Powers and Procedures, England and Wales, Year Ending 31 March 2017*. London: Home Office. www.gov.uk/government/uploads/system/uploads/attachment_data/file/658099/police-powers-procedures-mar17-hosb2017.pdf.

Harrison, M., & Phillips, D. (2010). Housing and Neighbourhoods: A UK and European Perspective. In A. Bloch & J. Solomos (Eds.), *Race and Ethnicity in the 21st Century*. Hampshire: Palgrave Macmillan.

Henry, A. (2007). Policing and Ethnic Minorities. In D. J. Smith & A. Henry (Eds.), *Transformations of Policing*. Hampshire: Ashgate.

Her Majesty's Inspectorate of Constabulary. (1997). *Winning the Race: Policing Plural Communities*. London: Home Office.

Holdaway, S. (1983). *Inside the British Police: A Force at Work*. Oxford: Blackwell.

Holdaway, S. (1997). Responding to Racialised Divisions Within the Workforce—The Experience of Black and Asian Police Officers in England. *Ethnic and Racial Studies, 20,* 69–90.

Holdaway, S., & Barron, A. M. (1997). *Resigners? The Experience of Black and Asian Police Officers*. Basingstoke: Macmillan.

Home Office. (2011). *Code of Practice for the Exercise by Police Officers of Statutory Powers of Stop and Search*. London: Home Office.

Home Office. (2014). *Stop and Search: Theresa May Announces Reform of Police Stop and Search*. Available: www.gov.uk/government/news/stop-and-search-theresa-may-announces-reform-of-police-stop-and-search. Accessed 30 April 2017.

Home Office. (2015). *Police Powers and Procedures England and Wales Year Ending 31 March 2015*. London: Home Office. www.gov.uk/government/publications/police-powers-and-procedures-england-and-wales-year-ending-31-march-2015. Accessed 1 February 2018.

Institute for Race Relations. (1991). *Deadly Silence: Black Deaths in Custody*. London: Institute for Race Relations.

Institute for Race Relations. (2003). *Roger Sylvester: Police Condemned for Black Death*. Available: www.irr.org.uk/news/roger-sylvester-police-condemned-for-black-death/. Accessed 21 January 2018.

Jefferson, T. (1993). The Racism of Criminalization: Policing and the Reproduction of the Criminal Other. In L. Gelsthorpe (Ed.), *Minority Ethnic Groups in the Criminal Justice System*. Cambridge: University of Cambridge.

Jones, T. (2011). The Accountability of Policing. In T. Newburn (Ed.), *Handbook of Policing*. Abingdon: Taylor & Francis.

Kapoor, N. (2011). The Advancement of Racial Neoliberalism in Britain. *Ethnic and Racial Studies, 36*(6), 1028–1046.

Kristina, M. (2009). Public Satisfaction with Police: The Importance of Procedural Justice and Police Performance in Police-Citizen Encounters. *Australian and New Zealand Journal of Criminology, 42,* 159–178.

Lammy, D. (2017). *The Lammy Review: An Independent Review into the Treatment of, and Outcomes for Black, Asian and Minority Ethnic Individuals in the Criminal Justice System*.

Lee, J. A. (1981). Some Structural Aspects of Police Deviance in Relations with Minority Groups. In C. Shearing (Ed.), *Organisational Police Deviance*. Toronto: Butterworth.

Lentz, S. A., & Chaires, R. H. (2007). The Invention of Peel's Principles: A Study of Policing 'Textbook' History. *Journal of Criminal Justice, 35,* 69–79.

Loftus, B. (2008). Dominant Culture Interrupted: Recognition, Resentment and the Politics of Change in an English Police Force. *British Journal of Criminology, 48,* 756–777.

Loftus, B. (2009). *Police Culture in a Changing World*. New York: Oxford University Press.

Long, L., & Joseph-Salisbury, R. (2018). Black Mixed-Race Men's Perceptions and Experiences of the Police. *Ethnic and Racial Studies*. https://doi.org/10.1080/01419870.2017.1417618.

Longstaff, A., Willer, J., Chapman, J., Czarnomski, S., & Graham, J. (2015). *Neighbourhood Policing: Past, Present and Future: A Review of the Literature*. London: Police Foundation.

MacPherson, W. (1999). *The Stephen Lawrence Inquiry: Report of an Inquiry*. London: The Stationary Office. Available: http://webarchive.nationalarchives.gov.uk/20130814142233/. http://www.archive.official-documents.co.uk/document/cm42/4262/4262.htm. Accessed 4 January 2017.

Mama, A. (1993). Black Women and Police: A Place Where the Law Is Not Upheld. In W. James & C. Harris (Eds.), *Inside Babylon: The Caribbean diaspora in Britain*. London: Verso.

May, T. (2015, July 23). Policing by Consent Is a Principle We Must All Fight for. Available: https://www.gov.uk/government/speeches/home-secretary-announces-review-of-deaths-in-policy-custody. Accessed 24 July 2015.

Miller, J. (2000). *Profiling Populations Available for Stops and Searches*. London: Home Office.

Mills, C. W. (1997). *The Racial Contract*. New York: Cornell University Press.

Ministry of Justice. (2011). *Statistics on Race and the Criminal Justice System 2010: A Ministry of Justice Publication Under Section 95 of the Criminal Justice Act 1991*. Available: http://www.justice.gov.uk/statistics/criminal-justice/race. Accessed 5 November 2014.

Murphy, K. (2013). Policing at the Margins: Fostering Trust and Cooperation Among Ethnic Minority Groups. *Journal of Policing, Intelligence and Counter Terrorism, 8*, 184–199.

Murphy, K. (2015). Does Procedural Justice Matter to Youth? Comparing Adults' and Youths' Willingness to Collaborate with Police. *Policing & Society, 25*, 53–76.

Murphy, K., & Cherney, A. (2011). Fostering Cooperation with the Police: How Do Ethnic Minorities in Australia Respond to Procedural Justice-Based Policing? *Australian and New Zealand Journal of Criminology, 44*, 235–257.

Office for National Statistics. (2013). *Unemployment Numbers and Rates for 16-24 Year Olds Within Ethnic Groups*. http://www.ons.gov.uk/ons/search/index.html?newquery=ethnicity. Accessed 19 May 2017.

Paoline, E. A. (2003). Taking Stock: Toward a Richer Understanding of Police Culture. *Journal of Criminal Justice, 31*, 199–214.

Pemberton, S. (2008). Demystifying Deaths in Police Custody: Challenging State Talk. *Social and Legal Studies, 17*, 237–262.

Phillips, C. (2011). Institutional Racism and Ethnic Inequalities: An Expanded Multilevel Framework. *Journal of Social Policy, 40*(1), 173–192. https://doi.org/10.1017/S0047279410000565.

Platt, L. (2009). *Ethnicity and Child Poverty*. London: Department for Work and Pensions.

Quinn, B. (2011). David Starkey Claims 'the Whites Have Become Black'. *Guardian*. Available: www.guardian.co.uk/uk/2011/aug/13/david-starkey-claims-Whites-black. Accessed 13 August 2017.

Quinton, P., & Morris, J. (2008). *Neighbourhood Policing: The Impact of Piloting and Early National Implementation*. London: Home Office.

Quinton, P., Bland, N., & Miller, J. (2000). *Police Stops, Decision-Making and Practice*. London: Home Office.

Reiner, R. (2010). *The Politics of the Police*. Oxford: Oxford University Press.

Reith, C. (1956). *A New Study of Police History*. Edinburgh: Oliver and Boyd.

Rowe, M. (2004). *Policing*. Willan: Race and Racism Devon.

Sanders, A., & Young, R. (2008). Policing Powers. In T. Newburn (Ed.), *Handbook of Policing*. Willan: Devon.

Scarman, L. (1981). *The Scarman Report: The Brixton Disorders 10–12 April 1981*. London: HMSO.

Shearing, C. D. (1981). Subterranean Processes in the Maintenance of Power: An Examination of the Mechanisms Coordinating Police Action. *Canadian Review of Sociology, 18*(3), 283–298.

Sivanandan, A. (1982). *A Different Hunger: Writings on Black Resistance*. London: Pluto Press.

Skolnick, J. (1966). *Justice Without Trial: Law Enforcement in a Democratic Society*. New York: Wiley.

Smith, D. J. (1985). *Police and People in London*. Aldershot: Gower.

Stone, V., & Pettigrew, N. (2000). *The Views of the Public on Stops and Searches*. London: Home Office.

Stone, V., & Tuffin, R. (2000). *Attitudes of People from Minority Ethnic Communities Towards a Career in the Police Service*. London: Home Office.

Storch, R. D., & Engels, F. (1975). The Plague of the Blue Locusts. *International Review of Social History, 20,* 61–90.

Sunshine, J., & Tyler, T. R. (2003). The Role of Procedural Justice and Legitimacy in Shaping Public Support for Policing. *Law and Society Review, 37,* 513–548.

Tate, S. A. (2016). 'I Can't Quite Put My Finger on It': Racism's Touch. *Ethnicities, 16,* 68–85.

Topping, A., Diski, R., & Clifton, H. (2011, December 9). The Women Who Rioted. *Guardian*.

Tyler, T. R. (2006). *Why People Obey the Law*. Princeton: Princeton University Press.

Tyler, T. R. (2003). Procedural Justice, Legitimacy, and the Effective Rule of Law. *Crime and Justice: A Review of Research, 30,* 283–357.

Tyler, T. R., & Huo, Y. (2002). *Trust in the Law: Encouraging Public Cooperation with the Police and Courts.* New York: Russell Sage Foundation.

Tyler, T. R., & Lind, E. A. (1992). A Relational Model of Authority in Groups. *Advances in Experimental Social Psychology, 25,* 115–192.

Virdee, S. (2010). The Continuing Significance of 'Race', Racism, Anti-racist Politics and Labour Markets. In A. Bloch & J. Solomos (Eds.), *Race and Ethnicity in the 21st Century.* Hampshire: Palgrave Macmillan.

Waddington, P. (1999). Police (Canteen) Sub-culture: An Appreciation. *British Journal of Criminology, 39,* 287–309.

Waddington, P. A. J., Stenson, K., & Don, D. (2004). In Proportion Race, and Police Stop and Search. *British Journal of Criminology, 44,* 889–914.

Wainwright, M. (2000). Christopher Alder Unlawfully Killed. *Guardian.* Available: http://www.guardian.co.uk/uk/2000/aug/25/race.world1?INTC-MP=SRCH. Accessed 25 August 2000.

Wainwright, M. (2003). Police Cleared of Station Death. *Guardian.* Available: http://www.guardian.co.uk/uk/2003/jun/25/prisonsandprobation.martin-wainwright?INTCMP=SRCH. Accessed 25 June 2003.

Ward, T., & Coles, D. (1998). Investigating Suspicious Deaths in Police Custody. In A. Liebling (Ed.), *Deaths of Offenders: The Hidden Side of Justice.* Waterside: Winchester.

Webster, C. (2008). Marginalized White Ethnicity, Race and Crime. *Theoretical Criminology, 12,* 293–312.

Part II

Erasing Race: Policing Diversity

4

'Babylon Remove the Chain, Now They're Using the Brain': Race and the Perpetual Suspect

The finding of the Stephen Lawrence Inquiry that the Metropolitan Police Service (MPS) were institutionally racist brought about a significant programme of reform for the police service and other institutions on a national scale. However, the efficacy of the reforms has been limited (Foster et al. 2005; Loftus 2009; Rollock 2009). This chapter will consider how Black and Black-mixed-race people experience policing contemporarily in the Post-Macpherson era. Through narratives of the policed it develops a counter story to the dominant police narrative which denies the existence of racism. Utilising the concept of the 'White gaze' (Yancy 2008; Fanon 1986) it illuminates the construction of Black bodies as the perpetual suspect. Through an analysis of their experiences of over-policing through surveillance, stop and search, arrests and excessive use of force, this chapter argues that in the post-Macpherson period very little has changed in relation to the racist effects of policing.

L. J. Long, *Perpetual Suspects*, Palgrave Studies in Race, Ethnicity, Indigeneity and Criminal Justice, https://doi.org/10.1007/978-3-319-98240-3_4

Planting the Seed of Fear

For Black and Black mixed-race people their negative experiences of policing begin in childhood-this was a consistent feature across research participants recollections of their encounters with the police. The awareness of police presence in the everyday context is striking, particularly for those who grew up in 'racially othered spaces'.[1] Several participants also recalled childhood memories of being stopped and questioned by the police. Childhood memories of being treated as suspect were recalled by both Marcus and Bianca;

> I was probably seven or eight my brother was probably ten or eleven and we had a bag with fish and chips in it and we got stopped [laughs] and searched and they took our fish and chip shop [bag]. (Marcus, 44, Black, British-born, male)

> I was stopped on my bike by a police officer and asked questions such as 'is this your bike?'… 'Can you prove it's your bike?'… 'Well have you got a receipt on you?' [laughs]. What a ridiculous question. 'Well I'm going to have to radio in to the station to see if this checks out'. (Bianca, 25, Black mixed-race, British-born, female)

These encounters occurred two decades apart, this highlights that little had changed in the intervening years. The laughter which punctuates both accounts reveals an incredulity at the treatment of children as suspect in the absence of any misbehaviour. Suspicion of Black bodies and the treatment of a child as suspect is counter to dominant societal narratives of childhood innocence and vulnerability. However, as Bernstein (2011) argues, these narratives were developed in relation to the White child. The age at which a child can be held criminally responsible for their actions in the UK is ten years old; however, children are often treated as criminally suspect before they reach this age. Goff et al. (2014)

---

[1]The term racially othered spaces is used here to refer to spaces considered to be spaces occupied by the black (and ethnic minority) Other. These are spaces which have acquired the shapes (Ahmed 2007: 156), or the skin, of those who live there and resultantly are imagined as dangerous, criminogenic spaces.

find that Black boys are not afforded the privilege of innocence. They are often perceived as older and seen to have a greater culpability for their actions than their White peers. This is evident in participants' accounts, for both young black boys and girls.

Overt racist abuse did not feature prominently in participants' experiences of police contact. The use of overt racist language is less prevalent in the Post-Macpherson context. This is one area in which police reform has had some positive impact (Foster et al. 2005). A comparison between the experiences of participants from different generations highlights these differences. Some of the older participants who took part in this research and who were children in the 1970s, were able to recall overt racism, harassment and gratuitous brutality in their encounters with the police. Levi (50, Black, British-born, male), recalled an occasion when he was racially harassed by two police officers in a patrol car when he was around nine years old;

> The police pulled up in a car, called me a coon and told me if I ever ran away from them they'd run over my legs. I was a little kid and I was pretty sort of like wow!

The experience understandably left Levi, then a child, feeling '*afraid*'. However, he did not attribute meaning to this encounter until his adult years;

> It's only as time passed on you would realise what it was about. They was actually planting the seed of fear in the children while they're young. You know it's only as time pass on and you look back and you say wow… It's a deep thing this power thing.

In this account the use of overt racist language, directed towards a child, and the threat of physical violence, underlines Levi's presumed racial propensity towards criminality. The threat of punishment is utilised to exert discipline and control. Whilst overt racist language is not a feature of participants' more recent experiences of police contact, the racialised power dynamics, inherent in the surveillance and control of children identified as 'police property' (Lee 1981), operate through 'social disciplinary' means of policing (Choongh 1998), which informally and routinely subjugate Black bodies. Levi's conclusion that police encounters with children 'plant the seed of fear' poetically elucidates the disciplining function of exposure to routine surveillance and control.

For Levi, his experience challenged his expectations of the police. He described being brought up to '*respect them*'. Also, there was one community police officer who was well known to the children in the local area who had already gained Levi's respect by '*getting on*' with them:

> There was a community officer that used to play football with us, and cricket. So, it just sort of left me a bit confused but that was the first time I had that sort of wait a minute. Cause, you were brought up to, say police officers, you respect them and then something like that happens. It just sort of like, it just confuses things. (Levi, 50, Black, British-born, male)

The confusion that he described is reflective of a broader emerging theme, that treatment as suspect was inconsistent with participant's expectations that the police would help and protect them. These expectations were developed through the family/parents inculcating a respect for the police in them, and also being exposed to positive police contact in primary years through school initiatives;

> I can remember in primary school the police talking to us about how to cross a road with demonstrations and maps of roads and vans and cars and traffic lights and all sorts of proper looking things. And I can remember going to see police horses and I remember a police dog coming to the school and you know like grabbing somebody's arm, not one of the pupils it was one of the police men and showing you what they do, there needs to be more of that. (Cynthia, 42, Black, British-born, female)

> Don't forget we were taught at school I gotta trust Mr Bobby. (Thomas, 55, Black, British-born, male)

These reflections suggest that encounters with the police in childhood have the potential to positively shape trust and confidence in the police. However, negative experiences have a long-lasting effect on perceptions of the police among black and black mixed-race young people.

When there is an incongruence between expectations of the police and their behaviour, it irrevocably alters their impression and sets the tone for their relationship with the police into adulthood;

> By the age of fourteen/ sixteen you did not trust Mr Bobby [laughs]. ...What you read about, what your friends told you about, you hear it every day on the news something untoward because of Mr Policeman. (Thomas)

> As you grow older you tend to find a lot of people who have gone through their own experiences and every one shares each other's experiences and you realise that the police ... they are not doing what they are supposed to do yea. (Levi)

The shift in the perception of the police from trustworthy to not trustworthy is shaped through a mixture of personal experience, exposure to the experiences of peers and, to some extent, high profile incidents in the news.

Another significant experience which impacts upon trust and confidence in the police is arrest. A number of the participants in this research had experienced arrest during their early teenage years. Further, in most of these cases no criminal charges were brought. This is significant as it suggests that arrest is used to effect social control, rather than crime control. Phillip, a 45-year-old African man who came to the UK as a young child, recollected his first arrest at the age of '*about thirteen or fourteen*'. Phillip recalled that he was '*shoulder barged* by another '*White*' teenager resulting in a fight. A passing policeman grabbed both parties by '*the scruff of their neck*' arrested them and took them to the police station in a police car. No charges were brought and Phillip was returned home to his parents later that day. Phillip was a recent migrant at the time of his arrest and one of the only Black children in the town. The police failed to take into account that Phillip had been the victim of an unprovoked attack to which he had reacted. As the perpetrator was White, the threat that is fixed in the Black body rendered him suspect (also, see Yancy 2012). Following the incident, the police frequently parked in the street where Phillip lived;

> When I walked past they'd say to me 'are you keeping out of trouble?' which was clearly an indication that they were keeping an eye on me you know. (Phillip, 45, Black, African male-resident in UK from age 10)

Despite being released without charge, the police made Phillip aware that they knew who he was and that they would be watching him. His Blackness made him a conspicuous presence in a White space. For Phillip, and other participants with similar stories, the denial of childhood occurs through their treatment as suspect. The threat is embodied in their blackness, even in the absence of deviance or criminality.

It is not only Black boys whose childhood is denied through racialised police contact. Some of the women who took part in this research, specifically those who grew up in racially othered spaces, had experienced arrest at a young age. Bianca was arrested at the age of thirteen when she reported a crime committed against her. She attended the police station with her mother to report being assaulted by an adult, the mother of another child from her school, when she got off the school bus. When she arrived at the police station to report the assault, her assailant had already reported the incident. Bianca was arrested and held in a cell at the police station. She reflected upon this experience;

> I'd been attacked by this woman… and I'm sat in a cell. Whoa, what? She attacked me, I'm like thirteen and I'm sat in the cell. And she was sat in the cell as well but she's an adult. I just felt that they made that assumption that what she [a White, woman] was saying was how it happened; therefore, this thirteen-year-old child is a criminal.

Bianca's sense that the police perceived her as the offender is instructive of the ways in which the Black victim is often misrepresented as criminal, particularly when the offender is White (also, found in Macpherson 1999). The racialisation of crime and criminality produces Black bodies as inherently criminogenic and in need of surveillance and control. In this context they become the (Un)Victim (see Chapter 5). Bianca was later released and the charges that had been made against her were dropped. However, this experience, which was discordant with her expectations, influenced her perceptions of the police;

> [I] didn't expect that to happen to me, didn't expect that of the police. We'd grown up from primary school, told that they're here to look after you and serve and protect you, and my first experience, I was taken in. And before that I'd never really seen them do any good for me... I've never had that comparison to weigh it up. So, I feel a bit abandoned by the police. (Bianca, 25, Black mixed-race, British-born, female)

Again, as for the young men whose experiences are discussed earlier in this section, Bianca's account suggests that one negative encounter with the police, can undermine the trust and confidence in them, instilled through the family and education, particularly when this is reified by the absence of a lack of positive comparison at an individual or community level. These early experiences are significant in understanding the demonstrable low levels of trust and confidence in the police. By their teenage years several participants had already concluded, based on their experiences, that the police were not there to help and protect them.

Policing Suspect Bodies

Stop and Search

Despite its prominence in political and academic debates on police and community relations, the issue of stop and search was surprisingly unremarkable in participant's narratives. There is an evident normalisation of being stopped by the police in the lives of heavily policed populations. The routine nature of stop and search in the every-day may explain why some participants did not recall this type of police contact unless prompted to do so. The extent of this normalisation is evident in Earl's account of his teenage years;

> If we go into the city centre we are being stopped, if we're walking from school we are being stopped, if we are out after a certain time we are being stopped, wherever we go we seem to be being stopped so it got to a stage where I no longer saw police because I see them so regular. (Earl, 54, Black, British-born, male)

The routine nature of being stopped by the police, for Black and Black mixed-race men in particular, underlines its disciplinary function in the policing of racialised bodies. It is a common perception that the police use '*excuses*' to constitute grounds for a stop (see also, Sharp and Atherton 2007). A lawful stop and search requires that the police officer has a 'reasonable ground' for the suspicion, based on objective factors e.g. intelligence or a description of the person, rather than individual factors such as race or gender. However, participants were often unable to identify objective grounds for their treatment as suspect, which led them to conclude that race was a factor in their treatment as suspect.

> They said that they were looking for two lads who'd done a burglary. Not sure I believed it. It was my area. I think if there was a burglary I would have heard about it and they would have had to have had a description of two guys, 6ft 4, one Black, one mixed-race. I don't think there's that many pairs going around like that in the area. (Lee, 23, Black mixed-race, British-born, male)

This account reveals one of the ways in which racial profiling operates through police discretion in stop and search. Lee described the area in which he lived as having a few Black families but not a '*massive community*'. In White spaces, Black bodies appear as '*bodies out of place*'. The use of police discretion to determine which bodies are suspect relies upon stereotypical constructions of Black male bodies as embodying the criminal threat. These bodies are read as a site of danger in the collective police imagination and this legitimates police suspicion of them.

Particular forms of criminality are heavily racialised, from the Black mugger of the 1970s, to the drug dealers and gangsters of today. Through the 'White gaze' (Yancy 2008; Fanon 1986), the Black body is interpellated as the criminal other. These criminal stereotypes are perceived to influence stop and search decisions, this is evident in Robert's perception of his first experience of being stopped and searched;

> I was 19[years old] and I was waiting for one of my friends. It was winter so I had on my big parka coat with fur lining and I had the hood up because it was cold. The police pulled up and basically asked me what

> I was doing, why I was waiting there. I just said I was waiting for my friend. They asked me if I'd ever been in trouble with the police before and they asked me who my friend was and why I was waiting for him...I didn't think I looked like criminal. I was dressed quite fashionably and I just thought why are they asking me? They were probably expecting me to be waiting for drugs or something. (Robert, 27, Black mixed-race, British-born, male)

Robert had not grown up in an area with a heavy police presence and this was his first experience of being stopped by the police—relatively later than those who had grown up in racially othered spaces. He described never having to be 'concerned' about the police in his younger years, believing that they 'protect us'. However, in the absence of a convincing objective ground for police suspicion of him, Robert is forced to confront himself anew through the 'White gaze'. This is compounded when the subject feels that they are 'not doing anything' and the police explanation simply does not make sense;

> At the time I was a bit shook up and I was really confused because I really wasn't causing trouble at that time. I can remember that probably changed my perception. it gave me an awareness of how I thought other people might see me. (Lee)

> I always hate to think that's [race] the reason why. You always say to yourself it can't be that reason, it's got to be something else... when you look at it and take everything else that's the only thing that it could have been. (Robert)

In both of these accounts, racism is not the first explanation that the participants look to in order to understand why they are considered suspect. However, as argued by Fanon (1986), when seemingly rational explanations cease to make sense the individual is forced to encounter themselves through the eyes of another. This finding is contrary to the police view that Black people play the race-card to their advantage in their dealings with the police (see Loftus 2009: 47–48). Conversely, racism was the last explanation considered, and even then tentatively so, after considering the other possible reasons.

Frequency of stop and search declines with advancing age. However, car stops were still experienced by participants' in the 30+ age bracket, albeit occasionally rather than routinely. The changing frequency is attributed to lifestyle changes such as no longer driving at night, changes to working patterns or having children in the car;

> Once I hit my 30s going forward, there wasn't that when you are out and about driving your car. Some of those social activities as well I'm not out and about late at night… that frequency is just not there now because I'm busy ferrying my kids around to their sports activities [laughs]. Dads taxis… (Andrew, 41, Black mixed-race, British-born, male)

Andrew, is a professional male who has moved from the racially othered area where he grew up, to the 'White' suburbs. Further, his work is now during the day time and he often has children in the car with him. As highlighted by Bowling and Phillips (2007), structural inequalities determine availability for stop and search through postcode/area, school exclusion, unemployment or employment in night time or shift work (pp. 946–948). For these reasons he is less likely to be available to be present in racially othered space where the police focus their resources. However, for some of the other participants car stops were a regular occurrence.

Police powers to stop a car are subject to less guidance than stop and search powers and therefore less scrutiny.[2] Research suggests that Black people are more likely to be subjected to routine car stops (see Chapter 3). In the absence of procedural guidelines governing this practice, car stops are left entirely to the discretion of the police officer.

> Every time I have been stopped in my car I don't see why they have stopped me. This guy [police officer] who told me that my exhaust was hanging down… I just agreed with him but there was nothing wrong with my car. (Jean, 40, Black, African, male)

---

[2]In the UK The Road Traffic Act simply states 'A person driving a motor vehicle on a road must stop the vehicle on being required to do so by a constable in uniform' (Road Traffic Act 1988; Sec. 163.1).

> They ask, is this your car? I just turn it into a joke because I've done nothing wrong. They give you a producer of course and you produce it [documents] and that's it. (Phillip, 45, Black, African, male)

As with stop and search, the absence of a legitimate reason for a car stop fuels mistrust of the police, and the subject of the stop is forced to question the motivation for police suspicion. The reliance on police discretion in the execution of policing functions is problematic, particularly where procedural guidance is subject to interpretation as to the nature of suspicion, or where this is lacking, as is the case for traffic stops. As Andrew stated, '*It's that inconsistency which is quite worrying. I don't know anybody else that's white that's been stopped twice in a night*' (41, Black mixed-race, British-born, male). When a clear, objective reason for the stop is not evident to the subject, the basis of suspicion is perceived to arise from the police recourse to stereotypes of black propensity to criminality.

Use of Force

Whilst use of force in recent times is generally by way of restraint, historically Black people have been the target of more overt forms of police brutality, as documented throughout the 1960s and 1970s (Hunte 1966; Institute for Race Relations 1979). For some of the older participants', their earliest experiences of policing included violence. Marcus recalled being arrested at the age of fourteen;

> I got stopped by the police and the policeman says 'well where are you going?' and I said 'I'm just going home, I live on [name] road just up there' and he punched me ... and he threw me in the back of the van and I got taken to the police station. (Marcus, 44, Black, British-born, male)

At the time of his arrest Marcus did not know the reason for this violent arrest. Following the incident, his parents complained. Marcus was interviewed at home along with his whole family '*as though we'd done something wrong*'. Similarly, Earl recalled an aggressive encounter with the police when he and his friends were caught throwing snowballs at a bus;

> I think the way the police dealt it was well over aggressive and the fact that I was twelve… And the way they pinned us to the wall and spoke to us and dealt with us was just atrocious. (Earl, 54, Black, British-born, male)

Both of these experiences occurred at a time when police brutality as a means of 'justice on the streets' (Weinberger 1995), was largely accepted. This was acknowledged by Thomas and Earl;

> It probably wouldn't be allowed today, but back in them days it was a lot harsher, you know. The police did give you a kick up your arse and the police did grab you roughly and throw you about a little bit. (Thomas, 54, Black, British-born, male)

> I think now, in 2014, if a young person was dealt with a police officer like that he would be reprimanded. (Earl, 54, Black, British-born, male)

The changing attitudes towards use of force and police brutality, reflected in these accounts, mean that overt brutality is no longer as common as in the 1970s and 1980s. The legal test for use of force is reasonable, proportionate and necessary (College of Policing 2013). As with other areas of policing e.g. stop and search, the police officers use of discretion to determine when force is necessary, is shaped through racialised stereotypes. Dominant stereotypes of Black people link them with crime, violence, mental illness, lower class background and hyper-masculinities. These stereotypes justify the police perception of an elevated risk of harm and subsequent perceived necessity of force in order to restrain a suspect (Angiolini 2017; Pemberton 2008; Ward and Coles 1998). This is evident through disproportionality in the use of force (see Chapter 3). The danger embodied in phenotypical signs of Blackness, legitimates excessive use of police force to control and punish the dangerous body. Andrew recalled a particularly memorable car stop which he described as '*harrowing*';

> My Mrs was in the car to the side of me and then me little one, my daughter was in the back… next thing you know a car sped around… it sped around the cul-de-sac, and it drove right up to the front of me and four, what can be described as burly White men jumped out and

> grabbed me and dragged me out of the car and told me to get over the car and put my hands over the car, padded me down, checked all under my car, tyres, checked in my car, checked in the back, asked me who was in the car with me.... it was an unmarked car that kind of came so I didn't know what were going on. (Andrew, 41, Black mixed-race, British-born, male)

After subjecting Andrew and his family to this ordeal the officers in question further inconvenienced him by imposing a requirement for him to produce his car documents at a police station—'*they made a point of giving me a producer as well*'. This measure which inconveniences the suspect is retributive, communicating that the lack of evidence does not prove an absence of criminality. Retributive measures, outside of crime control and due process, serve as a reminder that those considered 'police property' are under surveillance.

The British police are not routinely armed, unlike their American counterparts. However, there has been an increasingly militarised approach to policing, developed around the control of the Other (Fekete 2013). One of the measures in this increasing militarization is the police use of Taser. As with other measures of control, Black people are more likely to be subjected to the use of Taser in the UK. Black people are three times more likely to be the subject of Taser use-between 2010 and 2015, 12% of all discharge of Taser were towards Black people. The statistics also raise concerns about the increasing use of Taser against children (Gayle 2015). Described as 'less-lethal' force its increasing availability, and consequent increasing use, has resulted in the Taser being attributed as a factor in restraint related deaths (Bunyan 2015). Derek, had experienced incapacitation by taser and talked about this in his interview. Derek, in this case, was not the suspect. However, he had attended the home of his children, after his former partner had called him in distress as her house was surrounded by armed police. At the time of the incident Derek's soen was serving a prison sentence. The police were looking for another suspect and had linked Derek's son with the suspect. He described what happened when he arrived outside and asked the police what they were doing at the property;

> All of a sudden I get jumped by all five officers, so they've jumped me and I'm going like this 'what do you think you are doing?', 'what do you think you are doing?', 'what you doing'? All of a sudden one of them says 'let him go' and they've all backed off yea, and the man stood there and shot me in the chest with the Taser gun and dropped me to the floor…

The deployment of a Taser is legally justifiable by trained officers when there is an assessed threat of serious violence. Derek's account, that he was outnumbered five officers to one, suggests that the use of Taser in this situation not justified by the threat posed. Derek continued;

> …one of them there, he's going 'put your fucking arms out, put your fucking arms out'. And in my head I'm saying how the fuck do you expect me to do that when he's still got his finger on the trigger yea, I can't fucking move what the fuck do you expect and I'm saying all of this in my head, I said it three times, that's how long this man had his finger on the trigger. (Derek, 46, Black, British-born, male)

In this account, the police officer appears to have kept his finger on the trigger for longer than was necessary in order to achieve incapacitation. This is particularly concerning, the use of a Taser in a coercive or punitive manner amounts to torture which constitutes a breach of fundamental human rights (Smith 2009). Whilst this is just one experience, it reflects a broader pattern of excessive use of restraint techniques in encounters with black men, with Taser being the most recent concern (Gayle 2015) in a much longer history of brutalising policing.

Derek recalled that it was a wet day and after being incapacitated he was on the floor in handcuffs, he asked to be stood up. This request resulted in an onslaught of verbal abuse from one of the police officers;

> look at you, the fucking big man sat on the floor begging to be picked up right, I tell you what if you were my dad I'd be fucking ashamed of you, you are a fucking disgrace to this world, you're horrible, you're an awful person.

When Derek is contained and the threat that he embodies is no more, he is verbally degraded. Whilst the police officer does not overtly recourse to racialised language in this exchange, the metonym of the 'big man' is associated with stereotypes of Black masculinity. These stereotypes of the 'big Black man' construct Black male bodies as possessing superhuman strength which requires excessive force to contain. The 'big Black man' image provides the rationale for use of force which is disproportionate to the threat posed, this is undoubtedly a contributing factor in the disproportionate use of excessive force and restraint towards Black and Black mixed-race men.

'Us vs Them'

There was a commonly held perception, amongst participants, that the police service is racist. This is a significant factor in understanding why Black and Black mixed-race people describe their relationship to the police as '*Us vs Them*'. The extent to which they understand police racism to be a problem for them as individuals varies based on personal experience and level of exposure to routine policing. This perception was particularly pertinent for those who were residents of, or had grown up in, racially othered spaces. Overt racism by police officers, including the use of racial slurs, was almost wholly absent in the accounts of police encounters in the post-Macpherson period. However, covert or 'invisible' racism was evident to participants through comparison with the experiences of their peers. Communal narratives are based on shared experiences in common. These communal narratives, combined with personal experience, both validate and reinforce the perception that Black and Black mixed-race people cannot trust the police. Robert highlights the significance of shared experiences;

> My own combined experiences but also the experiences that friends have also told me… they've all kind of added up together to make me think actually, you know, I don't know if I trust you. (Robert, 27, Black mixed-race, British-born, male)

In addition to recalling the shared experience of friends and acquaintances, some drew upon the experiences of people who they did not know but had been made aware of through news reporting of high profile policing incidents. For example, participants made reference to high profile cases including the police shooting of Mark Duggan, the death in custody of Christopher Alder, and the failed investigation into murder of Black teenager Stephen Lawrence. This finding is consistent with the findings of *Reading the Riots* (Lewis et al. 2011), in which participants drew upon their knowledge of and empathy with high profile cases to express their anger at police. High profile cases can illuminate police racism and make it visible to those who have not experienced it. Alice spoke about feeling 'happy' when high profile cases of police racism were discussed in the media because it made her experiences appear more believable to others;

> My White friends don't understand how I feel but when they highlight it on the news you sort of feel happy that is out there so people do know that it [racism] does exist. (Alice, 38, Black mixed-race, British born, female)

These shared experiences reveal to the racialised Other that their experiences are different to those of their White friends and acquaintances. The perception that White people have more favourable experiences of the police than Black and Black mixed-race people was reflected by several participants;

> Listening to a lot of other people's stories you realise, especially when you've got a lot of Black friends and you've got a lot of White friends, you start to think well why are all the Black friends having all the problems whereas the White friends don't? (Marcus, 44, Black, British-born, male)

> I've got White friends who've never ever been stopped and questioned by the police that look a lot more dodgy than I do. (Robert, 27, Black mixed-race, British-born, male)

> It was as profound speaking to White people who hadn't been stopped and searched. I think that was as enlightening for me as speaking to Black people. (Lee, 23, Black mixed-race, British-born, male)

These shared experiences and the comparison in and between peer groups serves to not only reinforce a communal narrative but crucially to unmask the everyday racisms that are felt but not seen.

Communal narratives also shape the perceptions of those with minimal personal experience of police contact through a shared understanding of the experiences of other Black people, men in particular. This was discussed with reference to high profile media cases or the experiences of contacts and peers, as evident in Cynthia's reflections;

> I think being involved with [support organisation] has helped me [to understand] as well because I become aware of police complaints from different service users. Not necessarily of individual police or West Yorkshire police...but like physical happenings in the station. I've gone to the playhouse and I've watched plays about Black men or young Black men in prison, how they've been treated, how they've been isolated, how they've been cruelly treated, how they've been neglected. (Cynthia, 42, Black, British-born, female)

Cynthia is disabled and spends long periods of time at home. She accesses support services targeted at 'BME' communities. Through the support service she has developed her understanding of how police racism impacts upon the lives of Black men. Although Cynthia's personal experiences as a victim of crime were positive, this knowledge did give her cause to reflect on how her experience may be different to that of Black men.

Similarly, for Kenneth, his personal experiences of the police had not been sufficiently negative to alter his perceptions towards them. Although he had experienced stop and search on more than one occasion in his twenties, shortly after arriving in the UK, he felt that the police were just '*doing their job*' (see discussion of migrant perceptions in Chapter 7). It was the high profile shooting of Mark Duggan in Tottenham in 2011 that forced him to consider the racialised treatment of black people;

> The only thing that has affected me is the Mark Duggan case in London … Until now nobody is brought to justice…If they have seen him doing something bad they should have arrested him, not shoot him to death… So why they could have done it is something I don't understand. So, it makes you begin to wonder are these people just out to kill who they don't like sometimes. (Kenneth, 38, Black, African, male)

These accounts show how communal narratives, developed through the experiences of friends and contacts and high-profile cases in the media, impact upon perceptions of racial disparities in policing. However, personal experience is the most significant factor in determining perceptions of and trust and confidence in the police. For the majority of participants, their experiences of the police were overwhelmingly negative. Their negative experiences influenced their perceptions of how race shaped their encounters with the police.

Despite the finding in Macpherson (1999), that the police are institutionally racist, racism was generally perceived by participants to be a problem of individual racist police officers. A distinction is drawn in participant's accounts between good and bad police officers, as reflected in the oft made comment 'but *they're not all like that*' [racist]'. Several participants made reference to one police officer that they could remember because they were 'good' and, therefore the exception to the rule. Bianca recalled one police officer who worked in her community when she was a child who engendered the trust and respect of the community;

> He was the police officer who would sit down with you and say…you tell me your version of events …which is so rare. He used to come into our school, show his face, we all knew him, we all called him [nickname]. That's obviously not his real name but he let us have that relationship with him. I think he retired and that was the only decent police officer that I've ever known. (Bianca)

Here, Bianca's reflection highlights the importance of the police engaging with communities for developing trust and confidence in the police service. It was this police officer's willingness to be a part of the community that shaped Bianca's view of him as a '*good*' police officer. Bianca continued;

> I've never reported a crime to him or been arrested by him or anything like that he was just very present. Always at carnival and he did the full shebang at carnival. He did J'ouvert morning where you come out in your pyjamas so he'd let the whole community see him in his pyjamas. He was with us. (Bianca, 25, Black mixed-race, British-born, female)

Similarly, Cynthia reflected that the police service could be improved by engaging with communities in more positive ways;

> [They need] more fun-days and things like that where there's more community work. I can remember in primary school the police talking to us about how to cross a road with demonstrations and maps of roads and vans and cars and traffic lights. I can remember going to see police horses and I remember a police dog coming to the school and showing you what they do. There needs to be more of that and keep in contact with the community... There's nothing wrong with making a service a bit more unique or a bit more personalised or a bit more friendly. (Cynthia, 42, Black, British-born, female)

Both Bianca and Cynthia reflect that it is not the presence of the police alone that creates an 'Us vs Them' relationship. It is the treatment of those who live in spaces that are subjected to over-policing as suspect that shapes the perception that is it 'Us vs Them'. When the police routinely engage with the community in positive ways that are not tokenistic or for the purposes of gathering information, the officers engaged with the community are viewed positively. Unfortunately, for the majority of participants, their experiences of positive contact with the police were limited to the conduct of one 'good' officer who was considered to be different from the norm.

Conversely, Samuel thought that the majority of police officers were good with a few bad ones who would not treat citizens fairly- '*they still have bad tomatoes in there. Maybe the bad tomatoes are fewer than the good tomatoes*' (Samuel, 45, Black, African, male). Samuels hopeful reflection is evidently different to the perception of the majority of participants. Samuel had been in the UK for around eleven years since his mid-thirties. His lack of contact with the British police force in his formative years, and the evident decline in frequency of police contact amongst older participants, may explain his willingness to believe that there are more good police officers than bad ones. Further, research suggests that immigrants report more positive perceptions of the police (Bradford et al. 2017; also, see Chapter 7).

Those participants who had a generally more positive perception of the police had experiences of police contact outside of the 'suspect' context, including direct and regular contact with the police through work or acquaintances and friends. This aspect of familiarity led to more favourable perceptions for Janice who described a relationship of mutual trust and respect which allowed her to negotiate with police officers to the benefit of her service users. Similarly, for Carol, having a personal acquaintance who was a police officer increased her trust in the police more broadly. Carol described the officer as a 'role model'; she was able to draw upon her personal contact with him to reify her opinion that there are some good police officers—'*he's really fair, he's open, he's lovely, he's gentle.* It may be significant that these two participants were female professionals without an offending history (see Chapter 6). Their experiences of being suspect, though present, were not as frequent or as significant in defining their relationship to the police as some of the other participants-in particular men.

Whilst the publication of the *Stephen Lawrence Inquiry Report* (Macpherson 1999) ushered in a wave of reforms to policing, racism is still experienced by Black and Black mixed-race people. However, there is some evidence that it manifestations have changed. Over racist language and police brutality may be less common; however—'*It hasn't changed for the better, it's just different*' (Marcus). This difference is expressed in the accounts of Thomas and Levi; both were over the age of fifty and reflected upon the changes in policing over their lifetime. In both of their accounts, they expressed the view that the police no longer resort to physical violence routinely, rather they use their power through the criminal justice process to hinder life chances. This constitutes a psychological beating if not a physical one;

> No, they don't beat you like they used to do but they do other things that you may as well, you feel like you may as well have been beaten. (Thomas, 55, Black, British-born, male)

One of the ways in which the police are perceived to damage the life chances of Black and Black mixed-race individuals and communities is through corruption. The IPCC define police corruption as 'the abuse of a role or position held, for personal gain or gain for others' (IPCC 2010: 168). The belief that police corruption is widespread or endemic is found to be more prevalent amongst those for whom personal police contact has been negative and frequent, as opposed to people whose experiences are positive and infrequent (IPCC 2012a). It is therefore unsurprising that a number of participants expressed the view that the police are corrupt. Levi felt that the police had replaced overt use of brutality with more covert measures of violence, including the use of corrupt police practices to secure unfair convictions;

> The police literally couldn't wait to get you. I can name some…actually a few other experiences are coming to mind where police had me up in cells and beat me right. Nowadays they won't do that they would more use the system, lies deception and get you convicted. So, they've literally replaced the cosh with some cunning words and a conviction. (Levi)

This reflection is in respect to an occasion when Levi was arrested. During the arrest Levi was called a 'Nigger' and beaten with police batons before being handcuffed and put in the police van. Where, instead of being seated in the rear of the van, he was locked between the cage and the van door. Following his arrest, he was charged with assaulting three police officers. Through what Levi referred to as a '*culture of corruption*' in which those outside of the system are seen as '*game just for their police records*'. The police were perceived to, regardless of whether the charges are right or wrong, '*just fit it up and pass it through*'. He recalled that the statement he gave to the police about the incident was not reflected in his statement that was to be presented in front of the judge;

> It was hard to find the bits… I was saying where's the bits I put in? where's my contribution to this statement? (Levi, 50, Black, British-born, male)

The case against Levi went to court and, if he had been found guilty, he risked a lengthy prison sentence. On this occasion the case against Levi was unsuccessful. However, police officer solidarity, which remains a core element of cop culture (see Loftus 2009; Bowling et al. 2004), is a barrier to accountability. Levi made a complaint to the, then relatively newly established, Independent Police Complaints Commission.[3] He recalled that the police were not cooperative with the IPCC investigation and lost evidence (CCTV footage) from the police van. His experience of the IPCC was a positive one, he was kept up to date and his complaint was investigated. This resulted in disciplinary action against the police officers concerned. The accountability of the police is essential for the maintenance of trust and confidence in the police;

> I dare say the Independent Complaints Commission has got their own problems but the job that they do when they do it right is an important one. (Levi)

However, Levi's experience does not reflect the expectation that other research participants had of the police complaints process. Several participants expressed that they would not pursue a complaint, it was understood that the police would lie, close ranks to cover for each other or that a complaint would result in retribution against the complainant. This view is supported by research carried out by the IPCC (2012b), into confidence in the complaints process. In their study, 40% of respondents from 'ethnic minorities' feared police harassment if they made a complaint, compared to 17% of White participants. The lack of accountability for over-policing in the lives of those treated as perpetual suspects leads them to reject the police as a legitimate body and to adopt informal strategies to manage their experiences of racist policing.

---

[3]Now, the Independent Office for Police Conduct (IoPC).

Altered Lives: Living as the Perpetual Suspect

For Black and mixed-race people, particularly those who live in racially othered spaces, the extent and nature of police presence in their lives forces them to adopt strategies through which they manage their over-policing and under-protection. There are three key strategies that Black people use to manage their contact with the police; there are compliance, resistance and avoidance. Further the unburdening of shared experiences and the development of communal narratives, as discussed earlier, may be described as a protective strategy.

Compliance with the police is a common strategy in managing police-initiated encounters. One of the reasons why people comply with the police is when they perceive the encounter to be legitimate, for example when the subject of police attention knows that they have broken the law. In these cases, participants were less likely to feel that they were treated unfairly or that the police were biased in their assessment of them. Carol compared the way she felt about being stopped for a clear and valid reason with another occasion when she was stopped and asked to confirm ownership of her car, without any evidence to the contrary;

> There was once I was stopped but I did see a reason for that, because I did do a turn that I really shouldn't have been doing. I was a little bit lost and I was looking for somewhere at this turn and I thought oh I wonder, where am I, and they stopped me. But I thought that was valid so that wasn't a problem. But it was just about the car, that was the one that I thought, and the way he said it [is this your car?]. It does make you wonder doesn't it. Is it racism, because of race or…you do wonder that. (Carol, 49, Black, British-born, female)

On both occasions Carol complied with the police; however, the perceived validity of the police encounter is significant in understanding perceptions of fair treatment. This strengthens the rationale for increased accountability for police use of powers.

Participants' expressed that they would comply or had previously complied with the police, even when the contact was deemed to be unfair or illegitimate. The power that the police have is coercive and it is perceived that they are not accountable for its use;

> When you are stopped by the police, there is first of all fear… You feel that you are under threat even though you know you haven't done anything. It is not easy to remember that you can challenge that person who is stopping you cause they are powerful and, you know, you don't want to cause any trouble. You don't want to irritate them, you don't want too upset them, to cause any trouble because you know they've got the powers to do whatever they want. (Jean, 40, Black, African, male)

> I'm a nice man anyway, I'm always joking, and also because I haven't done anything. So if a policeman stops me when I'm driving, I can't think of anything why….so I just comply with them and cooperate and just laugh and say if you can't spell my name I will spell it for you officer, that kind of thing…It was an officer that said 'well you passed the attitude test'. (Phillip, 45, Black, African male)

Here, both Jean and Phillip show how the authority that the police have, to make things difficult for the suspect, facilitates cooperation even when the suspect has not behaved outside of the law. The perception that the police can behave with impunity—'*and they don't have anybody to answer to*' (*Jean*)—serves to enhance their power. In these encounters, compliance is a survival strategy. Passing the '*attitude test*' may prevent escalation to more formal procedures.

In the context of pedestrian or car stops, the police have the power to escalate the encounter; challenging them in this context may be risky. Taking part in police and community consultation was one way in which both Jean and Earl were able to challenge police racism. Jean was engaged as a scrutiny panel member[4]; in this capacity he found the police officers to be friendly and cooperative; however, this behaviour

[4]In the UK, scrutiny panels engage a panel of community representatives with the aim of providing transparency around policing. They review, in particular, issues which impact on marginalised communities such as investigation of hate crime and stop and search guidance.

and attitude is not reflected in his experiences of traffic stops. The rank structure of the police service may be relevant here; in his role with the Scrutiny Panel, Jean engaged with more senior ranking police officers. There are differences in police culture between those in managerial roles and those who occupy the lower status roles, such as police constables. When police officers are promoted to the senior ranks they adopt a more 'formal ideology of policing' that is more aligned with the values of society (Cockcroft 2013: 80), rather than the rank and file cop culture premised on isolation, solidarity and suspicion (Reiner 2010).

Earl had been involved in the 'riots' which occurred in response to over-policing in his community in the 1970s and subsequently spent time in prison for his role. He reflected upon how this had changed his approach to tackling unfair policing;

> One thing you have to accept; police are a necessary entity within society. You need to have them, so rather than fighting them trying to get fair policing and correct policing I figured that being around the table was a better way of dealing with them than fighting with them because you end up getting locked up. (Earl)

Similarly, to Jean, the nature of the contact between Earl and rank and file officers was different to contact with more senior ranking officers involved in community engagement. Whilst he has managed to form some good working relationships with more senior police officers, the respect he has gained from higher ranking police officers is seen as a threat to the rank and file;

> I've had to take out grievances against police officers. We had one a couple of years ago shouting me down in the street saying 'you think you're smart, you think that because you speak to my boss that I can't do this and that'. I'm like wow, at the end of the day you are damned if you do and you are damned if you don't. (Earl, 54, Black, British-born, male)

This extract illustrates the ways in which the rank and file police officers distinguish categories of people who have the potential to either support and align with police values or to challenge them. Both Earl and

Jean might be considered 'disarmers' with the capacity to 'neutralise' police work (Reiner 2010: 124–125) or 'challengers' through their roles which allow them access to information about the police (ibid.; Also, see Holdaway 1983).

Less frequently participants recalled challenging the police officer in an individual capacity; however, the view that this is a risky strategy for those considered 'police property' was acknowledged. Marcus recalled an occasion when he challenged a police officer who had pulled him over in his car for the second time. The police officer claimed that he had pulled him over for taking a junction in the wrong lane. Marcus knew the road well and it was his perception that the police officer had been in the wrong position to turn;

> I said to him 'if you want to do anything let's go to the police station. I've got time to go up there now. Let's explain to your sergeant what's actually happened here'…and he was the one that said after that 'oh well no it's alright we've got to go somewhere else' [laughs]. But at that point I was willing … if you can say that I've done something wrong let's go and sort it out. (Marcus, 44, Black, British, male)

Despite Marcus's victory on this occasion, the authoritarian approach of the police officer left Marcus feeling as though the officer had tried to bully him into admitting that he had made an illegal manoeuvre, using his position of authority—'*I'm [police officer] right because I've got the badge*'.

Challenging the police during an encounter or through an official complaints process could result in the police officer switching the blame on the challenger and is considered to be a risky strategy. Thomas was engaged in a campaign against joint enterprise as his son was serving a prison sentence, for murder, through charges brought under the joint enterprise principle. He felt that this would bring him to the attention of the police because he was challenging the police and criminal justice processes more broadly. The joint enterprise principle provides that more than one person can be charged with the main offence through association. Ironically this provision which enabled the killers of Stephen Lawrence to be prosecuted, almost two decades after his death, has been used increasingly to target racialised young men (Bridges 2013,

Williams and Clarke 2016). Over 11 times as many Black/Black British prisoners are serving a prison sentence under joint enterprise compared to the proportion of Black/Black British people in the general population (Crewe et al. 2014). The challenge that Thomas brought has led him to move out of the area for fear of becoming a police target;

> I am not in a hurry to go back to [town] to live, partially because I know I would just get grief from the police for standing up, speaking out, saying whatever we want to say. And that's sad that …

The campaign against joint enterprise, led by campaign group JENGbA (Joint Enterprise Not Guilty by Association), has had recent success in the Supreme Court ruling R *v Jogee (appellant)*, making it possible for some of those convicted under joint enterprise to appeal. Such victories, in the face of racialised criminal justice processes, would not be possible without the activism of people like Thomas. However, challenging the system places those considered 'police property' in a risky position, as Thomas recognised. The racial effects of persistent, negative police contact were further evident during the research interview with Thomas, when two police officers on patrol passed by the window. Thomas visibly froze and stopped speaking until they had passed. This interruption prompted him to explain his visceral response to the visible presence of the police;

> I'm always aware when the police pass me you know what I mean. And that comes from being a kid and growing up with that [police] attitude. Even though I've been out of being arrested and all of them sort of things probably for the last ten, eleven years, but yet I still have that conditioning within myself… so when does that leave ya? (Thomas, 55, Black, British, male)

The long-lasting effects of consistent, negative policing on the Black body and psyche is acutely evident here. Thomas's response to the visible presence of police officers, albeit on the other side of a window, is damning illustration of the physical and psychic toll resulting from a lifetime of being imagined as the perpetual suspect.

Avoiding the physical geographical space where the police had a persistent presence was a common strategy amongst participants'. Andrew, who had grown up in a racially othered area, described moving away to avoid the routine nature of police presence and encounters that he had experienced through largely car stops in his earlier years;

> I think you build up a level of resilience and just keep yourself out of the way. And that's probably one of the reasons I've kind of chosen the route that I've chosen and I don't live in the close Black community, I live in an affluent area, I stand out like a sore thumb on my street. (Andrew, 41, Black, British, male)

Andrew would rather have the experience of being a body out of place, as acknowledged in his claim that he '*stands out*', than to experience the day to day presence of the police in a community that is considered 'police property'. Whilst both Thomas and Andrew took extreme measures to avoid persistent police presence there is evidence that people strategize to avoid the police in their more routine day to day activities by avoiding particular places or people (Brunson and Miller 2006). This strategy was reflected upon in Roberts account;

> You see lots of police around the train station and things like that which sometimes makes me think I want to get the coach instead of the train [laughs]. (Robert, 27, Black mixed-race, British-born, male)

Communal narratives are the shared experiences of encounters with the police which are passed on, both inter and cross generationally, and form collective understandings of how race operates in the context of police contact, for both individuals and communities. Communal narratives of policing serve two functions, an individual unburdening in a safe space and protection. The form part of the arsenal of strategies developed in response to living with the reality of racialised policing encounters in the everyday. The protective function of communal narratives is evident in the passing down of experiential knowledge from generation to generation, by way of warning;

> I've drilled it into my kids you will be treat differently because you are Black and I've always told them that. My dad told me that and I didn't believe it, I thought no it can't be just because I'm Black but having experienced it I do believe it and I've passed it on to my kids. I've taught them that you will be treated differently you will be arrested and you will be charged and it will affect you in later life. (Alice, 38, Black mixed-race, British born, female)

> I've got a lot of grandkids and you know other people's kids who's around us and I find myself in a situation sometimes telling kids not to trust Mr Bobby, not to believe what they say. And that is sad because I shouldn't have to say that..., I should be able to be normal and say you know what if you're stuck go and have a word with them, they'll put you in the right direction and I can't say that, I can't say that, I really can't say that [emphasis]. I don't want to say that. (Thomas, 55, Black, British, male)

Here, Thomas laments not being able to pass on '*normal*' expectations of the police to subsequent generations. He recognised in his interview that this makes them more vulnerable to not knowing how to manage an encounter with the police and, also, to not availing themselves to the protection of the police. This produces racialised outcomes which prevent Black and Black mixed-race people from having recourse to equal protection. For the police these communal narratives are simply evidence of anti-authority pathology (Sanders 2005: 161); for those on the receiving end of racialised policing they inform and protect against the very real racial effects of over policing and under protection.

The psychic toll of encountering systemic racism through the experiences, analysed in the previous sections, is expressed viscerally in participant's accounts. Both 'frustration' and 'anger' were frequently recalled responses to encounters with the police. This was compounded by unequal power relations and the perception that there was nothing that the subject could do. Robert described an '*antagonising*' encounter with British Transport Police in which they confiscated a valid travel pass;

> I felt that they were accusing me. It was like they had all the power and they were very happy that they had all the power and there was nothing I could do. And I think they quite enjoyed that to be honest. (Robert, 27, Black mixed-race, British-born, male)

Roberts account reveals that whilst compliance may prevent escalation of the police encounter, to the detriment of the suspect, this strategy also renders the suspect powerless. When an unfair encounter denies the subject their rights, and the police behaviour remains unchallenged, this denial of justice produces 'racialised rightlessness' (Cacho 2012). This has a significant psychic toll and even in cases where the initial encounter could be considered minor, 'racialised rightlessness' compounds the effects of the encounter.

These effects are evident in Derek's account of the aftermath of being tasered by the police, discussed earlier. Following this incident, he made a complaint to the relevant police service. He met with a senior police officer and the investigating officer decided that his complaint did not have any basis. Derek referred his complaint to the IPCC and they failed to answer the questions he raised about his treatment. He had recently spoken with the elected Police and Crime Commissioner (PCC) and the issues he raised were ongoing (see Chapter 7 for further analysis-accountability). The physical and psychological effects of both the encounter with the police and lack of recourse to justice were evident in his recollection;

> It's affected me. Firstly, like I said the way that I feel about the police. And secondly it affected me in that particular way in terms of self-medicating [with alcohol]and dealing with it. And not being able to sleep and you know sitting up at night smoking sugar loads of cigarettes and all that kind of stuff. It had a proper effect on me.

This honest and emotive account excavates the trauma exacted upon the individual by racialised policing. This is exacerbated when the police are not held accountable. Derek expressed that he would not be happy until he had exhausted all avenues of complaint;

> Mentally I've dealt with it but now it's like, you know what, the fight continues. I may never get anywhere with it but until I feel satisfied in myself that Derek, you have done everything you can and there is nothing else you can do then I will leave it there. (Derek, 46, Black, British, male)

These accounts show that in order for subjects to heal from the trauma of racist policing, and have their confidence in the police restored, it is important that the police are held to account. Whilst there is a lack of faith in the processes of accountability, '*the fight*' for justice, in the face of 'racialised rightlessness', can empower those who are otherwise forced into accepting their construction as perpetual suspects.

Conclusion

This chapter powerfully illuminates the persistence of racism in the police institution. Whilst overt forms of racism are not a common feature of contemporary policing, not in public view at least, racism is felt through over-policing. This is manifest in practices of routine surveillance in racially othered spaces, stop and search and car stops, unjustified arrest and use of force. Racialised stereotypes which construct Black bodies as a threat, permeate the 'police imagination'[5] and this is significant in understanding the over-policing of Black and Black mixed-race people. Participants experiences are in common with that expressed by Yancy (2008) *I continue to live my body in Black within a culture where Blackness is still over determined by myths and presuppositions that fix my body as a site of danger (p. 59)*. Racialised forms of policing are experienced from childhood and interrupt childhood innocence for Black children. As articulated by Levi, these experiences serve to '*plant the seed of fear*' at an early age. The racialisation of space is fundamental to understanding police practices of surveillance and control of othered populations. Spaces which have acquired the shape of the bodies that inhabit them (Ahmed 2007: 156) are policed more intensively. However, the presence of Black bodies in both racially othered spaces and spaces racialised as White (where they are 'out of place') is suspect.

[5]See Chapter 7 for expanded discussion on concept of police imagination.

These experiences alter the way in which people live their lives. Black and Black mixed-race people adopt conscious strategies to manage the impact of living as the perpetual suspect. Avoidance of the police and compliance in encounters with the police, are two common strategies that can help to manage the risk perceived to be inherent in contact with the police. This shapes Black people's use of public space and, for some, their choice of area of residency as well as their willingness to avail themselves to the police for protection. Communal narratives are also important in understanding how Black and Black mixed-race people manage these experiences. Experiences in common with other Black and Black mixed-race people through storytelling contribute to a commonly understand narrative about how Black people are treated by the police. These communal narratives expose racism inherent in policing of Black communities and, when passed on, serve a protective function, warning others to be alert to the risk of contact with the police. Comparing their experiences with White peer's reveals differences in frequency and contact with the police which further illuminate the racialised nature of policing.

Levi's words, used in the title of this chapter, '*Babylon remove the chain, now they're using the brain*', succinctly capture the essence of racisms manifestations in policing in the age of equality and diversity speak. Racism in the police service has largely been made invisible, through a diversity agenda which has failed to eradicate racism from the police. As argued by Ahmed (2012) the diversity agenda is 'symbolic' (p. 29); its commitments are not experienced by those who embody diversity. Perhaps-counter-intentionally, it proliferates racism through its obscurity, and in the context of a post-race policing narrative which implicitly denies the structural nature of racism. It is no longer as common as it once was for police officers to single out those racialised as Black for a 'beating', and overt racist language is no longer routinely used in plain view. However, the racist effects of invisible racism are traumatic, taking both a physical and psychic toll on Black and Black mixed-race individuals and communities.

Chapter 5 will turn its attention to the under-protection of victims of crime.

References

Ahmed, S. (2007). A Phenomenology of Whiteness. *Feminist Theory, 8*, 149–168.

Ahmed, S. (2012). *On Being Included: Racism and Diversity in Institutional Life*. London: Duke University Press.

Angiolini, E. (2017). *Report of the Independent Review of Deaths and Serious Incidents in Police Custody*. London: Home office. https://www.gov.uk/government/publications/deaths-and-serious-incidents-in-police-custody. Accessed 20 January 2018.

Bernstein, R. (2011). *Racial Innocence: Performing American Childhood from Slavery to Civil Rights*. New York: New York University Press.

Bowling, B., & Phillips, C. (2007). Disproportionate and Discriminatory: Reviewing the Evidence on Police Stop and Search. *The Modern Law Review, 70*, 936–961.

Bowling, B., Phillips, C., Campbell, A., & Docking, M. (2004). Policing and Human Rights: Eliminating Discrimination, Xenophobia, Intolerance and the Abuse of Power from Police Work. *Racism and Public Policy*. Durban, South Africa: United Nations Research Institute for Social Development.

Bradford, B., Sargeant, E., Murphy, T., & Jackson, J. (2017). A Leap of Faith? Trust in the Police Among Immigrants in England and Wales. *British Journal of Criminology, 57*(2), 381–401.

Bridges, L. (2013). The Case Against Joint Enterprise. *Race & Class, 54*, 33–42.

Brunson, R. K., & Miller, J. (2006). Young Black Men and Urban Policing in the United States. *British Journal of Criminology, 46*, 613–640.

Bunyan, N. (2015, July 6). Police Taser Shooting Contributed to Man's Death, Jury Finds. *Guardian*.

Cacho, L. M. (2012). *Social Death Racialised Rightlessness and the Criminalization of the Unprotected*. New York: New York University Press.

Choongh, S. (1998). Policing the Dross: A Social Disciplinary Model of Policing. *British Journal of Criminology, 38*, 623–634.

Cockcroft, T. (2013). *Police Culture: Themes and Concepts*. Oxon: Routledge.

College of Policing. (2013). *Public Order: Police Use of Force*. www.app.college.police.uk/app-content/public-order/core-principles-and-legislation/police-use-of-force/. Accessed 1 February 2018.

Crewe, B., Hulley, S., & Wright, S. (2014). *Written Evidence: Submitted to Justice Select Committee*. Cambridge: Cambridge Institute of Criminology.

Fanon, F. (1986). *Black Skin, White Masks*. London: Pluto Press.

Fekete, L. (2013). Total Policing: Reflections from the Frontline. *Race & Class, 54*, 65–76.

Foster, J., Newburn, T., & Souhami, A. (2005). *Assessing the Impact of the Stephen Lawrence Inquiry. Home Office Research Study, 294*. Home Office Research, Development and Statistics Directorate.

Gayle, D. (2015). Black People 'Three Times More Likely' to Be Tasered. *Guardian*. http://www.theguardian.com/uk-news/2015/oct/13/black-people-three-times-more-likely-to-have-taser-used-against-them. Accessed 13 October 2015.

Goff, P. A., Jackson, M. C., Di Leone, B. A. L., Culotta, C. M., & Ditomasso, N. A. (2014). The Essence of Innocence: Consequences of Dehumanizing Black Children. *Journal of Personality and Social Psychology, 106*, 526–545.

Holdaway, S. (1983). *Inside the British Police: A Force at Work*. Oxford: Blackwell.

Hunte, J. A. (1966). *Nigger Hunting in England?* London: West Indian Standing Conference.

Institute for Race Relations. (1979). *Police Against Black People*. London: IRR.

Independent Police Complaints Commission. (2010). *Statutory Guidance to the Police Service and Police Authorities on the Handling of Complaints*. London: IPCC.

Independent Police Complaints Commission (IPCC) (2012a). *Corruption in the Police Service in England and Wales: Second Report – a Report Based on the IPCC's Experience from 2008 to 2011*. London: IPCC. Available at: https://www.gov.uk/government/publications/corruption-in-the-police-service-in-england-and-wales-second-report. Accessed 17 August 2016.

Independent Police Complaints Commission. (2012b). *Police Complaints: Statistics for England and Wales 2011/12-Research and Statistics Series: Paper 25*. London: IPCC.

Lee, J. A. (1981). Some Structural Aspects of Police Deviance in Relations with Minority Groups. In C. Shearing (Ed.), *Organisational Police Deviance*. Toronto: Butterworth.

Lewis, P., Newburn, T., Taylor, M., McGillivray, C., Greenhill, A., Frayman, H., & Proctor, R. (2011). *Reading the Riots: Investigating England's Summer of Disorder*. London: The London School of Economics and Political Science and The Guardian.

Loftus, B. (2009). *Police Culture in a Changing World*. Oxford: Oxford University Press.

Macpherson of Cluny, S. W. (1999). *The Stephen Lawrence Inquiry*. London: The Stationery Office.

Mills, C. W. (1997). *The Racial Contract*. New York: Cornell University Press.

Pemberton, S. (2008). Demystifying Deaths in Police Custody: Challenging State Talk. *Social and Legal Studies, 17,* 237–262.

Reiner, R. (2010). *The Politics of the Police*. Oxford: Oxford University Press.

Rollock, N. (2009). *The Stephen Lawrence Inquiry 10 Years On: An Analysis of the Literature*. London: Runnymede Trust.

Sanders, B. (2005). *Youth Crime and Youth Culture in the Inner City*. London: Routledge.

Sharp, D., & Atherton, S. (2007). To Serve and Protect? The Experiences of Policing in the Community of Young People from Black and Other Ethnic Minority Groups. *British Journal of Criminology, 47,* 746–763.

Smith, R. (2009). Police, the Public, 'Less Lethal Force' and Suspects: Deconstructing the Human Rights Arguments. *Police Journal, 82,* 194–211.

Tate, S. A. (2016). 'I Can't Quite Put My Finger on It': Racism's Touch. *Ethnicities, 16,* 68–85.

Ward, T., & Coles, D. (1998). Investigating Suspicious Deaths in Police Custody. In A. Liebling (Ed.), *Deaths of Offenders: The Hidden Side of Justice*. Waterside: Winchester.

Weinberger, B. (1995). *The Best Police in the World: An Oral History of English Policing*. Hampshire: Scolar Press.

Williams, P., & Clarke, B. (2016). *Dangerous Associations: Joint Enterprise, Gangs and Racism. An Analysis of the Processes of Criminalisation of Black, Asian and Minority Ethnic Individuals*. London: Centre for Crime and Justice Studies.

Yancy, G. (2008). *Black Bodies, White Gazes: The Continuing Significance of Race*. Maryland: Rowman and Littlefield.

Yancy, G. (2012). *Look, A White!* Philadelphia: Temple.

5

The (Un)Victim of Crime: Racialised Victims and the Police

Black and Black mixed-race people are significantly more likely to be victims of crime than Whites (Ministry of Justice 2015). The process of becoming a victim is an 'emergent process of signification' (Rock 2002: 17) which involves the individual perception, the response of the public, the media, and criminal justice agencies. The police are significant actors within this process as they are often the first person a victim of crime will come in to contact with. The *Code of Practice for Victims,* which applies to all police forces in England and Wales, enshrines entitlement to services provided under the code to a person who has 'made an allegation' that they have experienced criminal conduct. According to the Code of Practice, the victim should be treated with respect, sensitivity and professionalism and without discrimination (p. 1). However, Black and Black mixed-race people report lower levels of trust and confidence in the police (Office for National Statistics 2017), lower levels of satisfaction with police responses to their victimisation and are less likely to report victimisation when they experience it (Yarrow 2005; Sharp and Atherton 2007). Victimisation has traditionally been researched through a White lens, with the exception of work related

L. J. Long, *Perpetual Suspects*, Palgrave Studies in Race, Ethnicity, Indigeneity and Criminal Justice, https://doi.org/10.1007/978-3-319-98240-3_5

to racist violence and hate crime (see Bowling 1999). Black and black mixed-race people's experiences of victimisation more broadly, and police responses to it, have been overlooked. These experiences are the focus of this chapter.

From the perspective of Black and Black mixed-race people, it will be shown how they experience policing when they approach the police as victims. It argues that the processes of racialisation in the operation of police decision making, and the legitimisation of White fear, construct Black victims of crime as antithetical to the image of the 'ideal victim' which Christie (1986) describes as '*a person or category of individuals who, when hit by crime, most readily are given the complete and legitimate status of being a victim*'. This is evident through racialised policing which denies victim status to black bodies. Through the processes implicated in 'becoming' the victim, black and black mixed-race people become the (Un)Victim. It will show that the resulting denial of justice has a significant impact upon trust and confidence in policing and willingness to report crime, therefore preventing them from seeking support and protection from the state. This under-protection results in a racialised re-victimisation. This has brutalising racist affects which can trump the effects of victimisation, particularly in the context of minor crimes.

Becoming the (Un)Victim

In reality, the police do not investigate all crimes that are reported. Resources would not permit this, particularly in the context of the cuts to public services in the post-2008 austerity agenda. Local and national policing priorities (Tilley 2008) and the severity, or perceived severity, of the crime are influencing factors in the response to victims of crime. Police officers conceive of their role primarily as crime fighters (Reiner 2010). Incidents that do not require the performance of the crime fighter role, or tasks that involve paperwork and/or customer service, are not considered proper police work. However, these tasks form a large part of the day to day reality of policing (ibid.). These factors, which influence police responses to reports of crime, are oppositional to the expectation, created by the victims' rights agenda, that the victim of crime will be treated as such. Samuel, one of the participants' in this study, contacted the police after his car was hit and damaged by another driver who failed to stop. His initial impressions of the police response were positive;

> These staff who I talked to on the phone were willing to help. The police officer said "please come in I will be there". I went to the police station they inspected the car… he [police officer] was really nice. (Samuel, 45, Black, African, male)

As a recent migrant, at the time of the incident, the initial positive contact was Samuels's first encounter with the British police. However, 'what *happened after that [initial report] was a different story*'. Following the initial report of the incident the police failed to update Samuel on the progress of the investigation. Samuel persistently called and left messages and, after five months of not getting a response from the police, he gave up and contacted a local councillor. Even though the incident was minor, Samuel described feeling 'angry' and 'frustrated' at the police failure to communicate with him. His expectations of the British police based on their reputation were high. Samuel expressed that he would not have been surprised if this had happened in Denmark where he had lived previously. He felt that the Danish police had lower levels of understanding of 'diversity'—'*way behind where this country is*'. For Samuel, his expectation of the British police was that they would respond by completing a thorough investigation of the crime and that he would be treated fairly. This perception was in part, based on his knowledge of the changes in policing resulting from the Macpherson inquiry report.

There is a 'mythology' around the investigation of crime, reproduced through media and fictional representation of crime investigation, and the growth in the victim centered criminal justice discourse. Successful criminal investigation has become a determinant of perceptions of police effectiveness and legitimacy (see Maguire 2011: 430–464). When the police do not appear to prioritise evidence gathering, it can create a perception that the victim is not being taken seriously. Kenneth reflected on the failure of the police to catch the person who stole his bike;

> I thought they could have done more to catch up with those criminals because they just do it with impunity … The only thing that will have caught them is cameras and the police trying to investigate. Maybe because they know they don't bother with it like shoplifting and things they just do it, continue to do it.

When asked why he thought the police did not bother, Kenneth recognised that the prioritisation of more serious crimes may have been a factor. However, this did not change his belief that the police did not do enough to help him as a victim of crime;

> I don't know maybe because they are overworked or something they are dealing with major crimes like terrorism and things like that so they don't even bother with little crimes but all crime are crimes. (Kenneth, 38, Black, African, male)

The perception that the police do not thoroughly investigate reported crime, and that they are not always honest with the victim about the steps that they have taken to investigate, was a commonly expressed perception. This is reflected in both Robert and Charles's experiences of reporting a crime. In both cases the victim believed that CCTV would assist the police in their investigation. Robert was assaulted in a public place. Initially, when he reported the assault, the police attended his home and took a statement. Robert felt that he was treated well and that the police '*were very keen*' to get his '*side of the story*'. This initially positive response gave him the expectation that the incident would be investigated. However, he described several weeks of '*chasing them up*' to be told that the perpetrator had been '*cautioned*'. Robert questioned this course of action;

> I felt very frustrated because in the end they just said well we just cautioned him and nothing else happened. I said did you check any CCTV or did you do this or did you do that and they just kind of put me on hold and came back and said oh no there wasn't any CCTV which I took to mean that they hadn't actually bothered to look… There was no follow up [after the initial report]. I wasn't even sure what kind of investigation they had done and so for me it didn't feel very adequate. (Robert, 27, Black mixed-race, British-born, male)

Charles was the victim of a scam when he bought a laptop outside of a shop, after handing over the cash he discovered that the bag contained bottles of lemonade, rather than the laptop he had been shown earlier. Charles viewed the CCTV with the consent of the shop owner and the exchange could be seen clearly on the CCTV footage. However, when he requested that the police view the CCTV to identify the perpetrator the police officer told him '*there's no camera in the shop. I sent somebody there already and there's no camera in there*' (Charles). Because Charles had already viewed the footage, he was able to challenge the police officer's account of the steps they had taken to conclude the investigation. Afterwards, the police took a statement and gave Charles the impression that they were taking the investigation seriously. The offender was not identified; however, Charles was led to believe that the CCTV footage was considered as well as fingerprints left on the lemonade bottle. However, Charles remains skeptical about whether the subsequent communication reflected an honest account of the investigative process. Charles felt that his '*foreignness*' could have led to the police assumption that he did not understand the British system and therefore he could be afforded a lesser service;

> When you actually don't know what you are doing the police can take advantage. Not actually looking at, you know, into your matter properly because they believe you don't actually know what is, what is your rights. (Charles, 40, Black, African, male)

Charles experience reveals how a perceived absence of procedural fairness can communicate un-belonging for those with marginalised social identities (Bradford et al. 2014). Signs of foreignness can operate to racialise the police response, both communicating that the subject is not perceived to belong and that they are not worthy of victim status.

Keeping victims of crime updated on the progress of their case is attributed to improved satisfaction with policing and perceptions of procedural fairness (Kristina 2009; Wells 2007). Further, the expectation that the police will do so is set out in the *Code of Practice for Victims of Crime*. When the police fail to keep victims informed of the progress of the investigation this contributes to the perception that their report is not being taken seriously. When Kenneth reported the theft of his bike, a relatively minor crime, he was not kept informed in accordance with the information he was given;

> I thought they were a little bit relaxed with the issue … They said they were going to be getting in touch every week, they never did. I went [to the police station] after two weeks. It's like they've almost forgotten the case. She told me the person that was in charge of the case was not there… I should either come back or they would write to me, which they never did until after three weeks. That was when they wrote to say they closed the case. (Kenneth, 38, Black, African, male)

Kenneth did recognise that police resources are stretched in the context of austerity, and that cuts and reduction in staff could explain the failure to keep him informed. However, the way in which these routine procedures are carried out with an absence of care for the victim can compound the victim's perception that their report has not been taken seriously. When the police wrote to Kenneth, three weeks after his follow up visit to the police station, his name was misspelled in the letter. This seemingly minor detail heightened Kenneth's perception that the police had not taken him seriously—'*it tends to show some carelessness or not caring of who you are dealing with to even know their details*'—particularly as he had provided the correct spelling when he reported the crime. Similarly, to Charles's perception that his '*foreignness*' changed the police response to him as a victim of crime, the misspelling of Kenneth's surname highlights his otherness. As Sara Ahmed (2007) argues, through a name '*the stranger becomes a stranger because of some trace of a dubious origin*' (p. 161). Through this dubious origin, they become unworthy of the treatment afforded to the 'ideal victim'.

The decision to act upon a reported crime is influenced by the perceived worth of the victim. Worthiness is assessed in relation to socio-economic, structural and demographic factors (Loftus 2009) as well as the legitimacy and deemed innocence of the victim (Van Wijk 2013; Christie 1986). Eric reported a burglary at his flat, which he described as being in a '*deprived area*'. He expected that the police would investigate the crime and that they would provide him with reassurance. However, his account of what happened was met with skepticism;

> When I got burgled I was a suspect already rather than them trying to establish I was a victim. Nobody reassured me that you've been a victim of crime, they started asking me questions. Who do you think it was? Why did you take so long [to call the police]?

Burglary is often considered one of the 'rubbish crimes' (Grimshaw and Jefferson 1987), crimes which, for the police, constitute a '*paper exercise*' (Eric). However, the police response to the victim can signal their assessment of victim-worthiness. Eric described feeling like the '*perpetrator*' instead of the victim. On the basis of this experience, he reflected on how processes of racialisation shape police responses to the victim;

> I think if a White cop comes to a Black person house you're a suspect. You're guilty even before you know like they've asked the questions. They don't ask questions to ascertain who you were they ask you questions so they can catch you out. (Eric, 32, Black, African, male)

The gap between Eric's expectation and the police response forced him to reflect upon his Otherness—'*I think that's when I realised we were different*'. Reflecting on his perception that he would have been treated better if he had been dealt with by a Black police officer, Eric described Blackness, in similar language to DuBois (1994), as the '*line that divides us*'. Further, Eric perceived that shared cultural knowledge would negate some of the power relations which determine the police response to victimisation, '*somebody might have a crown on his head but if we are from the same colour or same kind of like background… that knowledge cuts barriers*'. Evident in this reflection is the ways in which the police response communicates to the victim the extent to which they are seen to 'belong' (Bradford et al. 2014; also see Chapter 7), their relationship to authority (Tyler and Lind 1992) and their capacity to recourse to the protective functions of the state.

Janice, who was born and has resided in the UK from birth, expressed more satisfaction with the police in relation to minor crimes. She did not expect an investigation when she was the victim of minor crimes but was satisfied that the police provided her with the service that she needed, for example, completing the relevant paperwork to enable the victim to claim on insurance. Further, Janice was satisfied with the way she was dealt with during these encounters;

> I've had like burglaries I've had criminal damage to my car probably cause of the area that I live in. And I think they've been nice and open minded and you know compassionate. (Janice, 37, Black, British-born, female)

Janice's perception contrasts strongly with both Samuel, Kenneth and Eric's expectations that the police would apprehend the offender and punish them appropriately. Perhaps, this can be explained by their migrant position. Recent migrants appear to have a more favourable perception of the police than those who have been in the UK for longer periods of time, particularly when compared with British born Black and mixed-race people (Bradford et al. 2017; also see Chapter 7). When this favourable perception is called into question by treatment that does not meet their expectations those perceptions are challenged. In relation to petty crime at least, British born participants appear to have lower expectations that the police would apprehend the offender, therefore this was less important in determining perceptions of police effectiveness and victim satisfaction. However, Janice was still forced to reflect upon racism as an explanation for the police failure to successfully investigate more serious crime.

In the context of more serious crimes, perceptions of police effectiveness are more likely to be premised on successful investigation of the crime and punishment of the offender. Janice talked about the way that her family was treated following the murder of her cousin. In this context, the treatment of the family was less important than the successful investigation of the crime;

> I lost a family member once and the support that they gave my family at the time was huge you know. As a victim of crime, they will support you.

Whilst the family were well supported by the police service, including Family Liaison Officers, the police investigation did not result in successful conviction of the suspected killer. Janice described feeling that the police '*didn't do right by us*'. The support that the family had received was not as significant, in the victim's family member's evaluations of the police, as their failure to convict anybody in respect of the murder. Central to this was the suspicion that the victim was not considered, by the police, as the 'ideal victim';

> He was a criminal I'm not going to deny it. Not a vicious vindictive criminal but he was not somebody they went to arrest without maybe ten or fifteen officers present because he wasn't going to give them an easy time.

Janice reveals how victim-worthiness is constructed drawing on the victim/offender dichotomy. This dichotomy separates the ideal victim from the offender and positions one as irreconcilable with the other. Thus, the fact that the murder is previously known to the police, places him at distant proximity from the ideal victim label and therefore unworthy. He is wholly defined by his criminal record by the police; however, for the family he is defined by his relationship to them;

> He was respectful at home, a good family member loyal, loving, and caring. He had a criminal history but uneducated, big in build, bit of a bully to other people and he wanted a better life for himself, whichever which way it came. Whether that was morally right or wrong that was his cross to bear but as a family member he was perfect in every way.

Here, Janice reflects upon both his role in the family and his involvement in crime, which she understands with reference to structural factors including a lack of education and a desire to improve his own life. However, he was unable to do so in legitimate ways. This is in contrast to the person suspected of killing him;

> The person who did kill him was a nice law-abiding citizen. Really good references from teachers, police officers, doctors. Good friends in high places and he [victim] was never going to win. (Janice)

This is instructive of the ways in which the victim of crime is constructed in relation to the perceived legitimacy of the offender/suspect. Black and black mixed-race victims of crime 'known' to the police through the 'fact of blackness' (see Fanon 1986); as the perpetual suspect they are already in conflict with the ideal victim image. These narratives shape their experiences of police contact and they become the (Un)Victim.

Justice Denied

The expectation that the police will provide reassurance, framed in the popular imagery of the police response to the 'ideal victim' (Christie 1986) is frustrated when the victim is disbelieved, questioned about their knowledge of the crime or their lifestyle. This is perceived by the victim to indicate that they precipitated their own victimisation or indeed deserved it. This is most conspicuous when a call for help results in the victim being treated as the suspect. Levi was able to recall two occasions when he had been the victim of an attack in a long running property dispute with his neighbours and a local housing authority. On one occasion, whilst entering the property, a neighbour threw bricks at him. Levi restrained his neighbour and called the police; however, when the police arrived '*I'm the one that gets arrested*' (*Levi*). On the second occasion Levi had a verbal altercation with another neighbour, in relation to the same dispute. Levi described what happened on that day;

> Me and him had a little altercation with words, I went out onto the pavement to challenge him he then drove his car up on to the pavement and ran in to me on the pavement ran in to me. Ah, fair do's, my reaction was, damage his car…

Levi smashed the car's window, in what he perceived as an act of self-defence. When the police arrived, they arrested him. Despite the evidence of two witnesses, which supported his account, he was charged and at the time of interview had an impending court appearance. Further, when he was arrested on this occasion, Levi recalled that it was a particularly aggressive encounter;

> I went back to my building and they called the police, the police came down and he literally pushed open the gate and jumped on me, put cuffs on me and started beating up on me. He's [police officer] now put in his statement that he cautioned me and he did everything by the book etc. He is saying that I obstructed him in his duty, that's not what happened. I've got a witness that was there and saw everything and she says clearly none of that happened…. If he was doing his duty, he wouldn't have cautioned me. He would have come to me and asked me what happened…he didn't ask me what happened. He came there, decided beforehand that he's gonna go in there and manhandle me and take me away. The fact remains that the amount of times the police have been down to arrest me never once have they had to fight me. (Levi, 50, Black, British-born, male)

On this occasion, a friend had filmed the incident on his phone; however, the police refused to accept this as evidence to corroborate his version of events. Levi could be described as a 'delinquent victim' (Miers 2000); although Levi does not consider himself in these terms he recognises that the police do. When asked if he would approach the police for help he responded, '*I believe my address is literally Blacklisted*'. This perception leads him to believe that the police would not help him and would approach him as a suspect.

Alice, who was known to the police due to previous offending, had similar experiences of being treated as the suspect when she contacted the police for assistance. She recalled that on one occasion a stranger knocked on her door to ask for help as her boyfriend was being attacked nearby. Alice called 999 and requested that the police attend. Following the call Alice waited at least an hour for a police officer to arrive, despite her stating it was an emergency situation. A police officer knocked on her door about one hour after her initial call and Alice was told that the reason for the delayed response was that they recognised her name;

> The policeman actually said "oh we heard your name and we thought oh". That's exactly what he said to me yea. "We thought here we go" that's exactly what he said. (Alice, 38, Black mixed-race, British born, female)

This illustrates how the victim-offender dichotomy, the assumption that the individual can either be one or the other but not both, shapes police responses to victimisation. When the victim of crime has a history of previous contact with the police or a name that the police recognise they become removed from the constructed ideal of the deserving victim.

The perpetrators' race is perceived by participants' to be significant in shaping police responses to Black victims of crime. When a Black or mixed-race' person is victimised, the White voice is often the one that is heard and prioritised. The *Stephen Lawrence Inquiry Report* found that, in relation to racist incidents, Black victims were, time and time again 'turned into' perpetrators, and that the White version of such incidents was 'all too readily accepted by police officers' (Macpherson 1999: 45.11). Marcus called the police when his neighbour began to kick down a fence he was in the process of erecting, as they claimed that the fence encroached the property boundary. The police arrived and immediately went to the perpetrator, a White woman, to ask her what had happened. Marcus recalled;

> the police came, and I'm waiting in the front garden for them to come, and they went into the next door neighbour's garden. So, I said 'excuse me I've made the complaint, can you come here' and he goes 'oh no, we're going here first'. I says 'well what you going there for cause I've made the complaint? You should come and speak to me and ask me what's happened and then go and speak to them afterwards'. He says 'no sorry don't tell me how to do my job, I'm gonna go see them first'...

A statement was taken from both Marcus and his neighbour. The police concluded that no further action would be taken as it was a case of 'your word against hers'. This led Marcus to reflect that the police had protected the perpetrator from the criminalising consequences of their behaviour, illuminating how the denial of victim status racially re-victimises the subject;

> I am actually the victim here and you are protecting the person that has actually committed the crime, and I want to know why you've [the police] actually done that. (Marcus, 44, Black, British-born, male)

Common stereotypes associated with, in particular, Black men, led to unfair treatment and unsatisfactory responses when they reported being the victim of crime. Shawn reflected on the way the police responded to him when his car was hit by a White, middle aged woman' in a queue of traffic. He pulled over in order to check for damage and exchange insurance details with the woman. However, as he got out of his car, she drove off. Shawn reported the incident to the police, including that the driver had fled the scene. When the police officer spoke with the female driver, she told him that the reason she left was that she felt threatened.

> I'm like what she felt threatened? I didn't even approach her, I didn't even see her, I didn't get to speak with her. So, he goes [police officer] 'well I can't tell you what she said to me but she said something that I can't repeat to you over phone'. So, to me, I thought okay yea, so she's seen a big Black guy, felt threatened even though it's the middle of [a busy area], broad daylight, there's gonna be cameras everywhere.

In this exchange, it is clear how in the 'police imagination' racialised common-sense understandings of the threat posed by the Black male legitimate White fear. The White perpetrator's fear of the '*big Black man*' was deemed to be a legitimate reason for driving away from the scene of the accident, resulting in the victim being treated as a threat. Shawn described how this made him feel;

> I find it totally out of order, you know how the police handled it as well. They didn't even tell me if it was something she could get done for or if I could pursue it further. For me that's not justice. I wasn't happy at all.

Shawn's experience reflects a pattern prevalent in participant's accounts. Several participants recalled an occasion when the police failed to follow up the report of an offence or closed the case on the basis that no further action could be taken when the offender was White and female, the most 'deserving' of victims. Further, for Shawn and for other participants', they recognised that if they had been the perpetrator the police would have dealt with them punitively;

> I'm fairly sure, if it was the opposite way around, me leaving the scene of an accident, have been prosecuted for doing that. (Shawn, 39, Black, British-born, male)

In a similar incident, Phillip's car was hit by a White female driver coming out of a side street. The driver left the scene of the accident and Phillip reported the accident to the police. He later received a letter informing him that the police would not be pressing charges. Like Shawn, Philip perceived that if he had been the perpetrator the police would have taken action against him;

> If it was me as a Black man … they would have done something about it. They wouldn't have let me off at all.

Phillip felt strongly that this was a reflection of inequitable policing and he made this clear in a letter of complaint, to which the police responded with a home visit:

> A commander came he was a very big man and he was impressive in the way he was dressed and I mean he came in a big patrol car so I thought that it was a courtesy thing you know. (Phillip, 45, Black, African, male)

In the context of the policing diversity agenda there is some police sensitivity to the potential for them to be accused of racism (Foster et al. 2005; Loftus 2009). Phillips experience reflects the symbolic nature of this police gesture in order to allay his claims to have been treated differently than a White victim—'*that was a bit of a courtesy that we had a commander came in his uniform with all his badges*'.

The police rely upon the public in order to investigate crime and secure convictions. In this context encounters with the police can be more positive. Phillip reflected on the police attitude when his neighbour was the victim of murder. Phillip spoke to the police during their enquiries. He was unable to help them, by providing any significant information. However, the police approached him '*sensitively*' on this occasion. Phillip reflected upon how this context shaped the encounter;

> I mean I think the fact that [detectives] knew me [helped]. But I mean it's different isn't it in different circumstances. Interviewing people to help the police, as opposed to you being you know the assailant or a victim, so you can assist the police by being their witness or you can be the persecuted or prosecuted or you can be the victim.

When the public can be of assistance to the police, in investigating crime, this appears to alter the power balance inherent in the encounter and a more sensitive approach may work in the police's favour. Further, to Philips advantage, he knew one of the officers on a personal level (an old school friend). However, ability to assist the police may not always operate in this way. Alice recalled an occasion when the police knocked on her door looking for two crime suspects. Alice did not know the men that the police were looking for. They had run away from the police close to her house and the police believed that one of them had sustained an injury in escaping and there was blood outside on the street, close to the entrance to Alice's block of flats. She described being questioned for a long time by the police officer, who made her feel as though she had '*done something wrong*';

> What's happened is they've chased a car; two Black guys have got out of the car they've run off. What they think has happened is one of them has gone on to a garage roof and fallen and badly hurt himself and they've… what was the word he used "deliberately" come to my house to seek help.

Despite Alice's insistence that she did not know who the people were and they had not come to her flat the police made repeated visits to Alice in pursuit of the two men.

> I don't know why they would come to that conclusion, like they would because I'm the only Black person in this block … he goes [police officer] 'all the other families are Polish and he hasn't been to see them. He's obviously come here you need to tell us where he is'. (Alice, 38, Black mixed-race, British born, female)

The assumed belonging to an 'imagined community' (Anderson 2006) of a homogenous, black and criminal other, positions all Black people as in opposition to the law. They cannot be relied upon to cooperate in the interests of crime investigation and they must therefore be suspect.

Marcus recalled calling 999 to request an ambulance and police attendance for one of his tenants who had been hit over the head with a hammer. The address was in an area of the city with a significant ethnic minority population, an area that has been framed in the media as crime-ridden and dangerous—a racially Othered place. After waiting almost an hour for the ambulance a police officer arrived. Marcus asked the police officer where the ambulance was as he was concerned for the deteriorating health of his tenant. Marcus recalled his conversation with the police officer;

> like 'where's the ambulance'. 'Oh, the ambulance aren't gonna come til we tell them to come'. I was like 'you what?'. I said 'there's a guy in there he's been hit with a hammer'. So, he goes 'you've got an attitude problem haven't ya'. I said 'hang on a minute, we phoned you nearly an hour ago, you've just turned up and you're telling me I've got an attitude problem. You better go in and have a look at this guy', so he went in and he goes 'fucking hell get an ambulance down here straight away'. (Marcus, 44, Black, British-born, male)

In this exchange, Marcus's frustration at having to wait for an ambulance for a man who was seriously injured was read as an attitude problem. Further, the reason given for the delay in dispatching an ambulance was rooted in the racialisation of the space. Marcus was told, '*we've [police] got to come because it's [area name]. We've got to come and verify that everything's alright for the ambulance*'. Those who occupy racialised spaces are constructed as a threat (see Chapter 7) based on their socio-cultural and geographical belonging and do not fit into the image of the 'ideal victim'. This is evident in the refusal to send medical assistance to a man with serious injuries before first conducting a risk assessment of the threat posed by the Other. Black and mixed-race people are 'known' as one body—'THE BLACK BODY' (Gordon 2005: 105). The response to their calls for help is to treat them primarily as a threat. This serves as a reminder, to those resident in that space, that they are perpetual suspects. In this context, both individuals and whole communities are rendered the (Un)Victim. The resultant effect is racial re-victimisation, through racialised responses to the victim as suspect.

Racial Re-victimisation

Minor crimes have a more significant impact when racial re-victimisation occurs through becoming the (Un)Victim. One of the ways in which this is manifested, is through the (Un)Victim's desire to understand the reason why their victimisation was not taken seriously by the police. For Samuel, who had been the victim of a collision with an uninsured driver (discussed earlier), the effects of what he perceived to be unfair treatment were being felt eight years after the relatively minor incident. Not being taken seriously on this occasion led to feelings of confusion and the desire to pursue the issue in order to understand why he was not afforded victim status;

> I would also like to revisit this case and try to hear what they have to say. I'm not really looking for an apology but asking them what the way forward is going to be. What lessons have you learnt? You know. What are you going to do differently so that someone else does not have the same experience? (Samuel, 45, Black, African, male)

For some research participants', the burden of racial re-victimisation, through becoming the (Un)Victim, formed part of their motivation for participation in this research;

> I just wanted to get it off my chest because I was so, so annoyed I was fuming with them. I was fuming, fuming. And as I say, I'm not of that nature I just take things with a pinch of salt usually but thinking that's not on that, that's just not on, just not on… so yea, really, really glad that I had the opportunity to air my feelings [laughs]. (Shawn, 39, Black, British-born, male)

Here, Shawn is referring to a minor hit and run, as discussed earlier. Shawn perceived that the incident was not taken seriously by the police. This was compounded through the construction of his blackness as a threat by both the White perpetrator, who left the scene of the (minor) accident, and the police. In both of these examples, a relatively minor incident has had long lasting emotional, racist affects which have impacted upon quality of life and recovery from victimisation (see also Elliott et al. 2014; Barkworth and Murphy 2016).

As Holdaway argues, racialised interactions with the police 'partially reconstructs their personal reality and the reality of race within the wider social terrain' (Holdaway 1996: 44). When racialised relations force the Other to view themselves through the 'White gaze', it serves to reproduces power relations. Further, when Black and Black mixed-race people are forced to consider that race is the reason that they do not have access to justice, they are re-victimised through race. This realisation that they are constructed as suspect, even when they are victimised, is a factor in determining whether or not they would approach the police for help in future. Both Levi and Marcus, two friends who lived in an area with a significant ethnic minority population, observed that there is a reluctance by Black people to contact the police to report crime;

Marcus: I mean I think that's why the police get away with a lot of what they are getting away with cause a lot of Black people or ethnic minorities don't phone the police do they?
Levi: I'm guilty of that.
Marcus: Yea, some things happen and you don't phone the police.
Levi: You're absolutely right.
Marcus: So, when they look at their official numbers they probably think oh well you know nothing's happening to this because we've not had anybody complaining or and that's because of the distrust that people have got about the police they won't phone up.

This reluctance to contact the police is reflected in participant's accounts;

> If it's something petty I'll just deal with it myself. Because that was about the first time I reported a police case. I thought they would deal with it but they didn't. (Kenneth, 38, Black, African, male)

> I mean, obviously if it was something serious like if someone had burgled my house or you know if I got seriously attacked or something then I probably would go to the police, but if it was just a minor thing, I'd probably think I can't be bothered with the hassle of dealing with the police. (Robert, 27, Black mixed-race, British-born, male)

For both Robert and Kenneth, their previous experiences of reporting crime had changed their expectation that the police would help them. This meant that they would assess their own experiences of victimisation in relation to a hierarchy of crimes, before contacting the police in future. For those who would contact the police, they rationalised this in relation to their entitlement to the service, rather than an expectation of a satisfactory response;

> The police are there. I pay taxes they've got a role to play… I'm a law-abiding citizen and if I need help I'm not one to shy away. (Eric, 38, Black, African, male)

> That's what we pay for as taxpayers. (Janice, 37, Black, British-born, female)

> You know I pay taxes and I pay council tax and all the rest of it and if something needs to happen then they need to do it. (Marcus, 44, Black, British-born, male)

Further, several participants said that they would contact the police because they had no other choice, regardless of their expectations of a helpful or satisfactory response;

> There is no other option; you have to talk to them. (Jean, 40, Black, African, male)

> Obviously, you don't have a choice; you won't go to the army, would you? You have to go to the police [laughter] …because at the end of the day they are the only people that you can actually go to. (Charles, 40, Black, African, male)

> I'd probably be anticipating their response but I'd still go… I don't see why I should have to change my story or not go at all or try to fit into their stereotype. I'm not going to fit into anybody's stereotype. (Shawn, 39, Black, British-born, male)

Here, Shawn reflects the ways in which opting to contact the police, despite low expectations, can negotiate the production of social identity through police interactions (Bradford et al. 2014). Whilst negative police contact can communicate exclusion through racialised responses, choosing to contact the police can be a way of reaffirming individual social identity and citizenship and challenging stereotypes of criminality and anti-police attitude.

One statement stood out as contrasting with the accounts of some of the other research participants'. Janice, when asked if she would contact the police for help, responded;

> There isn't one person that I honestly would think if something went wrong that you wouldn't think the first thing is to phone the police regardless of your situation. (Janice, 37, Black, British-born, female)

For Janice, the police were the first port of call without hesitation. Whilst Janice had negative experiences of policing in which she had been treated as suspect, her experiences as a victim had been satisfactory. She had relationships with the police in a professional context which allowed her to build up personal knowledge and trust relationships in that context. Whilst throughout her account she acknowledges police racism, she accepted that as a woman she was able to negotiate her position (also, see Chapter 6). This may explain her willingness to approach the police for help despite her previous negative experiences and her strong awareness of racism and its impact, in particular on Black men.

For some of the participants', the police were completely disregarded as a source of help. Some participants indicated that they would not contact the police for help regardless of the severity of the incident. The participants' who exercised complete avoidance of the police had in common that they had experienced extended and cumulative negative contact with police over several years and in various contexts, or alternatively, one significant and defining experience. For Derek, the experience of being tasered by the police (discussed in Chapter 4) led him to conclude that he would not contact the police if he was the victim of crime;

> There might be situations where I'd have to but right now in my head I'm saying whatever it is I would not get in touch with the police. No way, no way.

Derek was not alone in suggesting that it may be easier to try and deal with the problem, rather than contacting the police (also reflected in findings in Sharp and Atherton 2007). This is a risky approach that could lead the victim into offending, as he recognised;

> Honestly, I think about it, and I'm saying you know what just become a criminal because you've got legalised criminals out there in the shape of the police. But that's not me and I'm not looking to lower myself to those standards. I've talked about the kind of [criminal] behaviour that my son has got in the past. So, let's just say me and this man had a disagreement or this man stole something from me would I ring the police? Or would I ring one of my sons' friends and say, 'yo, can you come and deal with this for me?' (Derek, 46, Black, British-born, male)

Reporting a crime to the police is to 'put' the Black victim in a position where they would be treated unfairly because of their race.

> Why would I put myself there? Why would I encourage anybody to put themselves there? They've give me no reason to believe that I would be treat fairly. They've got this disease, I call it like a disease, where they have this belief that it's okay to treat Black people in the way they do'. (Thomas, 55, Black, British-born, male)

Similarly, Macpherson described institutional racism as a 'corrosive disease' (Macpherson 1999: 6.34), the police, in the collective sense, are infected. This finding is contrary to the police view that Black people are empowered by the diversity agenda and play the 'race card' to gain power in interactions with the police (Loftus 2009). Thomas went on to say '… *it's horrible to have to sit down and tell your sons and daughters and your grandchildren the truth*'. As illustrated by Thomas's account this disempowerment is felt both on an individual level and by whole communities. Community narratives passed from generation to generation convey that the police are not an organisation that can be trusted. Expectations of a less favourable response or fear of being treated as suspect preclude whole communities from the 'service' to which they are entitled. The fear of being the victim of crime is not as great as the threat posed by the police. Justice is relational in a system which under protects and over penalises the racialised other (also Cacho 2012; Hudson 2006).

It has previously been suggested that procedurally fair policing is not as effective in establishing trust and legitimacy in 'ethnic minority' communities, it is assumed that their opinions are fixed because of their knowledge of social identity and interaction with the state (Murphy and Cherney 2011). This approach risks blaming the '(Un)Victim' for their failure to trust the police, rather than considering how police behaviour informs these perceptions. Conversely, these findings suggest that people who have a generally favourable perception of the police and little previous contact with them in other contexts can have their perceptions changed negatively by unfair policing in victim contexts. Racialised response to victims of crime excludes the (Un)Victim from conventional routes to justice through both, the process of becoming the (Un) Victim and the subsequent racial re-victimisation, and self-exclusion from processes of justice because of a lack of confidence.

Conclusions

As this chapter has shown, the pervasive discourses of race which position Black and mixed-race people as Other, as threat, and linked to racialised discourses of criminality distance them from the image of the 'ideal victim' (Christie 1986) in the police imagination. The process of becoming a victim is shaped, in part, through these racialised discourses. Discretion in police decision making, about both the nature of the crime and the worth of the victim, opens up a space between the crime report and enactment of the 'entitlements' set out in the *Code of Practice for Victims*, for the victimised to become the '(Un)Victim'. As reflected in participants' experiences of victimisation, the perception of the victimised that they are a victim of crime creates an expectation that they will be treated as such when they make a report to the police. This is in the context of a justice process that makes claim, in the public domain, to center the needs of the victim, through their entitlements to 'service'. When these expectations are not met it communicates that they are undeserving of victim status and their relationship to the state and sense of belonging is called into question (Bradford et al. 2014).

For Black and mixed-race victims of crime the racialised processes of victim blaming and treatment as suspect damage trust and confidence in the police as a fair and legitimate institution. This has a significant impact on willingness to approach the police and/or levels of confidence in a satisfactory response. This delimits the boundaries of the deserving victim to the 'White, old, lady' (Van Wijk 2013; Christie 1986), the denial of victim status excludes the '(Un)Victim' from support mechanisms reserved for the deserving victim. Further, it disempowers them in the context of feeling safe and protected when they feel that it is '*a waste of time*' contacting the police for help, as when they do they will either be treated as suspect or have their victim status denied. As a result of their racialised position as '(Un)Victim', they unequal recourse to protection and/or justice.

The impact of police responses to victimisation for Black and mixed-race peoples trust and confidence in the police is a currently under-explored area. Over policing is often cited as the main cause of poor relations between the police and Black people. Whilst disproportionate stop and search remains a significant problem, as discussed in the previous chapter, the findings set out in this chapter suggest that police responses to victimisation are also significant in understanding trust and confidence in the police. Experiences of racial victimisation are addressed through some existing research (Bowling 1999), albeit scant. However, the White lens has hitherto been applied to victim experiences more broadly. The counter-story developed throughout this chapter begins to illuminate new ways of understanding race and processes of racialisation in the experiences of victimisation.

The intersection of race and processes of racialisation with gender, in both suspect and victim encounters with police, will be explored in the subsequent chapter.

References

Ahmed, S. (2007). A Phenomenology of Whiteness. *Feminist Theory, 8,* 149–168.

Anderson, B. (2006). *Imagined Communities: Reflections on the Origin and Spread of Nationalism.* London: Verso.

Barkworth, J., & Murphy, K. (2016). System Contact and Procedural Justice Policing: Improving Quality of Life Outcomes for Victims of Crime. *International Review of Victimology, 22*(2), 105–122.

Bowling, B. (1999). *Violent Racism: Victimization, Policing and Social Context.* Oxford: Oxford University Press.

Bradford, B., Murphy, K., & Jackson, J. (2014). Officers as Mirrors: Policing, Procedural Justice and the (Re)Production of Social Identity. *British Journal of Criminology, 54,* 527–550.

Bradford, B., Sargeant, E., Murphy, T., & Jackson, J. (2017). A Leap of Faith? Trust in the Police Among Immigrants in England and Wales. *British Journal of Criminology, 57*(2), 381–401.

Cacho, L. M. (2012). *Social Death Racialised Rightlessness and the Criminalization of the Unprotected.* New York: New York University Press.

Christie, N. (1986). The Ideal Victim. In E. A. Fattah (Ed.), *From Crime Policy to Victim Policy.* London: Macmillan.

DuBois, W. E. B. (1994). *The Souls of Black Folk* (2nd ed.). New York: Dover.

Elliott, I., Thomas, S., & Ogloff, J. (2014). Procedural Justice in Victim-Police Interactions and Victims' Recovery from Victimisation Experiences. *Policing and Society, 24,* 588–601.
Fanon, F. (1986). *Black Skin, White Masks.* London: Pluto Press.
Foster, J., Newburn, T., & Souhami, A. (2005). *Assessing the Impact of the Stephen Lawrence Inquiry* (Home Office Research Study, 294).
Gordon, L. R. (2005). *Bad Faith and Antiblack Racism.* New York: Humanity Books.
Grimshaw, R., & Jefferson, T. (1987). *Interpreting Policework: Policy and Practice in Forms of Beat Policing.* London: Allen and Unwin.
Holdaway, S. (1996). *The Racialisation of British Policing.* London: Macmillan.
Hudson, B. (2006). Beyond White Man's Justice Race, Gender and Justice in Late Modernity. *Theoretical Criminology, 10,* 29–47.
Kristina, M. (2009). Public Satisfaction with Police: The Importance of Procedural Justice and Police Performance in Police–Citizen Encounters. *Australian and New Zealand Journal of Criminology, 42,* 159–178.
Loftus, B. (2009). *Police Culture in a Changing World.* New York: Oxford University Press.
Macpherson of Cluny, W. (1999). *The Stephen Lawrence Inquiry.* London: The Stationery Office.
Maguire, M. (2011). Criminal Investigation and Crime Control. In R. Reiner (Ed.), *Handbook of Policing* (2nd ed.). Abingdon: Taylor and Francis.
Miers, D. (2000). Taking the Law into Their Own Hands: Victims as Offenders. In A. Crawford & J. Goodey (Eds.), *Integrating a Victim Perspective within Criminal Justice.* Aldershot: Ashgate.
Ministry of Justice. (2015). *Statistics on Race and the Criminal Justice System 2014.* https://www.gov.uk/government/statistics/race-and-the-criminal-justice-system-2014. Accessed 21 October 2017.
Murphy, K., & Cherney, A. (2011). Fostering Cooperation with the Police: How Do Ethnic Minorities in Australia Respond to Procedural Justice-Based Policing? *Australian and New Zealand Journal of Criminology, 44,* 235–257.
Office for National Statistics. (2017). *Confidence in the Local Police.* https://www.ethnicity-facts-figures.service.gov.uk/crime-justice-and-the-law/policing/confidence-in-the-local-police/latest. Accessed 21 December 2017.
Reiner, R. (2010). *The Politics of the Police.* Oxford: Oxford University Press.
Rock, P. (2002). On Becoming a Victim. In C. Hoyle & R. Young (Eds.), *New Visions of Crime Victims.* Oxford: Hart Publishing.

Sharp, D., & Atherton, S. (2007). To Serve and Protect? The Experiences of Policing in the Community of Young People from Black and Other Ethnic Minority Groups. *British Journal of Criminology, 47,* 746–763.

Tilley, N. (2008). Modern Approaches to Policing: Community, Problem-Orientated and Intelligence-Led. In T. Newburn (Ed.), *Handbook of Policing*. London: Routledge.

Tyler, T. R., & Lind, E. A. (1992). A Relational Model of Authority in Groups. *Advances in Experimental Social Psychology, 25,* 115–192.

Van Wijk, J. (2013). Who Is the 'Little Old Lady' of International Crimes? Nils Christie's Concept of the Ideal Victim Reinterpreted. *International Review of Victimology, 19,* 159–179.

Wells, W. (2007). Type of Contact and Evaluations of Police Officers: The Effects of Procedural Justice Across Three Types Of Police–Citizen Contacts. *Journal of Criminal Justice, 35,* 612–621.

Yarrow, S. (2005). *The Experiences of Young Black Men as Victims of Crime*. London: Criminal Justice Unit and Victims and Confidence Unit.

6
Gendered Experiences of Racialised Policing

The preceding chapters have illuminated the nature and effects of racialised and racist policing. However, there are evident differences between Black men's and Black women's experience of police contact. This chapter employs a gender lens in order to analyse the intersection of race and gender in the context of police encounters. It argues that the proliferation of racialised stereotypes, through reference to hegemonic and subordinate masculinities and femininities (Collins 2004), are crucial to understanding how race operates at its intersection with gender. Hegemonic masculinity is a key defining feature of contemporary police occupational culture (Reiner 2010; Loftus 2009). There has arguably been a small shift from a homogenous police culture centered on White hegemonic masculinity, towards plural cultures, owing to the diversification of the police service (Loftus 2009). However, the police rely upon hegemonic White masculinity and femininity to uphold the state interests invested in the 'White supremacist capitalist patriarchy' (Hooks 2004: 79).

L. J. Long, *Perpetual Suspects*, Palgrave Studies in Race, Ethnicity, Indigeneity and Criminal Justice, https://doi.org/10.1007/978-3-319-98240-3_6

A comparative analysis of the ways in which Black and mixed-race men and Black and mixed-race women experience and negotiate police contact in different contexts allows for a relational understanding of how oppression operates at the intersection of race and gender. This analysis highlights how intersecting oppressions of race and gender are organised, in relation to structures of power bound up with hegemonic forms of White masculinity. Through an examination of women's experiences of the police it will demonstrate that stereotypes attributed to Black women shape their experiences of police contact both as suspect and victims of crime. However, these stereotypes are not as inextricably tied up in discourses of criminality as those attributed to Black men. It will argue that some Black and mixed-race women are able to perform preferred versions of femininity, in the context of police contact, through recourse to social and cultural capital (Bourdieu 1986). This has the capacity to negotiate race to some extent in the police encounter. Black men are not able to negotiate race in the same way; Black masculinity is pathologized as hyper-masculine, hyper-sexualised and hyper-aggressive (Mutua 2006; Collins 2004). Therefore, Black men cannot perform a more desirable version of masculinity, they are the perpetual suspect and pose the ultimate threat to the White hegemonic masculinity of the police institution.

The Threat of the 'Big Black Man'

Racialised stereotypes attributed to Black men are perceived to impact significantly upon their experiences of policing. The news media has been a key source of constructing public perceptions of Black people and perpetuating racist tropes which link Black people with criminality. Media proliferated moral panics with Black males cast as the folk devil have perpetuated the criminal stereotype in the UK context. Take, for example, the image of the Black mugger (Hall et al. 1978), the Black drug user or dealer (Murji 1999; Gabriel 1998) and in more recent times the racialisation of the debate surrounding gangs and violent crime (Alexander 2008; Cushion et al. 2011; Smithson et al. 2013;

Williams and Clarke 2016). This race-crime link is significantly gendered and racialised images permeate discourses of masculinity (Connell 2005: 75–80). Further, these stereotypes shape bias against physical features associated with Black masculinity and related perceptions of strength and capacity for causing harm. Research finds that young Black men are perceived as taller, heavier and more muscular and more threatening than young White men (Wilson et al. 2017). Black women also have distinct negative stereotypes attributed to them which depict Black femininity as subordinate to White femininity. Stereotypes such as the welfare queen/welfare mother and the strong black woman, evident in both the US and the UK context (see Tate 2015), construct Black women as angry and their femininity as less desirable (Collins 2004; Walley-Jean 2009). However, these stereotypes are not inherently criminal. The image of the dangerous, criminal 'big Black man', is firmly entrenched in public consciousness and more significantly for suspect bodies, in the 'police imagination'.

Research participants perceived that their encounters with the police both as suspect, and as victims of crime, could be attributed, in part, to these racialised stereotypes. In both contexts Black and Black mixed-race men were treated as suspect and as a threat to the hegemonic White masculine authority of the police institution. There are significant assumptions about Black men that participants perceived to shape the police approach and response to them. The most critical is the assumption that Black men are inherently criminal. Further, their physical attributes—particularly height and size (or attributed height and size)—and cultural signifiers such as dress or hairstyle, symbolize a threat. Therefore, police officers expect Black men to react in non-compliant and potentially aggressive ways towards them (Bowling et al. 2008). On this basis they approach them preemptively in anticipation of an assumed threat. Kenneth described a police officer approaching him whilst he was sat on his bike fastening outside of his workplace;

> He just ran up to me so I was a bit shocked when he came and when he explained he was a police officer because he was a plain clothed. Then he explained why he has to come, that the camera picked me up behaving

> suspiciously [laughs]. I had to identify myself and that's fine. Yea, he was a bit harsh but finally he calmed down when he got my details and went... because of the way he approached me he thought I was going to react or something. (Kenneth, 38, Black, African, male)

Andrew was pulled over in his car by plain clothed police officers and aggressively restrained and searched (see Chapter 4). Here he reflects upon the reasons why he was approached in that manner;

> Just to be harassed like that is a bit of a unique experience... thrown over the car and that and the default being that I'm going to react. And, I didn't react in any way... But then the fact is I'm mindful as well that I'm a big guy as well, six foot two, six foot three, you know [sighs]. So, there's all that default stuff about, you know, Black people are aggressive, they're physical, they're violent. (Andrew, 41, Black mixed-race, British-born, male)

Andrew clearly understands how he is interpellated in the police imagination, the embodied threat represented in the 'big Black man' stereotype requires a particular response which assumes that there is an inherent threat created by simply approaching a Black man. This cannot be done without an immediate display of authority to remind the subject who is in control and to enforce compliance. Both Kenneth and Andrew know that the police expect them to respond to their approach in a defensive or aggressive manner. As argued by Hooks (2004), '...the Black male body continues to be perceived as the embodiment of bestial, violent, penis-as-weapon, masculine assertion' (p. 79). This perceived embodiment of 'subordinated Black masculinity' (Collins 2004: 187) operates through the 'White gaze' (Yancy 2008). These perceptions, which attribute hyper-masculine traits to individuals because of their physical attributes, position the Black body as a threat in the 'police imagination' creating an expectation of aggressive and threatening behaviours which shape police responses in pre-emptive ways.

This presumption of an aggressive response to being approached by the police, can potentially lead to a pre-emptive use of force which is not in accordance with the legal test of reasonable, proportionate and necessary. This is evident in the excessive use of police force and resultant restraint related deaths in custody (see, Chapter 3), increased complaints of police brutality (Gallagher 2015), discharge of firearms, more frequently in the US context, and recent UK evidence which suggests that Taser is being used disproportionately in the restraint of Black people (Gayle 2015). Derek was tasered by the police, as discussed in Chapter 4, he reflected upon his construction in the 'police imagination' in the course of his interview;

> I think some of the lads in my neighbourhood and I don't … I'm not knocking them yeah, but they've got a certain type of lifestyle that brings the police on them yeah, but the way they spoke to me yeah, gold tooth, black man, picky head yeah, they had an impression of me which is why they spoke to me like that. (Derek, 46, Black, British-born, male)

Here Derek acknowledges that meaning given to 'cultural signifiers' such as the styling of hair in particular ways and the wearing of gold teeth. These features, which are 'discursively constructed as Black' (Tate 2015: 15), have different meanings to those who employ them. When they are viewed from the outside, and have meanings attributed to them associated with 'Black culture', they are negatively attributed to a criminal pathology.

Several participants acknowledged that the police assume that Black people are involved in the supply of drugs. Marcus recalled with some amusement an occasion when the police knocked on his door to enquire about reports of a missing child being held at the property. Marcus assumed that it was a mistake and refused the police officer entry without a warrant, instead he allowed an accompanying paramedic into his house to look for the child. The paramedic confirmed to the police that the child in question was not in the house. She also reported to the police that she had seen a bag of White powder on the kitchen table. The police returned and '*burst into the house*', Marcus explained;

> There was a bag of white powder on the kitchen table. I'd run out of washing powder so I'd gone to my mam's house [laughter] … so I put some in to a plastic bag and I tied it up and I brought it back and left it on the kitchen table…He's [police officer] picked this White powder up

> and says 'what is it', he says 'washing powder', 'yeah' [laughter]. So, he says 'how do we know it's washing powder', 'I said well you better take it away and get it forensically tested [laughter] cause I'm not doing your washing for ya'[laughs]. (Marcus, 44, Black, British-born, male)

Marcus expressed obvious humour in his retelling of the event. However, his story highlights the extent to which Black men are cast, in the 'police imagination', as the enemy in the 'war on drugs'. The washing powder was taken away and Marcus heard nothing more from the police regarding the substance. However, such instances serve to perpetuate the cycle of mutual distrust.

For the most part, 'law abiding citizens' do not expect that they will be treated as a suspect by the police. For several participants', who self-identified in this way, the police response to them as suspect was a surprise. Participants' drew upon particular aspects of their identity to explain why they did not expect to be treated in accordance with the criminal Black male stereotype. Personality traits, area of residence, and level of education or being a 'law abiding citizen' were used by participants' to create distance from pervasive negative stereotypes. They also expressed surprise that they were treated in the same way that the police would treat somebody engaged in a criminal lifestyle. Andrew reflected on being roughly treated by the police during a car stop;

> I don't really see that there's much, kind of, questionable ammunition there to go in heavy handed with somebody. This is somebody that.... If I'd got a record of I don't know if I'd got a record of... being armed and having weapons previously and holding a gun or a knife, hey ho yea, yea maybe be a bit more heavy handed. (Andrew, 41, Black mixed-race, British-born, male)

In this extract it is clear that Andrew would have expected the police to react in a heavy-handed way and would accept this to some extent as justified if he had a criminal record or posed a risk due to being armed. Like other participants' Andrew expected that being a 'law abiding citizen' would prevent this kind of treatment at the hands of the police.

Unfortunately, as Andrew found out, the embodiment of threat, posed by the 'big Black man' stereotype, cannot be negotiated through compliance with the law.

Similarly having personality traits that do not fit with the hyper-aggressive stereotype associated with Black masculinity, does not protect Black and Black mixed-race men from the criminalising effects of the stereotype. This is evident in Shawn's experience, discussed in Chapter 4, when he was hit by a White female driver who then drove off from the scene of an accident. The woman was traced by the police and she told them that she had fled the scene because she was '*scared*';

> I've never attacked anybody; I've never hit anybody so you know it's out of my character. That is totally out of my character. Anyone that knows me would say that is not Shawn, he would never do that. So, to me it was like wow, in this day and age people still assume that because someone's stature and complexion that they're gonna be of a particular stereotype, I was stunned. (Shawn, 39, Black, British-born, male)

The White, female, driver's perception of him and the police readiness to accept this as a valid explanation for leaving the scene was a shock for Shawn. He had never before been confronted so starkly with the evidence that expectations of negative behaviour could be attributed to him on the basis of his appearance, despite the anti-racism rhetoric evident in '*this day and age*'.

Hypo-Masculinities and Race

There are some identities that intersect with race in such a way as to diminish the hyper-masculine threatening stereotypes associated with Black men. Eric, who described himself as disabled, perceived that the police responded to him differently to the way in which they would respond to a '*typical Black man*'. Perceptions of disability are synonymous with dependence and helplessness which is an antithesis to the characteristics ascribed by hegemonic masculinities

(Asch and Fine 1992: 141; Shuttleworth et al. 2012). The identification of individuals as hypo-masculine neutralises the threat attributed to the 'big Black man'.[1] Eric reflects upon how race intersected with disability, to negotiate embodied Black masculinity, when he was pulled over by the police for a driving offence;

> *Eric*: I would call myself a disabled person. And I think I don't look intimidating or a typical Black man. I've got a good speech and good manner from my upbringing. I think they felt sorry for me more than anything else.
>
> *Lisa*: It's interesting that you talk about seeing yourself as different to a typical Black man, what do you mean?
>
> *Eric*: I think when White people describe Black men they say it's a big Black man in that nature where we are deemed to cause trouble at any corner. I don't fit in a stereotype, so some people don't know how to handle me. (Eric, 32, Black, African, male)

Eric draws on his '*visible*' disability to explain the way that he was treated sympathetically, even when he had committed an offence. He perceived that his treatment was different to that of a '*typical Black man*' who might embody threatening Black masculinity. Eric also suggests that his speech and manner (compliance) are interpreted as evidence of his good character. Through a performance of respectability, he felt able to show that he was different to the stereotype. However, as will be argued in the following chapter, signs of respectability can be disregarded or misinterpreted through the inextricable race/crime nexus in the 'police imagination'. The police know how to handle people who they perceive fit into a stereotype that presents them as a threat. When the person they are dealing with does not present as the hyper-masculine stereotype that the police draw upon to determine threat, even when they have committed an offence, they are not treated in

[1]It should be noted that this point is made in relation to visible physical disability, there is evidence, particularly in relation to deaths in custody, that individuals with mental health vulnerabilities are constructed as particularly dangerous, legitimising the use of excessive force (Pemberton 2008) as was acutely evident in the death of Roger Sylvester at the hands of the state (IRR 2003).

the same manner. This thesis can be extended to the treatment of gay men who are attributed 'hypo-masculinity' in the context of a hetero-masculine police culture.

The police service is still dominated by a masculine ethos (Loftus 2010: 8). According to Bernstein and Kostelac, the maintenance of police status depends upon an 'organisational and cultural interest in heterosexism' (Bernstein and Kostelac 2002: 307). This makes it difficult for gay police officers to be open about their sexuality within a patriarchal society which views them as lacking in masculinity (Connell 2005: 143) and an institution that privileges masculine traits. This is particularly difficult for those who are already oppressed in the White police institution through race. Andrew, who has worked closely with police officers in the course of his employment, recalled his observations of police officers' attitude towards a gay colleague who was working in partnership with the police;

> I remember I was working with [colleague] who happened to be a gay guy. I overheard conversations; police members of staff laughing, trivialising him. I don't doubt for one minute, probably in his company, that they were doing the same about me from a 'BME' group you know. (Andrew, 41, Black mixed-race, British-born, male)

Andrew expresses how oppressions, race and sexuality, work together to produce injustices. This is achieved through the positioning of the othered, the hyper-masculine Black man and the hypo-masculine gay man, subordinately in relation to hegemonic White masculinities of the police institution.

Whilst the evidence suggests that race and 'sexuality' intersect to create different institutionalised oppressions for Black, gay police officers, the experiences at the intersection of race and sexuality in citizen contact with the public is under-researched. There is a perception that the police are discriminatory in relation to sexuality as evident in the finding that one in five people who had experienced homophobic hate crime did not report to police, due to an expectation of discriminatory treatment (Hunt and Dick 2008: 4). However, only one research participant talked about their own sexuality as it intersects with race in their experiences of policing. This was perceived to change the nature of the type of contact Black people have with the police and the types of crimes that they might be associated with in the 'police imagination' as expressed by Robert;

> If I was straight it would probably be slightly worse because I think that the kind of crimes they assume a gay person would commit and the crimes that they assume just a straight mixed-race or Black man would commit would be different. Perhaps I would be more likely to be singled out and spotted in the first place because of my race or my ethnicity but I guess once they assume that I'm gay or whatever then they might then assume different kinds of crime for me.

What is interesting here, is that Robert perceives that his sexuality may have altered the perception of him as an embodiment of the Black criminal threat in the 'police imagination'. The outcome may be a reduced frequency of contact with the police, that might have otherwise been routine and unpleasant on the basis of race;

> I probably might have been stopped and searched more in my everyday life if I was heterosexual.

Robert's perception illustrates how intersecting oppressions of race, gender and sexuality are organised through the 'structural domain of racism' (Collins 2000) in the police institution, an institution premised on the hegemonic power of White masculinity. Robert also expressed, through recounting the experiences of his friends, the ways in which the police single out sexual relationships between men for particular scrutiny;

> I don't feel that I've been any more picked on because of being gay but I know that a lot of friends do. I know that its cynical but at times they'll [the police] be marching in gay pride during the day time and then at night they go to cruising grounds and arrest loads of people because it's one way of getting the stats up. (Robert, 27, Black mixed-race, British-born, male)

The policing of casual sexual relationships between men is informed by embedded 'police cultural knowledge' of the practice as 'deviant' (Loftus 2009: 80). For Robert, this represented a betrayal by the police who used their attendance at the local *Gay Pride* event to perform diversity and then followed this with several arrests in the evening.

Hegemonic and subordinated masculinities are demonstrably significant in understanding the intersecting oppressions of race and gender. For Black and mixed-race men, the perceived criminal, hyper-aggressive threat that they pose, as communicated through prevalent stereotypes, places them as an enemy to the White police institution. Although it is clear that most of these men are not involved in criminal lifestyles, they are the perpetual suspect. It is only when they are perceived as hypo-masculine, such as in the case of Eric who identified as visibly disabled or Robert who identified as gay, that the Black man is no longer viewed as a perpetual suspect. Gay men may be considered sexually deviant and be punished through social control which targets the spaces that they frequent (Burke 1994; Bernstein and Kostelac 2002), as Robert opines. However, their perceived hypo-masculinity, viewed through the lens of the heterosexist police institution, does not pose the physical threat embodied by the 'big Black man' stereotype.

Black Women and the Police

Criminology, including feminist criminology, has been criticised for ignoring the experiences of Black women. Marcia Rice described this lack of attention as the 'other dark figure of crime' (Rice 1990: 58). The absence of Black women's experience is starkly evident in relation to the policing literature. This indicates that there is a need for a research focus on the treatment of Black and mixed-race women by the police and the Criminal Justice System more broadly. This section will focus on the accounts of five female research participants' and will explore the intersection of race and gender with reference to how the myth of Black criminality and subsequent threat is evident in Black and Black mixed-race women's experiences of policing.

Similarly, to Black and mixed-race men, Black and mixed-race women become the focus of police attention because of their race. Like men, female research participants also had experience of police contact and arrest at a young age, some in childhood, and are viewed with suspicion on the basis of popular and pervasive stereotypes, even when they are 'law abiding citizens'. In Chapter 4, it was shown how those considered 'police property' (Lee 1981) experience police context, as suspects, from an early age. This includes young women, as explored through Bianca's experience of being stopped by the police on her bike whilst playing outside with friends. However, there are some evident differences between men and women's experiences; for the women who had not been involved in offending behaviour, the frequency of contact with the police in day to day routine matters was less frequent than for men. Women do not experience stop and search in the same way as men. Even women who are known to the police—for example Alice, who was 'known' to the police for a significant period of her life—did not have personal experience of stop and search. However, research suggests that the changing perceptions of female offending is increasing stop and search for young women contemporarily, as highlighted in *Reading the Riots* (Lewis et al. 2011). The difference in frequency of contact and negative experiences of policing for women could also explain the small number of women who approached the project and the nature and length of interviews with female participants'. Interviews were shorter on average than those conducted with male participants' and experiences of the police more dispersed throughout their narrative.

Unlike male participants' 'accounts, female participants' did not view stop and search as a routine or inevitable part of their lives. In fact, none of the five women interviewed had experienced stop and search. However, Carol and Janice both recalled being pulled over and stopped by the police. Carol was keen to discuss a recent experience of being stopped in her car, a stop which did not appear to be justified. Carol is a Black health professional in her forties. Her contact with the police has been minimal and in relation to minor victim experiences which had elicited a satisfactory response. Carol had one previous experience of being pulled over in her car which she did not object to because she was in an unfamiliar location and had carried out an inappropriate manoeuvre. In this context Carol did not question the police response and accepted it as legitimate. The most recent incident occurred late at night when she was driving home from a friend's house with another friend in the passenger seat. Carol recalled being pulled over by two male police officers, one of the officers asked her if the car was hers. He followed his question with '*because nice cars like this are normally pinched*'. It was this statement that caused Carol to feel uncomfortable about the stop as the police officers alluded to a stereotype that when a Black person is driving a nice car they are doing so through illegitimate means. Carol said '*does he mean that a girl like me [Black] couldn't have a car like that?*'. Carol complied with the police officer and confirmed that the car belonged to her and she was allowed to carry on with her drive home. Carol made some observations about the police attitude towards her;

> They were polite; they weren't rough at all or nothing. No, they were polite in the way they asked. It's only the sort of the question that he asked that's why I just wondered [if the stop was motivated by racism]. But he wasn't at all, he wasn't threatening.

This experience is different to the nature of the car stops recalled in male participant's accounts, in which there were examples of the police officers testing participant's attitude to the police in what one officer described to Phillip as '*passing the attitude test*' (see Chapter 4). This was also evident through identity checks, issuing a 'producer' and aggressive restraint and search tactics. These behaviours were not prevalent in women's accounts of car stops. Carol reflected upon the different treatment of men and women;

> My friend was saying that, I bet if it was a Black fella he would probably have had a rougher time than me. They probably would have got him out and you know, asked for ID and some things like that. Because they didn't really ask me. I just said it was my car, that was it and then off I went. (Carol, 49, Black, British-born, female)

Carol complied with the officer's instruction to get out of the car, she answered his questions and was believed when she told the officers that it was her car. She was not asked to prove her identity, make further enquiries or issue a producer.

Similarly, Janice had cause to reflect on the differential treatment of black men when she was pulled over for speeding on the motorway. She was with her boyfriend, a Black man who '*is pulled up every time he enters Yorkshire*'. Janice got out of the car to meet with the police officer who was '*admiring*' the car. She apologised for her speed and explained how powerful the car was and that the speed had just '*crept up on her*'. The police officer did not issue a penalty notice on this occasion. Janice recalled how both her boyfriend and her brother, who she later told of the incident, were shocked that she had '*got away with it*' without any points. Janice discussed with her boyfriend the reasons for the absence of punitive approach by the police officer in question;

> When I got back in the car he was like 'did you get three points?'. I said 'no'. And he were like 'why? I would have got three points'. And I said 'cause you get out with attitude. I got out and confessed to exactly what I'd done'… I knew I'd done 82(mph). I knew exactly what I'd done. It's because of his attitude when he gets out the way he dresses, the way he looks. So, yea there is stereotypes because he gets pulled and it's the way he looks. He drives with his hood up, sat way back, so they're going to think it's being driven by bloody knight rider, no driver in there. But realistically this is genuinely how people feel that they do get stopped for wrong reasons because I've got a nice car'. (Janice, 37, Black, British-born, female)

Both Janice and Carol's accounts demonstrate that a display of appropriate 'feminine demeanour' (Collins 2004: 196) when confronted with the authority of the White hegemonic masculine authority of the police authority is advantageous for women. Their compliance with the police officer and their compliance with the law, evidenced through the absence of previous offending behaviour, demonstrates that they are not like the threatening 'big Black man' nor are they like the stigmatised working class Black woman who represents the 'least desirable form of femininity' (Collins 2004: 199). In this context, recourse to feminine traits negotiates the impact of racialisation.

The extent to which race can be negotiated through femininity is dependent on context. When a crime has been committed and the police are required to apprehend the suspect, Black women are more likely to be treated as suspect than White women. This is illustrated through Janice's account of an incident which occurred in the course of her paid employment as a youth worker. Janice described what happened when, in a professional capacity, she tried to break up a fight at a football match which incidentally had been organised to break down barriers between young people from two different estates;

> It turned out to be a fight with some Black boys and a White boy who was making racist comments. And they threw him on the floor, started kicking him. I obviously jumped in to try and save him because I knew that my clients wouldn't hurt me so I tried to jump in. By the time the police had got across the football pitch which was quite large they took us all [laughs]. (Janice)

Janice was alongside her White colleague at the time of her arrest yet Janice was the only member of staff who was arrested. She was later released without charge when she explained who she was and she received an apology. However, this experience illuminates how Black women's proximity to desirable forms of femininity leave them susceptible to being treated as suspect, even when they are engaged in 'respectable' activity, like paid, professional employment.

The differential treatment experienced by Black and Black mixed-race women, in comparison to their White peers, can have significant consequences for their life chances, particularly for young women. Alice's first arrest was at the age of fifteen, Alice recalled that on the occasion of her first offence the police charged her without any concern for the impact on her future whilst her White peers were 'cautioned'. During the interview Alice reflected on the longer-term impact of this decision and what this communicated to her about her position in relation to the police and to her place in society;

> *Alice*: I wish I'd just been a good girl and not had any but you know their treatment didn't help at all. If anything, it made me worse, a lot worse
>
> *Lisa*: Why do you say that it made you worse?
>
> *Alice*: I wasn't worth anything. I wasn't worth giving a second chance. I was kind of written off, that's how I felt. I've spoken to other [White] young girls and they've [police] said [to them] 'we don't want it to affect your future'. I never got that. I didn't matter I wasn't going anywhere anyway. I've got my criminal record and it dates back from when I was fifteen. (Alice, 38, Black mixed-race, British born, female)

The ability to compare her experiences with that of her White peers reveals the inequity in the police treatment of Black women. The knowledge that others had been given a second chance through alternatives to prosecution, and that the potential impact on their future had been a factor in the police decision to divert them from involvement with the Criminal Justice System, illustrates 'racism's invisible touch' (Tate 2016). In Alice's story there is no overt expression of racism; however, Alice knows that she was treated differently and viewed as not worthy of the opportunity to reform. In the 'police imagination' her future was already determined, by race, towards a propensity for criminality. It was in fact the police officer's decision that determined her path towards criminality which dominated twenty years of her life. At the time of her interview, Alice was studying Criminology and she hoped to develop a career as a criminal justice practitioner, using her experience to help others. However, her story, along with the narratives of other research participants', illustrate the racial effects of discriminatory policing on the life chances of young Black people.

A pertinent example of how police contact can escalate, resulting in criminalisation, is when charges of assault on a police officer are brought in retaliation for noncompliance or challenging the police. This can have a significant impact on the life chances of those charged. Bianca described an occasion when she was arrested for challenging the police use of force towards a black man who had been restrained on the floor outside of a nightclub;

> One officer had his knee in the man's head to pin him to the floor. His glasses had gone flying and his phones over there. Ones trying to get handcuffs on him and ones put the handcuff thing on his legs. He's just lying on the floor and it's freezing and it's snowing... he's shouting for help 'what are you doing? I haven't done nowt.'

A crowd gathered and asked the police to remove the pressure from his head. The situation escalated when the police refused to respond to the pleas from the crowd, including Bianca and her three friends, one black and two White women. Bianca described CS spray being discharged in the direction of the crowd, this led to some young men taking boxes from nearby shops and throwing them at the police. A number of police vehicles arrived at the scene and the police officers formed a line to push back the crowd. Bianca described being physically pushed by a police officer. In her frustration she verbally challenged the police officer; '*don't fucking push me, I think you are disgusting, you're devils... that man didn't deserve that*'. Whilst it can be argued that Bianca was indeed angry, her behaviour was in response to what she, and others, perceived to be the unfair and excessively forceful restraint of a Black man. Bianca expressed a strong awareness throughout her interview, garnered from the media and community narratives, of racism in policing. In this context, her response was a legitimate and humane response to perceived injustice. The way in which her response was racialised is evident through the treatment of her White friends, who were not treated in the same way despite their involvement in challenging the police officer. Bianca was arrested along with another Black friend, whilst her two White friends were told to move on and go home.

> My White friends like 'no, what the fucks going on, you can't arrest her, you can't do this, we are sleeping at her house'. And you see arms being waved and my White friend, you could see her physically pushing a police officer out the way. Maybe he didn't feel it or maybe he didn't want to feel it or whatever, but, you know, she pushed him just as [name of Black friend] had this interaction with her officer but she ended up in a cell and [White friend name] was told to move along.

Following the incident, the police proceeded to press charges of assaulting a police officer against Bianca's friend. These charges were later thrown out on the basis of CCTV evidence which disproved the police officer's version of events. This proof that the police officer had '*lied*' about what had happened served further to increase mistrust, particularly as the charges could have had significant consequences. Bianca reflected on the potential for the false charges to undo the hard work that the young women had undertaken to develop their career prospects;

> it was ridiculous to hear the stories that had been invented to get [friend] done for assaulting a police officer which in the long run would have been terrible for her, to have that on your record. And you know we are not criminals, we work, we do education like we've been told and we build up our careers. (Bianca, 25, Black mixed-race, British-born, female)

Bianca's story highlights how, even for Black and mixed- race women engaged in education and career development, their hard work can be jeopardised by criminalisation. Fortunately for Bianca's friend CCTV evidence disproved the allegation of assault made by the police officer; however, her life could have taken a very different turn if the allegation had been upheld. The victimization of Black women as punishment was a concern raised by Agozino (1997), who provides the example of a young girl who was arrested using significant force and subsequently charged with assaulting four male police officers at once (Agozino 1997: 79). Bianca's story has echoes of the treatment of the women of Broadwater Farm when they acted to protect Black men from racist policing in the 1980s (The Women of Broadwater Farm 1989). Solidarity with Black men both opposes the White patriarchal police institution and transgresses the norms of hegemonic White femininity against which conformity is measured.

Transgressing White Femininity

Feminist criminology maintains that women who break the law are doubly punished. Once for breaking the law and again for transgressing their gender roles (Heidensohn et al. 1985). For Black and Black mixed-race women, it can be argued that the stereotypes attributed to them are already in transgression of the norms associated with White hegemonic versions of femininity (Collins 2004; Walley-Jean 2009; Tate 2015). This explains why they are punished even when they have not broken the law. For women defined as criminal, race magnifies their transgression against desirable versions of femininity. Alice, a Black mixed-race woman, was the only female participant who was known by the police for her offending behaviour. Being known by the police defined the nature of her interactions and frequency of contact with them, which created a narrative of police encounters which were not dissimilar to those described by the Black and Black mixed-race men interviewed (the majority of whom were not criminally known to the police). For Alice, her lifestyle and behaviours renders her experiences as notably different to the other female participants'. She was unable to recourse to notions of respectability in order to negotiate the effect of race in the police encounter.

Minor criminal charges can escalate to more serious charges because of perceived stereotypes which position Black and Black mixed-race women as aggressive, particularly when they are 'known' for their offending. This was evident in Alice's account of her arrest during a shopping trip to buy goods for her daughter's birthday party with two White friends. Alice had placed some nappies on top of the pram which she forgot to pay for with the other shopping. She was apprehended by a security officer, the police who happened to be at the shop already intervened and arrested Alice, allowing her two friends to leave with Alice's daughter. Alice became concerned for her daughter and asked if she could make arrangements for her mother or sister to take care of her. Alice recalls not being allowed to make contact with her family;

> They shoved me straight in the police van and I'm saying 'well can I sort out my daughter and make some arrangements'. They said 'no get in'. So, I've kicked the door and as I've kicked the door I've touched his shirt with my foot and it wasn't like I've kicked him but he had a little mark on his shirt. I remember they didn't charge me with theft but they charged me with assaulting a police officer. (Alice, 38, Black mixed-race, British born, female)

Her frustration at not being able to make arrangements for her daughter was perceived as aggression. As Alice says '*If you are frustrated it doesn't mean you are being aggressive and they always used to say that I was being aggressive and restrain me*'. This incident led Alice to conclude that it didn't matter that she was a woman or a mother, she was treated in the same way that a man would have been treated. What is evident from Alice's account is that she was not charged with the offence for which she was arrested but rather for assaulting a police officer which resulted in a further conviction and a fine and an order for compensation to be paid to the police officer. Alice was punished for her perceived aggression, rather than theft, the transgression of gender norms carrying a heavier punishment than the minor crime for which the arrest was made. Gender is not a protection from mistreatment when women are seen to display behaviours which do not conform to the submissive traits expected of White hegemonic femininity. As argued by Collins (2004), 'just as hegemonic White masculinity occupies the most desired social script, an equally hegemonic Black femininity organized via images of bitches, bad mothers, mammies, and Black ladies coalesce to mark the least desirable form of femininity.' (Collins 2004: 199).

Even when Black women have been treated harshly by the police they understand that their bodies do not represent the same level of threat as embodied Black masculinity. Janice reflected on the way that she is perceived differently because of her gender;

> As a female I don't suppose I have that threat. I'm not small and I'm not tall and I'm not aggressive and I'm not extremely powerful, which genetically afro-Caribbean males are, and I don't have that aggression.

Janice clearly sees that, although she was arrested and treated differently to White women as discussed earlier, she is not perceived as possessing hyper masculine traits of physical strength and power. Whilst this may be the case when comparing perceptions of Black and Black mixed-race women with that of Black and Black mixed-race men, in comparison to White women, Black women are attributed strength and power through the strong Black woman stereotype (see Tate 2015). Further, Janice made reference to ideas of superior strength premised on biology, largely discredited in both the social and physical sciences. That they are reflected in participants' accounts, shows how negative stereotypes can be internalised within racialised groups, through exposure to them in the dominant culture. Whilst biological notions of race are discredited, race functions and endures through racialisation (see Garner 2010: 19–32). The aggressive traits attributed to Black men is one example. After reflection, Janice concluded that what is perceived by the police as Black, male aggression is actually a manifestation of frustration associated with their over policing;

> the aggression is not directed, the aggression is sometimes because people are sick of it. They are sick of hearing it, it might not have been them that you stopped yesterday but it could have been their brother, it could have been their nephew. (Janice, 37, Black, British-born, female)

It is the irritation caused by constant harassment from the police and an awareness of its racist effects on the lives of themselves and other men that can cause what is perceived to be an aggressive reaction in police contact. This obvious irritation and frustration when it converges with the images of Black masculinity in the police imagination, communicates a threat, which only serves to compound the stereotype.

For some Black and Black mixed-race women, it is possible to negotiate and redefine their position in relation to hegemonic White femininity with recourse to social and cultural capital. Through performing the alternative subordinated Black femininity of the 'Black lady' (Collins 2004: 139) the negative impact of racialised policing practices can to a limited extent be minimised or negotiated through social and cultural capital (Bourdieu 1986). When Janice was arrested she was able to draw on her professional status as well as her knowledge of local police through her work and she was respected in this capacity. Similarly, when Bianca was arrested as a teenager (discussed in Chapter 4) she was released from custody without charge when a family friend who was a lawyer represented her at the police station. The outcome for the teenager could have been very different if she did not have these resources. The difference in her experience and that of Alice, who was criminalised with life-changing consequences, is evident. Social and cultural capital are resources that can be drawn upon, in some contexts, to reaffirm compliance with gender norms of respectability and preferred versions of (White) femininity (Collins 2004).

Recourse to either social or cultural capital does not protect from over-policing, mistreatment or mistaken arrest, it merely affords redress for mistreatment. If Black women are able to perform, through symbols of respectability, a version of femininity that is more closely aligned to the desired 'hegemonic (White) femininity' (Collins 2004: 193), race can to some extent be negotiated. The following section will address the negotiation of race through femininity in relation to the victim experience.

Performing Deservingness

As was argued in Chapter 5, the 'ideal victim' will be accorded victim status more readily than the unworthy victim. This is, to some extent, dependent on the gender of the victim and the extent to which they perform in relation to preferred versions of masculinity and femininity. When compared with the experiences of men, women more frequently expressed satisfaction with the police response to their victimisation. This was particularly tangible when the reported crime was 'low level', for example burglary or theft, and did not result in physical contact or harm. Carol had been the victim of burglary she was left satisfied with the way that the police had dealt with her report of the crime;

> Somebody broke in and pinched the television and I had to call the police just to report it and they were okay about it, it was nothing, there was no problem. They checked it out; I can't remember whether they found it. (Carol, 49, Black, British-born, female)

Similarly, Cynthia recalled the police being responsive and reassuring after a burglary at her flat;

> After college…I realised I had been burgled, looked around the flat, it wasn't a mess they'd picked up the video player and they'd dropped it in the same room near the door and it was damaged and they'd gone with the TV, a massive TV… I asked my friend if I could use her phone because I don't know if they'd done something to the phone, maybe cut the wires on my phone and she said yes so I phoned the police from her home and explained everything including that I didn't have anywhere secure to stay that night and they either came first thing the next morning or that night I can't remember which.

This experience left her feeling vulnerable and unsafe. She felt the police response was good as, although they didn't recover her belongings or apprehend the perpetrators, they put her in touch with Victim Support, who helped her to deal with the aftermath of the burglary;

> They gave me information. They gave me the number [for victim support] and a crime number. It was them [Victim Support] that worked with the housing association to get the lock and the key and the door sorted out. (Cynthia, 42, Black, British-born, female)

Both Cynthia and Carol were not previously known to the police, their favourable impressions were on the basis of minimal police contact. As victims of relatively minor crimes, the police had responded to them in a satisfactory manner and in line with their expectations.

A history of offending, which transgresses norms of desirable (White) femininity, shapes police responses to the victim in less favourable ways. Alice contacted the police for help when there was a violent incident outside of her property (not related to Alice or anyone in her home) and the police failed to send anybody to the scene. When the police officer arrived, sometime after the incident was over, the police officer told Alice '*well we heard your name*'. This is illustrative of the victim-offender dichotomy discussed in Chapter 5, which discursively constitutes the victim and offender in binary terms, one worthy and the other unworthy. Those deemed criminal are therefore in contrast to the 'ideal victim' (Christie 1986) image and following victimisation are treated as suspect or have to prove their victim status. Further, as can be seen from Alice's story, being a Black mixed-race woman and being known to the police is at distant proximity to both the most desirable form of hegemonic White femininity and the vision of the 'ideal victim'. Eighteen years prior to the interview Alice was subjected to a serious sexual assault in front of her young daughter. She reported the assault to the police; however, she was advised that her complaint was not worth pursuing. She described the way in which the female police officer dealt with her report;

> She basically said [police officer] 'it'll be his word against yours, they'll rip you apart in court and I don't think it's worth pursuing'. I don't think they took me seriously or took the incident seriously, that's how I felt. They took me up to this rape suite they didn't even examine me or anything. (Alice, 38, Black mixed-race, British born, female)

Alice, is once again made to feel that she is not worthy of a chance in the eyes of the police. Whether as a suspect or a victim of crime Alice feels that she does not matter enough to be taken seriously. The failure to examine her, despite being in a purpose-built facility for dealing with sexual crimes, compounds this perception. Further, the evidence Alice supplied was not pursued, Alice was asked to provide the clothes she was wearing, which she did. However, '*they never did anything with them*'. Alice has been the victim of subsequent crimes in the intervening years and has not reported them to the police, she explained '*I just don't feel there's any point you know, I just don't feel there's any point*'. The perception of women more broadly is that reports of rape are not taken seriously (Westmorland and Brown 2012). This is borne out in the police failure to record reported rapes. A recent report found that 26% of sexual offences reported to the police are not recorded (HMIC 2014: 18). Further, it is evident that views surrounding sexual deviancy shape police 'cynicism' (Loftus 2009). Stereotypes about Black women discursively construct them as sexually deviant (Collins 2000), this positions them in opposition to the image of the 'ideal victim' when they are victimised through sexual assault.

Similar findings are evident in relation to the police response to domestic abuse. The police have historically been criticised for their failure to take domestic abuse seriously as a crime. It has been considered, from the perspective of a police service dominated by a masculine ethos, as a private/domestic matter or a 'rubbish crime' (Reiner 2010, Loftus 2009). Reforms in relation to police responses to domestic abuse does not appear to have changed how the police view these crimes as a 'crock of shit' (Loftus 2009). Loftus found some evidence of sensitivity to victims at the scene, though the manner of policing informed by 'masculine sentiments' is detrimental to the quality of service women receive (ibid.: 130–132). Women who are experiencing domestic abuse therefore expect that the police will not take their plight seriously and this is cited as a factor in the under reporting of domestic abuse to the police (Mama 1993).

The fear of racist treatment from the police directed towards the victim or their partner compounds the issue of under-reporting for Black women. Further Amina Mama found that some women had been assaulted or arrested by the police when they called them for help (Mama 1993). The fear of racism that Mama identifies in her influential research is reflected in Alice's account;

> I've been in domestic situations, like domestic violence situations, and I just won't report it. Because I know they are more interested in, well this is how I feel and what I perceive, they are more interested in locking Black people up more for being Black not for what they've actually [done]. That's my opinion so I don't want to give them that satisfaction to be honest.

Alice's reluctance to call the police highlights how racism intersects with gender to differentiate her treatment from a woman who is oppressed by gender but not by race. Alice is both the victim of domestic abuse at the hands of her partner and a victim of racism in the White police institution which means that as a Black woman she fears that she will not be taken seriously and that her perpetrator will be treated harshly. Again, the 'matrix of domination' (Collins 2000) is a useful tool here to understand the hierarchy of intersecting oppressions in the context of domestic abuse directed towards women. In this context, the woman is oppressed on the basis of gender as the victim of male partner violence but at the intersection of race she is under-protected by the racist police institution which will also over-police the perpetrator of the violence. Both gender and race intersect across 'domains of power' (ibid.: 287) to leave her without recourse to protection.

Conclusion

This chapter has discussed the intersection of gender with race in the context of contact with the police. Blackness is a unifying identity in the face of oppression from the White police institution; however, there is not one homogenous 'Black experience' of policing. The data suggests that the experience of police contact for Black and mixed-race people is shaped by the intersecting oppressions of race and gender. The 'matrix of domination' facilitates an understanding of how these intersecting oppressions are organised in relation to domains of power (Collins 2000).

Black women's relationship to the police and their experiences of policing are under-researched. This chapter illuminates the ways in which Black and mixed-race women experience policing and finds that similarly to Black and mixed-race men they are over-policed and under-protected. Their experiences are shaped by dominant stereotypes which proliferate in the 'police imagination'. However, the findings of this research suggest that, for Black and mixed-race women, their behaviour and lifestyle choices have a greater impact on their experience of police contact than that of Black and mixed-race men. Whilst they may come to the attention of the police because of racist stereotypes, it is evident that for some women, non-offending women in particular, performing a desirable version of femininity (Collins 2004) provides some respite from the racist effects of police contact.

This negotiation of race, through the performance of desirable femininity, is not possible for criminalised women. Through Alice's experience this chapter has illustrated that when women do not conform to desired forms of femininity, which includes complying with the law and displaying submissive traits in the face of police contact, they are treated more harshly and their experiences begin to resemble narratives of male participants'. They become the frequent target of police attention, are treated harshly and with force and are not protected as victim of crime. It should be noted that this finding is based on the experiences of one participant and should not be taken as evidence of a broader trend. Black and mixed-race women's experience of the police are wholly absent from the criminological and sociological literature. These findings based on the experiences of five Black and mixed-race women suggest that this is an area of research which is in urgent need of development.

Both race and gender intersect to produce 'subordinate masculinities' (Collins 2004) that are essential for the maintenance of the White hegemonic masculinity of the police institution. Dominant negative stereotypes that coalesce to produce the dominant image of the threatening big Black man position him as the ultimate threat to the White hegemonic masculine police institution. As demonstrated in the accounts of research participants' this results in their perpetual treatment as suspect even when they are the victim of crime. Whilst 'hypo-masculinity' can be ascribed, as shown in relation to disability and sexuality, there is no alternative version of Black masculinity that they can 'perform' in order to negotiate the impact of their over-policing and under-protection.

Over-policing has been attributed to social position, the following chapter will analyse the impact of class as it intersects with race in the context of police contact.

References

Agozino, B. (1997). *Black Women and the Criminal Justice System*. Aldershot: Ashgate.

Alexander, C. (2008). *(Re)thinking Gangs*. London: Runnymede Trust.

Asch, A., & Fine, M. (1992). Beyond Pedestals: Revisiting the Lives of Women with Disabilities. In M. Fine (Ed.), *Disruptive Voices: The Possibilities of Feminist Research*. Ann Arbor: The University of Michigan Press.

Bernstein, M., & Kostelac, C. (2002). Lavender and Blue: Attitudes About Homosexuality and Behavior Toward Lesbians and Gay Men Among Police Officers. *Journal of Contemporary Criminal Justice, 18*, 302–328.

Bourdieu, P. (1986). The Forms of Capital. In J. Richardson (Ed.), *Handbook of Theory and Research for the Sociology of Education*. New York: Greenwood.

Bowling, B., Parmar, A., & Phillips, C. (2008). Policing Ethnic Minority Communities. *Handbook of Policing.* Devon: Willan.

Burke, M. (1994). Homosexuality as Deviance: The Case of the Gay Police Officer. *British Journal of Criminology, 34*, 192–203.

Christie, N. (1986). The Ideal Victim. In E. A. Fattah (Ed.), *From Crime Policy to Victim Policy: Reorientating the Justice System*. London: Macmillan.

Collins, P. H. (2000). *Black Feminist Thought: Knowledge, Consciousness, and the Politics of Empowerment*. New York: Routledge.

Collins, P. H. (2004). *Black Sexual Politics: African Americans, Gender, and the New Racism*. New York: Routledge.

Connell, R. W. (2005). *Masculinities*. Cambridge: Polity Press.

Cushion, S. Moore. K., & Jewell, J. (2011). *Media Representations of Black Young Men and Boys: Report of the REACH Media Monitoring Project*. London: Department for Communities and Local Government.

Gabriel, J. (1998). *Whitewash: Racialised Politics and the Media*. New York: Routledge.

Gallagher, P. (2015). Over 3000 Police Officers Being Investigated for Alleged Assault—And Almost All of Them Are Still on the Beat. *Independent*. Available: http://www.independent.co.uk/news/uk/crime/over-3000-police-officers-being-investigated-for-alleged-assault-and-almost-all-of-them-are-still-on-10220091.html. Accessed 1 May 2016.

Garner, S. (2010). *Racisms an Introduction*. London: Sage.

Gayle, D. (2015). Black People 'Three Times More Likely' to Be Tasered. *Guardian*. Available: http://www.theguardian.com/uk-news/2015/oct/13/

black-people-three-times-more-likely-to-have-taser-used-against-them. Accessed 13 October 2016.
Hall, S., Critcher, C., Jefferson, T., Clarke, J., & Roberts, B. (1978). *Policing the Crisis: Mugging, the State, and Law and Order*. London: Macmillan.
Heidensohn, F., Silvestri, M., & Campling, J. (1985). *Women and Crime*. London: Macmillan.
HMIC. (2014). *Crime-Recording: Making the Victim Count. The Final Report of an Inspection of Crime Data Integrity in Police Forces in England and Wales*. London: HMIC.
Hooks, B. (2004). *We Real Cool: Black Men and Masculinity*. New York: Routledge.
Hunt, R., & Dick, S. (2008). *'Serves You Right': Lesbian and Gay People's Expectations of Discrimination*. London: Stonewall.
Institute for Race Relations. (2003). *Roger Sylvester: Police Condemned for Black Death*. Available: http://www.irr.org.uk/news/roger-sylvester-police-condemned-for-black-death/. Accessed 21 January 2018.
Lee, J. A. (1981). Some Structural Aspects of Police Deviance in Relations with Minority Groups. In C. Shearing (Ed.), *Organisational Police Deviance*. Toronto: Butterworth.
Lewis, P., Newburn, T., Taylor, M., McGillivray, C., Greenhill, A., Frayman, H., & Proctor, R. (2011). *Reading the Riots: Investigating England's Summer of Disorder*. London: The London School of Economics and Political Science and The Guardian.
Loftus, B. (2009). *Police Culture in a Changing World*. Oxford: Oxford University Press.
Loftus, B. (2010). Police Occupational Culture: Classic Themes, Altered Times. *Policing and Society, 20*, 1–20.
Mama, A. (1993). Black Women and Police: A Place Where the Law Is Not Upheld. In W. James & C. Harris (Eds.), *Inside Babylon: The Caribbean Diaspora in Britain*. London: Verso.
Murji, K. (1999). White Lines: Culture, 'Race' and Drugs. In N. South (Ed.), *Drugs: Culture, Controls and Everyday Life*. London: Sage.
Mutua, A. D. (2006). *Progressive Black Masculinities?* New York: Routledge.
Pemberton, S. (2008). Demystifying Deaths in Police Custody: Challenging State Talk. *Social and Legal Studies, 17*, 237–262.
Reiner, R. (2010). *The Politics of the Police*. Oxford: Oxford University Press.
Rice, M. (1990). Challenging Orthodoxies in Feminist Theory: A Black Feminist Critique. In L. Gelsthorpe & A. Morris (Eds.), *Feminist Perspectives in Criminology*. Milton Keynes: Open University Press.

Shuttleworth, R., Wedgwood, N. & Wilson, N. J. (2012). The Dilemma of Disabled Masculinity. *Men and Masculinities, 15,* 174–194.

Smithson, H., Ralphs, R., & Williams, P. (2013). Used and Abused: The Problematic Usage of Gang Terminology in the United Kingdom and Its Implications for Ethnic Minority Youth. *British Journal of Criminology, 53,* 113–128.

Tate, S. A. (2015). *Black Women's Bodies and the Nation: Race, Gender and Culture.* Basingstoke: Palgrave Macmillan.

Tate, S. A. (2016). 'I Can't Quite Put My Finger on It': Racism's Touch. *Ethnicities, 16,* 68–85.

Walley-Jean, J. C. (2009). Debunking the Myth of the "Angry Black Woman": An Exploration of Anger in Young African American Women. *Black Women, Gender and Families, 3,* 68–86.

Westmarland, N., & Brown, J. (2012). *Women's Views on the Policing of Rape, Domestic Violence and Stalking Within the Cleveland, Durham, Northumbria and Cumbria Police Force Areas.* Durham and Newcastle Upon Tyne: Durham University and Northern Rock Foundation.

Williams, P., & Clarke, B. (2016). *Dangerous Associations: Joint Enterprise, Gangs and Racism. An Analysis of the Processes of Criminalisation of Black, Asian and Minority Ethnic Individuals.* London: Centre for Crime and Justice Studies.

Wilson, J. P., Hugenberg, K., & Rule N. O. (2017). Racial Bias in Judgements of Physical Size and Formidability: From Size to Threat, *Journal of Personality and Social Psychology, 113*(1), 59–80.

Women of Broadwater Farm. (1989). Broadwater Farm Defence Campaign: Into Our Homes. In C. Dunhill (Ed.), *The Boys in Blue: Women's Challenge to the Police.* London: Virago.

Yancy, G. (2008). *Black Bodies, White Gazes: The Continuing Significance of Race.* Maryland: Rowman and Littlefield.

7
Race, Class and Belonging

This chapter will address the intersection of race with class in police responses to Black people, in doing so it will question the notion that Blackness is incidental to class in the police mapping of populations as 'police property' (Lee 1981). Firstly, it will address the power of the police institution through an analysis of the class values of the police institution. It will go on to analyse the experiences of over-policing in what participants referred to as '*Black areas*'. It argues that race and class coalesce in these spaces to create racially othered spaces, these spaces signify danger and serve to justify an oppressive police presence. Drawing on the experiences of Black professionals it will illuminate the ways in which race disrupts capital acquired through professionalism. This point underlines the significance of race in participant's encounters with the police. In this context, race is drawn upon as a 'symbol of inferiorisation' (Anthias 1999); the Whiteness of power operationalises Blackness as such a 'symbol'. Regardless of the individual's social identity, or context, the 'fact of Blackness' (Fanon 1986) constructs those who embody it as suspect. Finally, the chapter will analyse the importance of belonging in how migrants experience and understand their encounters with the police in

L. J. Long, *Perpetual Suspects*, Palgrave Studies in Race, Ethnicity, Indigeneity and Criminal Justice, https://doi.org/10.1007/978-3-319-98240-3_7

England. Drawing on the 'matrix of oppression' (Collins 2000), it will conclude that race and class are intersecting oppressions. However, in the context of police contact, race is the predominant trigger for imagining the suspect. Race is both the signifier of lower class and of criminality. The 'thin blue line' is not the only colour line which stands between order and disorder in the police imagination.

Constructing 'Police Property'

The working class are often conceptualised as a homogeneously White. However, as argued by Virdee (2014) the working class was a 'heterogeneous, multi ethnic formation from its inception' (p. 162). In the post-war period the class position of newly arrived commonwealth migrants was structured through colonial and post-colonial relations. The use of migrant labour, in the manufacturing industry in particular, operated to fit these migrant groups into an economic system which reproduced racial inequalities (see Virdee 2014; Anthias and Yuval-Davis 2005). Histories of migration, bound up with the historical context of Britain's role in slavery and colonisation, featured prominently in participant's reflections upon the structural inequalities faced by Black people in Britain contemporarily. Phillip clearly sees that there is a link between the histories of slavery and colonialism and Black people's structural position in contemporary society;

> The White British dealings with Black people has been one of slavery and colonialism. When they invited Black people over to this country we ended up being housed in poor areas because that is how we've evolved from Africa to the West Indies in poor housing in the slave plantations… That's been consistent in keeping down the people of Black race. When, as a result of the shortage of jobs in this country, they invited West Indians to come over…you house them in an area that is no longer desirable. Perpetrating this sense of poverty and lack of education, that is inadequate really. But it's alright for the Blacks because they are not worth anything. (Phillip, 45, Black, African, male)

His reflection invokes the notion of 'conditional hospitality' (Bell 2010: 241; Derrida 2000), through which the presence of Black people is on the terms of the 'host' nation. This is instructive of how tolerance on the 'hosts' terms reproduce systems of inequality premised on the maintenance of White power. As Phillip recognised, '*they [Black communities] have no employment and there is no investment in their community*'. The resulting structural inequalities which manifest in the overrepresentation of Black people in the lower socio-economic groups is a factor in their identification as police property. This provides a rationale for the disproportionate police focus on both Black individuals and communities, premised on their structural position. The analysis of how White power has shaped structural inequalities both historically and in contemporary context, illustrates the ways in which race and class intersect to produce Black bodies as poor, whatever their social status and as suspect regardless of their behaviour.

The police service is majoritarily White and male, this is perceived to contribute to the racialising processes which define Black bodies as 'police property'. Like many of the participants, Bianca reflected upon the impact that this has upon their relevance to the communities that they serve;

> They need to get some Blacks and ethnic minorities in the police force. They need some women in there. They need to think about taking their uniforms off once in a while. They need to start making themselves relevant, they need to start helping us be able to relate to them. Because you know a lot of the officers that are sent in they come in with their big hats and their handcuffs and their batons and you know they're White and thirty and male and from [White area]. (Bianca, 25, Black mixed-race, British-born, female)

Bianca's suggestion that an increase in diversity of police officers in the service would help to instil confidence is tempered by her subsequent reflections on the barrier that is created by the police uniform and equipment worn about the body. The role of the uniform in both the embodiment and display of state power was reflected upon by several participants. Here Bianca equates the inability of individual police officers to relate to communities with the symbols of authority which reinforce their power over the communities in which they are present. The police uniform is infused with symbolism which extends beyond the individual wearing it to represent the stability of the state (Holdaway 1983: 46). The wearing of a uniform is one way in which de-individualisation of the police officer occurs and relocates them as an agent of White institutional power. The shift that occurs through the wearing of the uniform is evident in Earls perception that '*police officers… are just like me and you*' until they put on the uniform. '*When they put on that police uniform it gives them a power*' (Earl). This power is implied regardless of the social status or class of the individual police officer. The symbols of law enforcement, which can include the police uniform, badge and body worn policing equipment including handcuffs, and batons, delineate the boundaries of the state and increase the power of the officer through positioning the subject as subordinate to the superordinate state actor.

Rank and file police officers have broadly been drawn from the working classes. In this context, it can be argued that on an individual level their power, in relation to the state, is not dissimilar to those groups considered 'police property'. However, as Anthias (1999) suggests, power is not individualized but 'institutionalised'. Whilst power is not exercised by all "Whites" over all "Blacks" it is 'about the power of the dominant group represented in the state to reproduce its own values and practices on its own terms' (4.4). Race has become a symbol of both 'inferiority' (Anthias 1999) and powerlessness, in the context of a global system of 'White supremacy' (Mills 1997). This defines Black bodies as 'police property' regardless of whether they are working class or middle class. This is manifest in their unequal policing;

> It's about how they utilise that power. And we've always argued as long as you are distributing that power equally then we have no problems but if it's disproportionately because we're Black then there is an issue with that. (Earl, 54, Black, British-born, male)

Despite the social status of individual police officers, when they put on their uniform, in the eyes of the public, they become middle class. This is evident in participant's perceptions of their interactions with the police;

> If I needed to, not that I should have to or that I want to, If I needed to speak in a more middle-class kind of language then I could do that. I could engage with them on their White middle-class level. But if I'd never moved out of a working-class area and never continued in education, then I guess the way that I talked, the way that I'd act … so class would have an impact as well [on the police encounter]. (Lee, 23, Black mixed-race, British-born, male)

Here, Lee reveals the ways in which the police are perceived to represent middle class value systems. The assumption here is that the police align themselves more closely with those who have shared values resulting in more favourable treatment. For Lee, this meant that he felt better equipped to engage with the police because of the cultural capital that he has acquired through upward social mobility.

The middle-class value systems that the police institution embodies align them more closely with powerful groups. Those without possession of the privilege inherent in White, middle class, normativity, understand that the police represent these values and that they will be judged relative to them. Alice was the victim of a sexual assault which she reported to the police around twenty years ago. At the time the police did not respond to her complaint and no action was taken against the perpetrator. The experience of both the sexual assault and not being taken seriously by the police still takes a toll on Alice. Recent media coverage of the Jimmy Saville abuse scandal prompted her to reconsider the way that her case was dealt with and she has recently considered whether to pursue justice through re-investigation of the crime or by raising a complaint against the police;

> I wouldn't be taken seriously because it happened so long ago and there's no evidence, but then you see in the media similar situation and with Jimmy Saville. And, these people are being taken seriously. But they do happen to be White middle-class people that are making complaints, they are being taken seriously. Whereas I don't think that they [police] would take me seriously. (Alice, 38, Black mixed-race, British born, female)

Alice expressed that she would not be taken seriously because she does not fit with the image of the deserving '*White middle class*' victims of Jimmy Saville. Whether or not the victims of Jimmy Saville were necessarily middle class, Whiteness was attributed, through Alice's narrative, to middle class social status. Similarly, to Lee's equivalence of police officers with middle class values, for Alice, respectability, as defined through Whiteness and aligned to middle class police values, assured that the victims would be taken seriously. Further, when Blackness intersects with signifiers of lower social status such as residence in areas of deprivation and a lack of material goods, this evidence of economic powerlessness, can lead to an unsympathetic response to victims who are positioned as 'scrotes' (Loftus 2009: 177). This is evident in Eric's experience of a visit by the police to follow up a report of a burglary at his flat;

> The police don't really care and don't take people seriously who live in deprived areas because there's a higher crime rate anyway. I live in a deprived area and I was Black. I was getting back on my feet I don't have any fancy furniture. I'd moved in not so long ago so I was just trying to get it all sorted. Some of the walls were not painted and I had a cheap carpet and I think with that they could tell that I wasn't well off and probably wasting their time because I had nothing. (Eric, 32, Black, African, male)

Similarly, to Alice, here Eric reflects that he is not taken seriously as the victim of crime. Drawing on both his residence in a deprived area and the absence of signs of wealth in his home, class deems him an unworthy victim, whilst his Blackness links him to both lower class status and to criminality. It is this intersection of race and class that constructs both individuals and communities as 'police property' in need of surveillance and control.

Policing in Racially Othered Space

In the UK context, there are very few examples of residential segregation, where the majority population of the area are from an ethnic minority (Jivraj and Simpson 2015). However, Black and other Ethnic Minorities are more likely to live in deprived, high crime areas. These spaces inhabited by racialised bodies are constructed as spaces of the Other (also, see Slater and Anderson 2012; Wacquant 2008). Such racially othered spaces can be found in most major towns and cities. Farrar's (2002) work illuminates how the multi-ethnic area of Chapeltown in Leeds has been constructed as a space of the other, through histories of migration, entrenched poverty and state neglect of housing, proliferation of crime and media narratives of moral decay. Similar narratives operate with reference to the notorious 'St Pauls area of Bristol' (Slater and Anderson 2012). The residents of these racially othered spaces become the focus of police attention by virtue of both economic powerlessness and race.

A common theme in participant's accounts was the significance of the concentration of Black communities in inner city areas. For migrants, in the post-war period, the availability of affordable accommodation forced them into substandard housing in areas which were reputationally associated with criminality through the narratives linked to previous migrant groups who had occupied these spaces (see Lambert 1970; Farrar 2002). Housing Black people in already racially othered spaces was a deliberate strategy in retaining colonial power relations and '*White superiority*' (Phillip) in the 'colony within' (Sivanandan 1982). This is described by Earl whose parents came to England from the Caribbean in the 1950s;

> Even though the Caribbean's were invited here, they were put into areas that were postally negative, had a bad reputation… Jewish people were here then the Irish came and then the Blacks came and then the Indians came. So, it's historically been an area of migration. (Earl, 54, Black, British-born, male)

Structural racisms have created and continue to perpetuate spaces racialised as '*White areas, Black areas and Asian areas*' (Janice) in towns and cities across the UK. This is not to suggest that residents of racially othered spaces are lacking in agency. Some participants described these spaces as areas of community, family and cultural ties and places of safety. Janice, a degree educated professional, who could be described as upwardly mobile, continues to live in the racially othered area where she grew up, with her children;

> People tend to live where they feel comfortable. And not only that you have local supplies. I wouldn't expect to go to [area] which is a predominantly White area and expect to get some hot pepper sauce or a patty. (Janice, 37, Black, British-born, female)

Here, Janice reframes the racially othered space as desirable, providing some respite from the impact of living in a racially predicated society. This understanding of the space contrasts with the construction of these 'reputational ghettoes' (Slater and Anderson 2012) as spaces of danger in need of surveillance and control.

Within these spaces, a heavy police presence serves as a reminder to the inhabitants that they are a suspect population;

> They are here to control us, not to get an idea of what our community is about. They're there as the authority to keep an eye on us. For the majority of us that are not committing crime it's like 'oh just go away, why are you even looking at me?' Even when they drive past and they look at you it's like don't look at me because I'm not doing anything. (Bianca, 25, Black mixed-race, British-born, female)

Like Janice, Bianca recognises the space that is racialised by outsiders as 'our community'—a space of belonging. Here, she identifies a familiar problem for those who live in racialised spaces and who are law abiding when they are produced as suspects through police practices of surveillance. Bianca compared this to the experience of young people in areas which are not the subject of routine police attention;

> We are not doing anything the sun is shining we are sat on a friend's back wall… I have White counterparts that live in [area] side, they all sit out and do the same thing, but there are no police vans circling them, you know.

The area Bianca referred to is a relatively affluent, predominantly White area. In White spaces, young people can sit outside in the sunshine without causing the police to question their reasons for doing so.

One of the most significant and contested ways in which police attention is manifest in racially othered spaces is through stop and search. Black men in particular are considered suspect bodies in the context of preventing and detecting crime. This was apparent for both bodies out of place in White spaces and those present in racially othered spaces. However, race operates at the intersection of its relationship to class to determine which bodies are suspect. Visible signs of lower social status are perceived to influence police decision making in this regard. One sign of lower social status which attracts police attention, discussed in participant's accounts, is particular types of clothing (see also Quinton et al. 2000; Stone et al. 2000). Sportswear and the infamous hoodie were perceived to be particularly problematic;

> It was on the morning and I'd missed my coach at night so I was very tired in the morning. I had to put my coat on because it was cold all night. The police came and walked up to me and said I should identity myself. Maybe because the hood was up in the station, which I did… they tend to have that impression that since you are wearing a hoodie you could be kind of deranged… that you can do anything. But like that hood doesn't make me bad. (Kenneth, 38, Black, African, male)

> I'm not saying that a middle class Black person wouldn't be stopped. But I would say that a working class White person who dresses in tracksuits say, that's associated with being working class, would be stopped more. But I guess if it was a more affluent area then maybe the police wouldn't be there in the first place at all. And if they were driving through a middle-class area would they have stopped to search a kid that wasn't looking really suspicious? Probably not. (Lee, 23, Black mixed-race, British-born, male)

For both Kenneth and Lee, the idea of particular forms of clothing as being linked with crime or being working class, leads the police to make particular assumptions about their propensity to criminality. This draws police attention to young people who wear casual clothing, such as the hoodie, which has come to represent the scourge of youth delinquency in contemporary times. As well as a symbol of class status, clothing can be attributed to particular forms of criminality. Most significantly for Black men, their clothing can be attributed to gang membership (Keeling 2017). This is an example of the ways in which cultural signifiers such as particular forms of dress, are both racialised and criminalised and serve as a visual code for a racialised threat.

Residents in racially othered spaces spoke more frequently about an awareness of heavy police presence in and surveillance of the community. Earl recalled that when he was growing up in the 1970s a heavy police presence was a constant and expected part of daily life;

> It was a constant, constant living in [area]. Wherever you seemed to turn there was a police officer. If I see a police car or a police officer it didn't faze me because I was so used to seeing them. I got saturated by police. (Earl, 54, Black, British-born, male).

This can be compared with Bianca's reflections on growing up in the same area two generations apart;

> The area that I live in there's always quite a lot of police presence, whether it be community support officers on foot or on bike or the big massive vans with the cameras on the back patrolling the area. (Bianca, 25, Black mixed-race, British-born, female)

The same themes are evident in both accounts. The prolific and saturating police presence that Earl recollects does not appear to have declined in the intervening years. The proliferation of technology utilised by the state contemporarily is a further layer, identified in Bianca's account, of intensification of the routine surveillance and collation of evidence against 'suspect' individuals and communities (see O'Neill and Loftus 2013).

The inextricable link between Blackness and both lower status and criminality leads to a disproportionate focus on Black criminality and the racialisation of particular crimes. Drug related offending is one crime type in which Black people are stereotyped as the usual suspects. Earl reflected on how poverty contributes to both offending behaviour and the formation of racialised criminal stereotypes through the intersection of race and class;

> If I said to all the kids you bring me a bag of dead leaves [in autumn], I'll give you a tenner… do you know how many kids I'd have trailing around here to get a bag of leaves. So, it's about money, it's not about being drug dealers. But the police have perpetuated this mentality that all Black people were drug dealers or have the potential to be drug dealers or know somebody who's a drug dealer.

Here, Earl highlights that when Black people do break the law, it is structural inequality rather than a pathological tendency to drug related crime which is to blame. However, this explanation is accepted more readily for White people, who are not linked with criminality by their race. Both Phillip and Earl further reflected on the way in which particular crimes, when carried out by White people, are not constructed and policed as a problem relating to the cultural or pathological proclivities attributed to a particular racialised group;

> Crimes are crimes. It doesn't have to be a stereotypical crime. I mean White people do drugs. There is something about race that police can't seem to put to one side and deal with the crime. (Phillip, 45, Black, African, male)
>
> The majority of people buying drugs are indigenous [White] people. I was born and educated here, when I was a kid White kids were sniffing glue doing all of this stuff, not something we engaged in. Alcohol is the biggest drug out there and it is the biggest drug that gets young people involved in other things but they never talk about alcohol but they'll talk about cannabis because cannabis is seen as a Black thing. (Earl, 54, Black, British-born, male)

These extracts provide some insight into how Black and Black mixed-race people conceive of their differential treatment in relation to the evidence that White people are more likely to be drug offenders, but less likely to be targeted for police attention in relation to drug offences (Eastwood et al. 2013). Through the discursive production of drugs as a 'Black thing', those racialised as Black are disproportionately policed, whilst for White people the problem is located with the individual and not attributed to race. This is instructive of the ways in which crime is racialised as not White. Further contributing to this is the discourses surrounding high crime, deprived estates inhabited by Whites who are considered 'police property'. Rather than constructing the problem of crime in these spaces as a 'White thing', they are attributed racialised features in discourses surrounding their incivility (Webster 2008; Wray 2006), serving to distance Whiteness from criminality.

The way in which the police respond to the threat of criminality in racially othered spaces, as a threat posed by a whole community, is instructive of the way in which whole communities are policed through race and class. Derek talked about a particularly aggressive armed police search for a suspect in his neighbourhood, in which several households were targeted. Derek compared the behaviour of the police officers to what would be acceptable in a predominantly White middle-class suburb;

> It's up in [area] that I live … would you go to [area] to do it… Predominantly White neighbourhood, would you go over them men's and do it? I don't think you would because doctors, lawyers, people who's got cash that can fight the police live at that end, yeah. … We're the lower class, yeah or the dregs of the community yeah so you know or believe that you can treat us and do anything with us. (Derek, 46, Black, British-born, male)

It is significant that Derek is a managerial professional yet he perceives that in the 'police imagination' he is in the lowest class, considered the 'dregs'. The space which he inhabits is lacking in power to challenge police behaviour. For Derek, the communities inhabited by those considered the '*dregs of the community*' are an easy target for the police. The upper middle-class professionals inhabiting 'White spaces', and with access to resources which would enable them to challenge the police, are not seen to be a target of aggressive police tactics. In contrast, as argued in chapter four, Black bodies in White spaces attract the attention of the police as it is assumed that they are 'bodies out of place' (Puwar 2004).

Black Professionals—'Out of Place'

As has been shown, race is a trigger for class assumptions in police interactions with the public. This section will consider the experiences of participants who had professional jobs and/or associated professional or educational qualifications. Similarly, to the participants in (Rollock et al. 2014), those who had mobilised between working class and middle-class status, based on objective professional class indicators, had done so through university education or professional career and their class position was likely to be different to that of their parents. Participants in this research were not asked to position themselves in relation to their own perception of class. However, the way in which participants compared their own experiences with that of White colleagues, and also more generally the experience of the White middle class, is indicative of the complexities inherent in locating racialised bodies within class systems which are racially structured. The resulting dissonance that has been identified in previous studies (Rollock et al. 2011, 2013; Daye 1994), between identity and identification as a professional, occurs when professional status is undermined through racialising discourses which position Black and Black mixed-race professionals as 'space invaders' or 'bodies out of place' (Puwar 2004). As argued by Rollock et al. (2013), 'There is not a straightforward way to be Black and middle class' (p. 253). As participants did not refer to themselves as middle-class, the term professional is used here to describe those who are upwardly mobile.

Black bodies are constructed in reference to both lower class status and inherent criminality in the police imagination. Signs of professional status, including being present in the workplace, do little to rupture this imaginary. Some research participants were engaged in employment in which they were required to have frequent contact with the police in professional context. Even in this context participants perceived that they were still viewed as criminal. This is reflected in Andrew' account of his work with the police, which relied upon having a working relationship with individual police officers in specialist roles;

> In the line of work that I'm in I have a lot of contact with the police but then they first are kind of weighing you up. I know that they'll then go and do the PNC check, check my background, ah he's not got a criminal record and then it's alright we can deal with him now. (Andrew, 41, Black mixed-race, British-born, male)

This reveals the ways in which the lack of trust in the relationship between the police and Black individuals and communities, discussed throughout, traverses class boundaries. Manifestations of mistrust were expressed both covertly, as Andrew suspected above, but also in more obvious and overt ways. Eric talked about an occasion when the police were called to report a break in at the offices of the local authority building in which he worked. One of the police officers expressed suspicion towards members of staff who were not White;

> We were a group of mostly Black and ethnic minorities [staff] in our office and a couple of White people. And he said we need to check fingerprints and he looked at us [two members of 'BME' staff] and said if you've got a criminal record we will come and knock on your door. (Eric, 32, Black, African, male)

There is further evidence to support this point in Janice's account, discussed in Chapter 6, of being arrested and treated as suspect when she was supervising a youth football match in a professional capacity. Janice noted that her White colleague, who was alongside her, was not arrested at that time. Whilst she was able to negotiate her professional position on arrival at the police station, and avoided being placed in a cell, race disrupted Janice's 'cultural capital' to the extent that she could not have been imagined as a professional, but only as a suspect body in the police response to the situation. These examples serve as a reminder that the Black body is always under surveillance and control, even when they are engaged in 'respectable' activity. This is instructive of the ways in which, 'skin colour acts as a form of embodied capital that disrupts and lessens the worth of the cultural capital held by Black middle classes' (Rollock 2014: 4).

Skin colour is not the only symbol of racialised otherness. Outward signs of un-belonging or 'foreignness', such as accent, were perceived to effect police willingness to respond to calls for help in professional context. Charles is employed in the security industry and is in frequent contact with the police in the course of his work. Charles recalled more than one occasion when he had needed police support in dealing with situations in his workplace and they failed to provide assistance. One particular occasion stood out when Charles was fearful that somebody would lose their life;

> There was a massive kick off at least fifteen people was involved, fifteen people. Drug dealers you know. It was two of us as a bouncer…they just turned against us. So, I called the police. It was a situation where there was a bottle, a knife, everything was involved. So, I called the police over the phone, this guy starts asking me my date of birth, where were you born… everything. You can't actually ask me all of those questions when somebody is getting killed in front of me. (Charles, 40, Black, African, male)

For Charles, his accent provided a reason for the police call handler to establish his legitimacy before responding to his call for help. As found in Hussain and Bagguley (2005) a perceived lack of fluency in English can be a factor in racism and negative stereotyping (p. 418). His professional capacity was not enough to communicate 'respectability' or ensure that police back-up was provided before first proving that he belonged.

Cultural capital embodied in professional status may be drawn upon to confer worth in particular contexts. Returning to Derek's story, discussed in chapter four, Derek made a complaint to the police service following an incident in which he was tasered and restrained by five armed police officers. Derek requested that the officer dealing with his complaint met with him at his workplace, rather than at his home. This was a deliberate strategy in anticipation of the police perception that as a Black man he was a '*hoodlum*' and that he would be treated as such;

> Their chief inspector or whoever it is that came and spoke to me knows full well fucking hell I'm in deep shit now because this is not a hoodlum from the community, this is somebody who actually has a good standing within the community. I wouldn't say he made any reference to that fact but I could just see it in his body language. I could see it in his approach when he came to meet me. I'm dressed smart, I'm not dressed like some hoodlum, yeah. He was actually quite surprised when I turned up in reception. (Derek, 46, Black, British-born, male)

In Derek's account his social position and associated cultural capital as evident in his position within the organisation, the community and his style of dress becomes a negotiating tool for re-asserting his respectability and affirming the legitimacy of his complaint. This enables him to situate himself as neither 'police property' nor powerless. This would appear to challenge the evidence presented in chapter six, in which it was argued that Black men do not have recourse to alternative forms of masculinity. However, context is key to understanding the intersection of race, class and masculinity in police contact. Here Derek is no longer in the position of 'suspect' or threat attributed to him through race. He is, in the context of the policing diversity agenda, a potential 'disarmer' (Reiner 2010: 125). Complaints made against the police by a person from a vulnerable group, for example those considered vulnerable to racist policing who are able to signal respectability, may be treated particularly carefully. This shifts the position of Derek into a more powerful position in which he can negotiate his class position in relation to the White police institution.

Signs of respectability associated with professional employment may negotiate or neutralise the race-crime nexus in the police imagination where there is evidence of this professional status. Jean described one of several car stops whilst travelling to work;

> I remember once I was stopped not far from here, by a police officer. He basically wanted to double check to know who I was and I remember that I was wearing my badge from work and then he saw my badge and then he kind of backed up a bit. (Jean, 40, Black, African, male)

When Jean was prompted to expand on the point, he went on to explain that the behaviour of the officer had initially been '*apprehensive or aggressive*' but his demeanour changed and he became a little more '*friendly*' when he saw Jean's badge—an outward sign of respectability. As argued by Reiner, mistaking a member of higher status group for police property is a major pitfall of the police and one which is particularly 'reinforced' in encounters with ethnic minority groups 'where the police officer is not as attuned to the signals of respectability' (Reiner 2010: 124).

Evidence of wealth associated with successful career have the potential to be misread as a sign of criminality. This is particularly significant in relation to the ownership of luxury cars. The offence of Driving While Black (DWB) is colloquial for police profiling of Black drivers in US and has made its way into extensive academic research in the US context (Harris 1999; Lundman and Kaufman 2003; Russell 1998) and more recently in the UK (Liberty and StopWatch 2017). In the United Kingdom, those from a Black or other ethnic minority background are significantly more likely to be stopped by the police under the Road Traffic Act (Liberty and StopWatch 2017). Further, research conducted in Oslo found that driving a BMW car and having dark skin precipitates car stops (Sollund 2006). There are several examples in participant's accounts of car stops, also discussed in previous chapters. The purpose of the car stop was either to confirm ownership of the vehicle or to allay police suspicions of involvement in criminal activity. Marcus described an incident that occurred with an acquaintance from the area in which he lives;

> There's a footballer, his mother lives a few streets down from here. He's got a Mercedes, so he went to visit his mother, parked outside her house. When he was driving home, he's driven from [here] all the way to [suburb name] he's pulled up outside his house, he's jumped out of his car and when he's got out of his car three other cars have come and he's got a gun at his head. Now some police officer has seen him driving down the road and mistaken him for a drug dealer and they've followed him in his own car all the way to his house and when he's got out of his car on his own drive he's got a gun to his head. (Marcus, 44, Black, British-born, male)

Here, Blackness cannot be reconciled with the legitimate ownership of luxury items in the police imagination. Further, for the suspect, the armed police response suggests that his ownership of the car was associated with violent or drug-related crime. This is illustrative of the ways in which economic capital is disrupted by race (Rollock 2014) and racialised images of crime.

The potential for professional Black or Black mixed-race people to risk their professional status and acquired cultural capital through contact with the police is greater than for professional White people. As evidenced throughout, they are subjected to oppressive police practices which can provoke or necessitate a response. Such challenges to the police can have long-term damaging consequences on career prospects. Bianca reflects upon this, *any sort of encounters with the police that go badly, it's basically ended my career for the sake of running my mouth to a police officer.* This has implications for the ways in which both individuals and communities can resist oppressive police practices, having an impact on the capacity for solidarity in the face of oppressive policing. As Andrew said, *I'd rather just keep away. I've got too much to lose. House, investments, family, kids. I don't want police beating down my door.* He reflected on how this could be perceived by others;

> Some of the Black community will probably say it's a little bit sad really. I kind of see it as I've got bigger fish to fry in my agenda, my own family. And being part Black is just one part of my identity. I'm not willing to take them risks. (Andrew, 41, Black mixed-race, British-born, male)

Andrew reconciled his unwillingness to get involved in openly challenging the police, with reference to the work that he does in a professional context. He felt that this might provide him with a more legitimate channel to address some of the harms caused by oppressive policing. However, to openly challenge the police, was considered too much of a risk to the forms of capital he had acquired through professionalism.

Whilst race may be a sign of class in police mapping of policed populations, it is not simply the attribution of class that can explain disproportionate policing. Race intersects with class to produce racialised forms of policing. Not only is skin read as a sign of lower class status

(Lea 2000; Anthias 1999), it also disrupts cultural capital acquired through professional status (Rollock 2014). The individual class identity therefore, is not as relevant in understanding racialised police contact as the ascribed class identity, read through race, which shapes interactions with the police. Further, as argued by Lea (2000) the 'Black-middle classes are not seen to hold sufficient power to pose a serious challenge to the police, it is therefore not in the police interests to accommodate their needs' (Lea 2000: 225).

Policing 'Heaven': Immigrant Responses to the Police in Britain

Imagined political communities, defined through the concept of 'nation' (Anderson 2006: 6) operate through processes of exclusion, both boundary exclusion and those who do not fit within the scope of ideas which delimit who can and who cannot belong. Immigrants to the United Kingdom, particularly but not exclusively immigrants of colour, in the post-war period have been constructed as 'the enemy within' (Gilroy 1982, 1987). Further, the idea that Black does not equate with Britishness is perpetuated through discourses of racialised otherness as reflected in the title of Paul Gilroy's seminal text, *There ain't no Black in the union jack* (Gilroy 1987). This means that even for Black Britons, their identity can conflict with their identification through the White gaze (Yancy 2008; Fanon 1986).

Participant's narratives demonstrate the ways in which notions of belonging/un-belonging operate to position the individual in relation to the state and by extension the police and policing functions. Perceptions of belonging and un-belonging are negotiated through social identity to shape expectations and perceptions of the police. This is acutely evident in the comparison between the perceptions of British-born Black people and those who were born outside of the UK and migrated to England in their adult years. One of the evident points of difference in non-UK born participant's narratives is the absence of regular police contacts throughout childhood and the teenage years which are evident in the accounts of British born participants (see Chapter 4). As explained by Eric;

> I came to the UK as a late teenager and it was a bit different because I didn't have many friends and I didn't go out a lot and I worked. I didn't hang around street corners or malls. I went home, I woke up carried on with my business and went home. I didn't hang around or go to the pub so there was no occasion of contact with me and the police. (Eric, 32, Black, African, male)

This observation suggests that not growing up in the UK, and therefore not being exposed to the police practices which '*plant the seed of fear*', may lead to a different expectation of the police. The racist effects of disproportionate and oppressive policing, which have longer term consequences for trust and confidence, have not been experienced. This could partially explain the more positive perception of the police expressed by Eric, Kenneth and Samuel. This perception prevailed in spite of their recollections of negative responses to victimisation and for Kenneth being stopped and searched. Overall, they believed that the police do '*a good job*'.

Additionally, non-UK born participants had a point of comparison with their country of origin, these were predominantly countries within the African continent. The ability to compare experiences of the British police with a service that was perceived to be worse would appear, in participant's narratives, to mitigate the impact of negative experiences in the UK. This is illustrated by Kenneth;

> I don't see it [institutional racism] as a problem because when I compare it to other experiences I've had, even in my own country that I call my own, this place [England] is heaven in terms of police dealing. (Kenneth, 38, Black, African, male)

There is a striking difference in the way that Kenneth describes the police when compared with the perceptions held by British born research participants (discussed in earlier chapters). Kenneth acknowledged that institutional racism exists within the police and felt that he had been treated unfairly both as a victim and in the course of routine policing; nevertheless, he did not view this as problematic in relation to his own contact with the police. He felt that he would be given the opportunity to prove himself when stopped and questioned, as long as he maintained a lifestyle that would not bring himself into contact with the police through criminal behaviour, and that he complied with the police in stop and search.

The notion that the police respond in different ways to those who comply with both the law and with the police during routine police contact, such as stop and search and car stops, was evident in non-British participant's perceptions. Eric, who has resided in the UK for around fourteen years, and is a citizen through naturalisation, mentioned at several points throughout the interview that he considers himself to be a '*law abiding citizen*'. This was not exclusive to the narratives of non-UK born participants; however, the notion of obeying the law as preventing harsh treatment from the police was more salient in the narratives of those who were not born in the UK. For the majority of UK born, male participants in particular, they knew through experience, that complying with the law was not enough to protect them from being on the receiving end of negative police attention, as was revealed in Chapter 4.

A failure on the part of the police to provide equal service and protection to Black people implied, to those born elsewhere, that even those born in the UK had not been accepted into the 'imagined community' (Anderson 2006) of the 'nation';

> This [Britain] is what they are born to accept as their own place and yet they can't feel okay to fit into the system. It's terrible isn't it because it's not like they have got to be able to go somewhere else and find a better option. That's why if they are having problem its more stressing to them. (Kenneth, 38, Black, African, male)

> I can understand where they are coming from especially those who were born in this country because they feel they are not, are they part of the society or are they not? And if they are not and they were born here where do they go? (Samuel, 45, Black, African, male)

These extracts illuminate that for those with 'hybrid' identities the negotiation of belonging, through contact with the police, may not be as significant as for those who identify as British by birth. For both

Kenneth and Samuel, negative police contact was understood as evidence of their [Black Britons] acceptance, or lack thereof, as part of the 'nation' (also, see Bradford et al. 2017). This relationship between police contact and belonging was not as strong for recent migrants.

The 'double alienation' (McAuley 1996) that Kenneth and Samuel reflect upon, in relation to Black British people, is evident in Thomas's narrative. Despite being born in England and spending all fifty-five years of his life in the country, he said, I *consider myself British because that's my place of birth. If they decided to kick out every Black person in this country I'd be a refugee [laughs], it's that drastic.* Here, Thomas reveals the dissonance between his identity and sense of belonging to Britain, through birth, and the possibility that race could negate his belonging through his identification by the state. As Ratannsi (2000) argues, when the Black male is constructed as a threat the 'conjunction of Black and British' is also threatened (p. 126). For Thomas, being 'British-born' did not have any advantage in relation to his treatment within the criminal justice system. Thomas spoke about the time he had spent in the prison system and the over representation of Black people that he had observed on prison wings, in particular in London but also in West Yorkshire.

> You know saying you're a British born Black doesn't alter the fact that it's a Black man in jail. When they are going into prisons and they're filling in these forms that say do you regard yourself as British, sometimes I put down I'm not even gonna answer that question because it feels insulting and offensive. (Thomas, 55, Black, British-born, male)

This illuminates the disjuncture between his identity as a British born citizen and his identification, through racialised othering in the criminal justice process. This differed from Kenneth's position, that '*I don't exactly call this place my home so I think I have a choice, an alternative*'. Kenneth mentioned in his interview that ultimately, he planned to return to Nigeria, he did not plan to settle permanently in the UK. This is instructive of the way in which the police's power to affirm or deny identification and belonging can be shaped through the individual's identity (see Bradford et al. 2014). If the individual does not identify with the dominant social (national) identity, as in Kenneth's case, this negates the power of the state actors (police) to reaffirm or deny identification with the dominant social group. It can be argued that this makes the police perception of the subject of policing less important for migrants and this may explain why Kenneth was not concerned about experiencing police racism, although he did accept its existence.

Skin colour was not the only marker of foreignness in the context of police contact. Accent and names were perceived to signify the bearer as not belonging and therefore not deserving of equal treatment. Charles had experience of police contact in a variety of contexts-as a security professional in a role that required frequent contact with the police to request back-up, as the victim of crime and in car stop and other routine policing contexts. Charles recalled several scenarios in which he had called the police for support in potentially dangerous situations and, rather than provide the requested support, the police questioned him about his identity, including his place of birth. Charles located his treatment as stemming from the fact that he was identified as 'foreign' through both his accent and his name;

> I don't see why people might, from the first word of the first sentence, [think] oh he's not from here, he wasn't born here… and maybe think that because I don't know the law in this country that's why you want to take advantage of me. That is unfair…As long as you've got the right to live in this country I don't see why you should treat me differently because I'm [an] immigrant. (Charles, 40, Black, African, male)

In all three contexts of police contact and on more than one occasion in each context Charles perceived that his treatment was inferior because he was marked as 'foreign'. Whilst he recognised that race and skin colour was also a marker of not belonging, it was that he was identified as '*not from here*' that determined the police response. For Charles, his accent communicated that he was an easy target for unfair treatment as it would be expected that he did not know or understand the UK legal system; therefore, he would be afforded unequal protection.

In contrast, for Eric, it was skin colour that precipitated unequal protection. He said *'I've got British nationality [naturalised]. I would align with being more British than African'*(Eric, 32, Black, African, male). On paper he could call upon the concept of belonging to the 'nation'. Nevertheless, he did not expect that the police would respond to a call for help as quickly as to that of '*an ethnically British [White] person*'. This statement provides further evidence for the claim that police contact can reaffirm or deny a sense of belonging. However, significantly for understanding the relationship between communities and the police, the attribution of race delineates who can and who can't belong to the 'imagined community'. The Other, who does not belong, becomes 'police property' (Lee 1981) by virtue of their racial otherness.

Conclusion

This chapter has illuminated the ways in which race serves as the predominant 'symbol of inferiorisation' (Anthias 1999) in the police imagination. Regardless of the subject's social position, race usually trumps class in identifying them as suspect. This is most apparent through the experiences of those whose social status is in contrast with the expectation that Black people embody lower social class status. For Black professionals, race operates to disrupt forms of capital (Rollock 2014). This was evident in participant's accounts of being treated as suspect through the reading of signs of wealth, such as luxury car ownership, as evidence of criminality and the suspicion of professionals in the course of their work, including mistaken arrest. Social status does not result in an improved experience of policing, Black middle-class people experience racist and racialised policing. This finding is counter to the dominant assumption that race is not as significant as class in understanding racial disparities in policing.

Racist policing is more pronounced for those residing in racially othered spaces, participants referred to these spaces as 'Black areas'. Whilst the residents of these areas are not predominantly Black, the presence of Black bodies in these spaces operates to constructs the space as dangerous through the skin of those who inhabit it (Ahmed 2007). Racially othered spaces are policed intensively and police presence, surveillance and stop and search is the norm. Race and social class intersect in these places, which suffer from high levels of unemployment, economic and social deprivation and resulting higher crime levels. All residents in these spaces, regardless of ascribed race, are considered 'police property' (Lee 1981). However, for Black residents it is the intersection of race with class and not class alone that explains their over policing and under protection.

Migrant populations generally report more positive perceptions of the police than British—born Black people (Bradford et al. 2017). Whilst the findings presented here accord with this, there are some caveats. The participants who had migrated to Britain recognised that racism is a problem within the British police, through exposure to 'community narratives', high-profile cases and their own experiences they were able to identify racism as a problem. However, in contrast to British-born Black people, they appeared less concerned with the impact that this might have on them. This appears to be shaped by their desire to either settle in England or return to their country of origin and, therefore, the extent to which belonging was important. Further, a point of comparison in the form of police services in other countries, both in European countries and in their home country,[1] serves to improve perceptions of UK police where the comparator is less desirable. Migrant participants also differed to British born participants in their perception that law abiding behaviour would mitigate against negative police attention. It is shown that, for those who had been in the country for a longer period of time and/or had been exposed to more negative encounters with the police, these perceptions could change.

It is concluded that race does intersect with class to produce specific outcomes in terms of policing; however, these oppressions are organised in relation to the 'structural domain of power' (Collins 2000). In the mapping of populations to be policed, it is race which acts as the primary 'symbol of inferiorisation' (Anthias 1999) to which the police respond. This has racial effects for both working class and professional Black and Black mixed-race people who are all treated as 'police property'.

---

[1]For participants in this study, these were all countries on the African continent.

References

Ahmed, S. (2007). A Phenomenology of Whiteness. *Feminist Theory, 8*, 149–168.

Anderson, B. (2006). *Imagined Communities: Reflections on the Origin and Spread of Nationalism*. London: Verso.

Anthias, F. (1999). Institutional Racism, Power and Accountability. *Sociological Research Online*, 4. www.socresonline.org.uk/4/lawrence/anthias.html. Accessed 13 July 2017.

Anthias, F., & Yuval-Davis, N. (2005). *Racialised Boundaries: Race, Nation, Gender, Colour and Class and the Anti-racist Struggle*. London: Routledge.

Bell, A. (2010). Being 'at Home' in the Nation: Hospitality and Sovereignty in Talk About Immigration. *Ethnicities, 10*, 236–256.

Bradford, B. (2014). Policing and Social Identity: Procedural Justice, Inclusion and Cooperation Between Police and Public. *Policing and Society, 24*, 22–43.

Bradford, B., Murphy, K., & Jackson, J. (2014). Officers as Mirrors: Policing, Procedural Justice and the (Re)Production of Social Identity. *British Journal of Criminology, 54*, 527–550.

Bradford, B., Sargeant, E., Murphy, T., & Jackson, J. (2017). A Leap of Faith? Trust in the Police Among Immigrants in England and Wales. *British Journal of Criminology, 57*(2), 381–401.

Collins, P. H. (2000). *Black Feminist Thought: Knowledge, Consciousness, and the Politics of Empowerment*. New York: Routledge.

Daye, S. J. (1994). *Middle-Class Blacks in Britain: A Racial Fraction of a Class Group or a Class Fraction of a Racial Group?* Basingstoke and London: Palgrave Macmillan.

Derrida, J. (2000). *Of Hospitality: Anne Dufourmantelle Invites Jacques Derrida to Respond* (R. Bowlby, Trans.). Stanford, CA: Stanford University Press.

Eastwood, N., Shiner, M., & Bear, D. (2013). *The Numbers in Black and White: Ethnic Disparities in the Policing and Prosecution of Drug Offences in England and Wales*. London: Release.

Fanon, F. (1986). *Black Skin, White Masks*. London: Pluto Press.

Farrar, M. (2002). *The Struggle for 'Community' in a British Multi-Ethnic Inner-City Area*. Wales: Edwin Mellen Press.

Gilroy, P. (1982). Police and Thieves. In CCCS (Ed.), *The Empire Strikes Back: Race and Racism in 70s Britain*. London: Hutchinson.

Gilroy, P. (1987). *There Ain't No Black in the Union Jack*. London: Hutchinson.

Harris, D. A. (1999). The Stories, The Statistics and the Law: Why "Driving While Black" Matters. *Minnesota Law Review, 84*, 265.

Holdaway, S. (1983). *Inside the British Police: A Force at Work*. Oxford: Blackwell.

Hussain, Y., & Bagguley, P. (2005). Citizenship, Ethnicity and Identity: British Pakistanis After the 2001 'Riots'. *Sociology, 39,* 407–425.

Jivraj, S., & Simpson, L. (2015). *Ethnic Identity and Inequalities in Britain: The Dynamics of Diversity.* Bristol: Policy Press.

Keeling, P. (2017). *No Respect: Young BAME Men, the Police and Stop and Search*. London: Criminal Justice Alliance.

Lambert, J. R. (1970). *Crime, Police and Race Relations: A Study in Birmingham*. Oxford: Oxford University Press.

Lea, J. (2000). The Macpherson Report and the Question of Institutional Racism. *The Howard Journal of Criminal Justice, 39,* 219–233.

Lee, J. A. (1981). Some Structural Aspects of Police Deviance in Relations with Minority Groups. In C. Shearing (Ed.), *Organisational Police Deviance*. Toronto: Butterworth.

Liberty and StopWatch. (2017). *"Driving While Black": Liberty and StopWatch's Briefing on the Discriminatory Effect of Stop and Search Powers on Our Roads*. London: Liberty. https://www.libertyhumanrights.org.uk/sites/default/files/Liberty%20Driving%20While%20Black.pdf. Accessed 3 March 2018.

Loftus, B. (2009). *Police Culture in a Changing World*. New York: Oxford University Press.

Lundman, R. J., & Kaufman, R. L. (2003). Driving While Black: Effects of Race, Ethnicity, and Gender on Citizen Self-Reports of Traffic Stops and Police Actions. *Criminology, 41,* 195.

Mcauley, J. W. (1996). Under an Orange Banner: Reflections on the Northern Protestant Experiences of Emigration. In P. O'Sullivan (Ed.), *Religion and Identity*. London: Leicester University Press.

Mills, C. W. (1997). *The Racial Contract*. New York: Cornell University Press.

O'Neill, M., & Loftus, B. (2013). Policing and the Surveillance of the Marginal: Everyday Contexts of Social Control. *Theoretical Criminology, 17,* 437–454.

Puwar, N. (2004). *Space Invaders: Race Gender and Bodies Out of Place*. Oxford: Berg.

Quinton, P., Bland, N., & Miller, J. (2000). *Police Stops, Decision-Making and practice*. London: Home Office.

Rattansi, A. (2000). On Being and Not Being Brown/Black-British: Racism, Class, Sexuality and Ethnicity in Post-imperial Britain. *Interventions, 2,* 118–134.

Reiner, R. (2010). *The Politics of the Police*. Oxford: Oxford University Press.

Rollock, N. (2014). Race, Class and 'The Harmony of Dispositions'. *Sociology, 48*, 445–451.

Rollock, N., Gillborn, D., Vincent, C., & Ball, S. (2011). The Public Identities of the Black Middle Classes: Managing Race in Public Spaces. *Sociology, 45*, 1078–1093.

Rollock, N., Vincent, C., Gillborn, D., & Ball, S. (2013). 'Middle Class by Profession': Class Status and Identification Amongst the Black Middle Classes. *Ethnicities, 13*, 253–275.

Rollock, N., Gillborn, D., Vincent, C., & Ball, S. J. (2014). *The Colour of Class: The Educational Strategies of the Black Middle Classes*. London: Routledge.

Russell, K. K. (1998). Driving While Black: Corollary Phenomena and Collateral Consequences. *Boston College Law Review, 40*, 717–731.

Sivanandan, A. (1982). *A Different Hunger: Writings on Black Resistance*. London: Pluto Press.

Slater, T., & Anderson, N. (2012). The Reputational Ghetto: Territorial Stigmatisation in St. Paul's, Bristol. *Transactions of the Institute of British Geographers, 37*(4), 530–546.

Sollund, R. (2006). Racialisation in Police Stop and Search Practice—The Norwegian Case. *Critical Criminology, 14*, 265–292.

Stone, V., & Pettigrew, N. (2000). *The Views of the Public on Stops and Searches*. London: Home Office.

Virdee, S. (2014). *Racism, Class and the Racialised Outsider*. Basingstoke: Palgrave Macmillan.

Wacquant, L. (2008). *Urban Outcasts: A Comparative Sociology of Advanced Marginality*. Cambridge: Polity Press.

Webster, C. (2008). Marginalized White Ethnicity, Race and Crime. *Theoretical Criminology, 12*, 293–312.

Wray, M. (2006). *Not Quite White: White Trash and the Boundaries of Whiteness*. Durham, NC: Duke University Press.

Yancy, G. (2008). *Black Bodies, White Gazes: The Continuing Significance of Race*. Maryland: Rowman and Littlefield.

Part III

Theoretical Implications and Conclusions

8

A Critical Race Theory of Racialised Policing?

This chapter illustrates the utility of Critical Race Theory in understanding the problem of racism in policing. First, it addresses the denial of racism in the police institution which believes it is post-race and makes the case for countering the denial of racism. The chapter goes on to argue that a Critical Race Theory of racialised policing offers some hope of resistance through the emergence of the counter story. It draws together the counter-story which emerged through the data in Chapters 4–7 and emphasises the radical possibility of the counter-story as a strategy for challenging dominant representations of Black bodies, their relation to criminality and how they experience policing. Further, it illuminates how racism is experienced and in doing so counters the denial of racism within the institution.

Within the spirit of Critical Race Theory research, this chapter employs participants voices to consider ways in which experiences with the police could be improved for Black and Black mixed-race people. Ultimately, this chapter challenges those within and outside of the police institution, to accept the inevitability of racism within a racially predicated society, rather than engaging in strategies of denial. It shows how Critical Race Theory can be employed within criminological research to unveil the operation of Whiteness and concludes that this is one way in which the longevity of racism within the police can be challenged.

L. J. Long, *Perpetual Suspects*, Palgrave Studies in Race, Ethnicity, Indigeneity and Criminal Justice, https://doi.org/10.1007/978-3-319-98240-3_8

Countering Denial: A Case for Critical Race Theory in Criminology?

The discipline of Criminology and the criminal justice practices which it seeks to understand are undoubtedly shaped by the imperial enterprise (Moore 2015). However, there has not been a sustained interest in understanding criminalising processes through a race lens (with some notable exceptions, see Glynn 2013; Gabbidon 2010). Racism, in the post-race institution, remains invisible to those who are privileged enough not to have to confront its effects. As argued by Goldberg (2009), '*raceless racism operates in denial, anywhere and anytime*' (p. 25). This is evident in the findings of this research, which has identified a shift in the manifestations of racism in contemporary policing. Whilst more overt forms of racist behaviour are no longer considered acceptable in the police institution, racism is felt by Black and Black mixed-race people in their encounters with the police. Levi summarised the nature of this shift from overt racism to 'raceless racism' in Chapter 4, when he said '*Babylon remove the chain, now they're using the brain*'. This statement speaks to the invisibility of racism in the context of the dominant narrative of post-raciality. Rather than overt forms of racism—for example, racist slurs, which are easy to identify—covert forms of racism, that manifest in the everyday practices of the institution, are invisible to those who do not feel them (see Tate 2016). This enables racism to flourish whilst it is simultaneously denied. The denial inherent in Post-race logic turns racism into a problem of deficient individuals. As Eddo-Lodge (2018) argues '*we tell ourselves that racism is about moral values, when instead it is about the survival strategy of systemic power*' (Eddo-Lodge, p. 64). Racism, in this context, becomes a behaviour to be punished, rather than a system of power implicated in control of the other. When, albeit occasionally, racist police officers are punished, their punishment is merely symbolic. It communicates a commitment to anti-racism whilst engaging in denial of the systemic nature of the problem.

One of the drivers of denial is the erasure of the language of race through the proliferation of 'diversity' within institutions. This has accelerated through the legal and policy changes, as well as training interventions, brought about by reform within the police (and other institutions) as a result of Macphersons (1999) recommendations within the *Stephen Lawrence Inquiry Report*. The denial of racism and the erasure of the language of race is observable in the immediate aftermath of the publication of Macpherson's (1999) report which found London's Metropolitan Police Service (MPS) to be institutionally racist. Paul Condon the then MPS commissioner, initially refused to accept Macpherson's finding of institutional racism. Both defensiveness and denial were evident in the 'white backlash'[1] (Toynbee 1999) which followed in the media, and the police were constructed as victims of the inquiry. However, the MPS swiftly introduced their *Protect and Respect* diversity agenda which aimed to increase ethnic minority police officers, develop strategies to deal with hate crime and improve race and diversity training (*Guardian*, 25 February 1999). By 2002 the new MPS Commissioner, Sir John Stevens, was able to confidently claim that the Metropolitan Police Service was no longer institutionally racist (discussed in Mclaughlin 2007: 24). In the post-race policing era the conflation of race with other diversity strands in awareness training and, more recently, in legislation (see Equality Act 2010), renders the language of race both unnecessary and undesirable. Members of the public, and police officers alike, who claim that they have experienced racism at the hands of the police institution are accused of playing the 'race card' (Loftus 2009). Rather than challenging racist practices, the focus on 'diversity' engages in denial, facilitating 'racism without racists' (Bonilla-Silva 2010).

The denial of racism continues to blight the police service, even when it is faced with evidence of its existence. In 2014, the *Ellison Review* found that the Metropolitan Police Service had illegally spied on the

[1]The response to the Stephen Lawrence Inquiry Report findings, in the right-wing press, was described as 'White Backlash' by Toynbee (1999). Through a racialised and overtly racist response to the finding of institutional racism, it engaged in a process of denial and represented the inquiry as an attempt to undermine the Whiteness of nation by challenging the 'quintessentially English' police institution.

Stephen Lawrence family during the course of the investigation into the racist murder of their son. In the wake of the revelations, Janet Hills, the Chair of the National Black Police Association (NBPA) claimed that fifteen years after the publication of the *Stephen Lawrence Inquiry Report*, the Metropolitan Police Service is still institutionally racist. Citing disproportionality in stop and search and underrepresentation of ethnic minorities within the MPS, Hills called upon the then Commissioner, Bernard Hogan- Howe, to concede that institutional racism is still present in the Metropolitan Police Service (Halliday 2015). To deflect the claim made by the NBPA, the Commissioner recoursed to the position that the police cannot be viewed in isolation as wider society is institutionally racist (ibid.). This position does not overtly deny the existence of institutional racism; however, it engages in denial of responsibility for the manifestations of racism within the institution. To accuse the police of institutional racism therefore, is to make them the scapegoat for societies racism problem. Whilst the debates pertaining to institutional racism are predominantly UK focused, denial is evident in the narratives around race and policing in the global context. One example is the response to the Black Lives Matter protests, particularly in the US context. According to Smith (2017), the backlash to the Black Lives Matter movement is couched in terms of white victimhood. Nowhere is this more apparent than in the Blue Lives Matter campaign which presents the police (who are majoritarily white) as the real victims.

The failure of the diversity agenda to eliminate racism from the police service has led to the growing popularity of psychological concepts to explain why racism is still evident in police practice. Unconscious and implicit bias have recently gained popularity in understanding racist practices and outcomes in institutions (see Equality Challenge Unit 2013, for comprehensive review). These terms are used to refer to biases that the individual has but that they are unaware of, and that have been shaped through socialisation and individual experience. UK police services are increasingly drawing upon these concepts to develop training targeted at reducing unconscious or implicit bias in police decision making (see Quinton and Packham 2016). The premise of Unconscious Bias Training (UBT) is that it exposes the individual to their own biases and in doing so will make them aware of how these biases can shape their behaviour. However, there are several problems with this approach to addressing racism within the institution. Some are of a practical nature, as identified in the Equality Challenge Unit (2013) review, most significantly that UBT is not shown to change behaviour in any sustained way. Similarly, Quinton and Packham's (2016) evaluation of the introduction of unconscious bias into police stop and search training finds that any initial behavioural changes are no longer evident after three months. Further, the concept of unconscious bias enables denial of knowledge at both an individual and an institutional level, therefore facilitating the evasion of responsibility for racist practices. As argued by Tate and Page (2018), '(Un)conscious bias is a strategy to distance the White self from the charge of racism and, indeed, that one can be implicated in its perpetuation' (p. 151).

Challenging the denial of racism, which is deeply ingrained in the police psyche, and unveiling the operation of Whiteness within the police institution is fundamental to holding the police accountable for racist practices. A Critical Race Theory approach can counter the denial evident in the contemporary post-race police narrative. The following section will analyse the counter-story that emerged through the voices of participants and illustrate the utility of the counter-story in countering post-race denial.

Centering Race—The Emerging Counter Story?

This book has facilitated the development of a counter-story to the dominant narratives about black bodies and their relation to crime and processes of criminal justice, specifically in the context of policing. Whilst the data is specific to UK experiences, the broader issues that emerge from the counter-story are relevant to racialised policing in the international context. In the post-imperial nations, policing operates to control the racialised other and maintain White power. Whilst policing policy and practice varies between jurisdictions, policing is shaped through their imperial histories (Cole 1999). Inevitably, policing is racialised in these contexts. The title of the book speaks to the overarching finding that Black bodies are the 'perpetual suspect'.

The counter-story exposes, through a race lens, how they come to be constructed as such. Black and mixed-race people experience policing as the perpetual 'suspect'. This is evident in police-initiated contact, predominantly stop and search (Long and Joseph-Salisbury 2018), car stops, arrest and use of force and also in the context of citizen-initiated contact, including experiences of victimisation.

The control of Black bodies through routine exposure to police stops is a common and unsurprising finding of this research. These experiences begin in childhood, as was revealed in Chapter 4. These experiences '*plant the seed of fear*' (*Levi*) in children and set the tone of their relationship with the police into their teenage years and early adulthood. Another significant effect of routine encounters with the police is the denial of innocence. Black bodies are perpetually suspect even when they are children. This has a determining impact upon their perceptions of the police and their trust and confidence in them. Further, the routine nature of surveillance of young Black bodies denies them their innocence. As both Bernstein's (2011) and Goff et al. (2014) show, the concept of innocence is reserved for White children. Often, Black children are forced to confront their interpellation through the White gaze, for the first time, through encounters with the police.

The counter story emerging from this research suggests that stop and search is a normalised experience, this is the case for Black men in particular. Because stop and search is a normalised experience, their experiences of policing in this context are unremarkable. This was evident in the interview process when participants frequently spoke at length about police encounters in other contexts, most commonly as victims of crime, but did not mention stop and search until prompted to do so. Further, as revealed in Chapter 4, race is the last explanation that they consider, rather than the first. Comparison with White peers is an important process in illuminating 'raceless racism' in this context (see Chapter 4; also Britton 2000; Sharp and Atherton 2007). This finding challenges the police narrative that Black people are anti-police and their claims of police racism can be attributed to this anti-authority pathology. This assumption contributes to the silencing of racism as Black people's claims of racist treatment are read as an attempt to gain an advantage by playing the 'race card' (Loftus 2010). Further, it shows that, whilst stop and search is significant in determining the nature of relationships with the police, other experiences are important and should be considered within research and policy agendas, in particular experiences of victimisation.

One of the most significant themes emerging from this research is that police treatment of victims of crime, an area frequently ignored in studies of police/community relations, has serious consequences for levels of trust and confidence in the police. As shown in Chapter 5, when the victim of crime is not attributed victim status they become the (Un)Victim. When they are forced to consider that race is the reason for their treatment, because they were not taken seriously, or treated as though they are suspect, the effects of the police response can be greater than the effects of victimisation. Becoming the (Un)Victim takes a psychic toll. When the police do not afford victim status to the subject of crime, and they are forced to consider that race is part of becoming the (un)victim, the effects of 'racisms invisible touch' (Tate 2016) are greater than the effects of the initial victimisation. This triggers the process of racial re-victimisation; the (Un)Victim is victimised once more because of race. This has multiple racist effects. First, as this research has shown, it delimits access to justice and prevents or prolongs the process of recovery from victimisation (see Chapter 5). Further, it can impact upon the sense of belonging to the nation (see Chapter 7; also, see Bradford et al. 2014). This finding is important as there is an absence of research which addresses Black victim's perspectives of policing through a race lens. Policy responses to the low levels of trust and confidence in the police among some ethnic minority communities, black communities in particular, are focused on stop and search as the key to improving perceptions of legitimacy. For example, the introduction of the *Best Use of Stop and Search Scheme* in 2014 (see Chapter 3). Whilst disproportionality in stop and search undoubtedly has a significant impact on trust and confidence in the police, the perception of discriminatory policing following victimisation is shown in this research to have significant racial effects. This results in the adoption of a strategy of police avoidance which, by proxy, excludes Black and Black mixed-race people from police protection.

Over-policing, including stop and search, arrest and use of excessive force as well as under policing in the context of victimisation, changes how people live their lives. The findings of this research have been instructive in revealing the strategies that Black and Black mixed-race people use in order to manage the routine threat of policing in their everyday lives. In Chapter 4 it was shown that avoidance and compliance are the two key strategies that Black people utilise to manage the threat of policing. One of the ways in which the perception of this threat is realised is through previous personal experience; this is the most important factor in determining how the police are perceived. However, communal narratives also have a significant function. These narratives emerge predominantly from the stories that people share about their own police encounters with family and friends and, to a lesser extent, high profile cases featured in the media. The communal narrative has become part of a lexicon which is understood by Black people, even those whose experiences of the police are different, and it shapes their adaptive strategies for managing the threat posed by police contact. Negative perceptions of the police are commonly understood by the police to be evidence of an anti-authority pathology (Loftus 2010), or rumour and conjecture that serve to damage the relationship between communities and the police. However, when race and racism(s) is central to the analysis of the problem, it is evident that they emerge from experiential knowledge. They can be understood as another of the essential protective strategies that Black people use to manage their treatment as perpetual suspect and the risks that this poses in terms of over policing, use of force, brutality and becoming the (Un)Victim.

The debate within criminology proposes a dichotomous race or class approach to understanding race and policing. To some extent the intersectionality between race and class is acknowledged (for example, see Bridges 1983; Jefferson 1993; Bowling and Phillips 2007; Webster 2008; Medina-Ariza 2014). However, the mainstay of criminological theorising prioritises class-based explanations and the disproportionate representation of ethnic minorities in the lower classes. Further, it is often focused on working class background, educational failure and family structure as drivers for offending. The counter story which has emerged in Chapters 4–7, challenges the underlying assumption that ethnic disproportionality in police statistics is a result of elevated offending. Further, it shows that regardless of social status or behaviour/lack of offending behaviour, Black people are perpetually suspect. Racialised contact with the police is not a phenomenon experienced only by poor, Black, youth. Rather, it persists throughout the life-course and is experienced by people across the social class spectrum.

Chapter 6 shows how Black and Black mixed-race women experience policing at the intersection of race, gender and professional status. By comparing their experiences with those reported by men, and their knowledge of how the men they knew had experienced police contact, it argued that racialised stereotypes impact negatively on both men and women's experiences of policing. Both men and women reported similar experiences of childhood encounters with the police and were treated as suspect; however, there is some evidence that in adulthood women had more capacity than men to negotiate their position in relation to notions of respectability. The intersection of race with gender constructs subordinated masculinities and femininities which are necessary for the maintenance of hegemonic forms of White, male, power (Collins 2004). Femininity operates as capital for some Black women to diminish, to a degree, the operation of the skin as a 'symbol of inferiorisation' (Anthias 1999). However, this is not the case for all women and relies upon their conformity with preferred norms of White femininity. These are performed through law abiding behaviour, submissiveness and compliance in police encounters and respectability evident through professional status. Through this analysis it is evident, as argued in Chapter 6, that the 'big Black man' poses the ultimate threat. Whilst Black men may be interpellated in the same way and their treatment accorded on this basis, their perceptions of the police are determined, to some extent by the intersection of their experiences with their subject position in relation to the state. This is evident through the perceptions of Black men who had migrated to the UK, as discussed in Chapter 7. Length of residency in the UK has a significant impact upon perceptions of the police and the extent to which participants would be prepared to trust the force as an institution. The research finds that recent migrants had a more favourable perception of the police than the participants' who were born and had lived in England throughout their formative years. This favourable perception relies upon the absence of frequency of contact, particularly from a young age, as experienced by British born participants'. Further, having a less favourable point of comparison, through experiences of policing in other countries, both in Europe and in the continent of Africa, placed particular expectations on the British police through their global reputation. In particular, the traits associated with the British police were a lack of corruption and a well-publicised diversity agenda which created an expectation of equality of treatment. For some, this expectation when it did not match with experience was confusing and ran counter to positive expectations. This contrasts with their British born peers whose expectation, based on personal experiences in youth and comparative experiences in community narratives, was that they would be treated unfairly. As Bradford (2014) suggests, the perception of unfair treatment by the police shapes identity formation, and sense of belonging to the majority group or society. However, what is interesting in this research is the finding that the power of the state to delimit agency, through a sense of unbelonging and/or Otherness, is limited when the subject's preferred national identity does not correspond with the dominant identity. When belonging is hybrid or located within another boundary, the nature of police contact is less important in the construction of identity. In these instances, even when the presence of racism in the police is acknowledged, it is not considered as problematic as it is for those who have an investment in belonging to the nation.

This counter story provides some original insights into the relationship between the police and Black communities which challenges dominant understandings. Crucially, it offers some evidence, through a race lens, towards untangling the race versus class debate prevalent within the discipline of Criminology. Class does matter. However, in the construction of the suspect, it matters more for Whites. The police rely upon race as a 'symbol of inferiorisation' (Anthias 1999). In a racially ordered society, Blackness is both a symbol of inferior race and inferior class in the police imagination. It is ultimately Blackness that defines the perpetual suspect.

A Critical Race Criminological Theory for Understanding Policing?

A Critical Race Theory framework for understanding policing crucially takes a racially ordered society, which favours Whiteness, as it starting point. In his paper *Racial Realism*, Derek Bell (1991), positions racism as an endemic part of life, which cannot be attributed simply to the prejudices of individuals. He claims that, '*This mind-set or philosophy requires us to acknowledge the permanence of our subordinate status. That acknowledgement enables us to avoid despair and frees us to imagine and implement racial strategies that can bring fulfilment and even triumph*' (ibid.: 373–374). This position is helpful in understanding how to both understand and resist racialised policing. The current 'diversity' focused approach expects the police to uphold a set of values which run counter to their role in upholding a system of racial ordering, premised on 'White supremacy' (Mills 1997). It is no coincidence that Carmichael and Hamilton (1967) define institutional racism in the context of colonialism. They argue that Black people in the US were colonial subjects in relation to the state. In this context institutional racism is described as a form of colonialism (p. 5). Similarly, Sivanandan (1982) referred to the status of Black people in the UK as the 'colony within' the 'mother' country (p. 61). This neo-colonial configuration produces communities as the Other, not by accident but by design. It is the role and function of the police to control racially othered populations in order to uphold this system of White power and they draw on policing practices developed in the colonies to do so (Bell 2013; Sinclair and Williams 2007).

This book has used the term 'police imagination' to describe a particular occupational consciousness which derives from the mapping of populations according to their power/lack of power. The most powerless in society are disempowered further through the narrative of risk and worthlessness and they become 'police property' (Lee 1981). The concept of the 'police imagination' can be utilised in order to understand the over-policing and under-protection of Black people. To some extent it borrows from the police culture literature (see Reiner 2010, Chapter 4), insofar as it proposes that the nature of the occupation shapes particular understandings of the world. As Chan (1996) posits, police culture develops its understanding of communities through interaction between the field of policing and institutional knowledge and practice (habitus). However, the 'police imagination' has a much longer genealogy. As argued in Chapter 3, the police services in the post-imperial nations are bound by their 'imperial linkages' (Cole 1999). The extent to which state forms of policing developed directly from the control and punishment of Black bodies during times of slavery and in the colonies, varies between nations. However, it is shown that, in all of these contexts there is a link between colonial forms of policing and the emergence of the police (see Bell 2013; Cole 1999; Sinclair and Williams 2007). In this context, the 'police imagination' has developed as an occupational consciousness that, drawing on skin as a 'symbol of inferiorisation' (Anthias 1999), gives racialised meanings to individuals, whole communities and the spaces where Black bodies reside (see Chapter 4). Through processes of racialisation and criminalisation (see Chapter 2), racialised meanings operationalize racist practices in policing.

For individual police officers, this imagining of Blackness as representing a threat may not be an overtly conscious process of determining who is the suspect. Whilst for others, overt racialised stereotypes do influence their policing. Take for example the police officer who pulled over a London DJ in 2017 and told him that '*predominantly, the criminal profile of people who do it [commit crime] are black people. So, naturally, if you see a car full of black lads, maybe dressed in gangster-style clothing or whatever, when they're driving down here, they're getting stopped.* For the police officer concerned, his perception *'isn't racist' it is simply a 'fact'* (*Guardian*, 27 January 2017). Whilst this is an overt example of racial stereotyping, for the police officer it is common-sense understanding of who is a natural suspect. Whilst not all police officers will draw on such overtly racist stereotypes to rationalise their understanding of the suspect, the police are trained to be suspicious-to look for conspicuous threats. Which types of bodies represent this threat is bound up with longer imperial histories which are predicated on 'White supremacy'. The narratives which position Black bodies as in need of containment endures and through the 'police imagination' Black bodies are produced as neo-colonial subjects. Whether police officers see this, as in the example above, or are unaware of its influence on their decision-making processes, it informs them nonetheless. It is an act of coloniality. This is not to deny the very real problem of individually racist police officers. However, to focus on individual failings de-centers racism as a lens through which the problem can be understood. Further, it facilitates institutional denial and reproduces the myth of a post-race police service. As Tate and Page (2018) affirm, we have to continually be alert to 'signs of anti-black racism' within institutions. A Critical Race Theory framework which prioritises race and racialised voices gives us the tools to constantly engage in this process, excavating racisms which have been denied allowing them to be challenged. As Goldberg (2014) argues, portability is 'racisms' contemporary modality of expression' (p. 178), the urgent task is to contest the post-racial myth, and challenge institutional denial.

The inevitability of racism in policing that these insights reveal, should not deter criminologists from attempting to propose practical solutions that both recognise the inevitability of racism whilst simultaneously working to ameliorate its effects. In the spirit of Critical Race Theory research, racialised voices are crucial in developing strategies to manage and improve their experiences of racialised policing. The next section will draw on participants voices in order to offer some recommendations for the improved policing of Black communities.

Recommendations: Minority Perspectives

As shown in Chapters 4–7, the programme of reform resulting from *the Stephen Lawrence Inquiry Report*, has made very little difference to Black and Black mixed-race peoples experiences of the police. As David said, *they've done a report [Stephen Lawrence Inquiry] they know what they are doing wrong. But it's [still] institutionally racist.* Opinions differed on whether racism within the police was institutional or limited to the individual behaviour of one or two '*bad tomatoes*' (Samuel). However, all participants recognised that racism shapes their encounters with the police and that there are things the police could do differently to improve their experiences.

Manner, Behaviour and Stereotyping

An improvement on how the police approach people at an individual level, is one way in which participants felt that their experiences of policing could be improved. Most of these reflections are about the behaviour of one particular police officer; however, there is a pattern of similar behaviours reflected across participants accounts, for example an unfriendly and authoritarian manner, as expressed by Eric and Jean;

> I think the way they approach me as a person, I've had both experiences [suspect and victim] and I think the way they question me rather than having this stereotype and you know they bulldoze. I was there asking for help. They can work on their technique to make me feel like I'm not bothering them as if they had better things to do. (Eric, 32, Black, African, male)

> They need to be more friendly basically. They need to connect with people and they need to show that they understand people… It needs to be more humane and not just abuse their power. They know they are powerful but I think that they abuse their power. It's not on. … You need to show respect to people. (Jean, 40, Black, African, male)

Evident in both of these accounts is a sense that the police deal with Black people in an unfriendly manner because of the stereotypes associated with them. This creates the impression that they use the power that they have unfairly when they encounter Black people, either as suspects or as victims. Encounters with the police could be improved by simple changes in communication style which would make the subject feel respected. This recommendation finds support in the procedural justice thesis, which proposes that when people feel that they are treated fairly and with respect their perceptions of the police are altered favourably (see Tyler 2003; also Barrett et al. 2014). A change in the behaviour and manner of individual police officers cannot reverse the impact of decades of mistreatment that Black communities have suffered at the hands of the police. This requires more sustained effort from the police service to show that they are working towards reversing the entrenched manifestations of institutional racism within the police.

Black and Minority Ethnic Representation in the Police Service

One of the most common suggestions in participant's interviews, for improving their experiences of policing, was the recruitment of more Black and Ethnic Minority (BME) police officers;

> I think they should have more of a reflection of the communities that they work in so that people could identify with... it would be a cheaper quick route solution because people feel safer communicating to people that are of their own identity and I think that areas need to reflect that. And I know people would say ah that's against the law but I would think that would be...able you to not have people say ah but it was a racist. (Janice, 37, Black, British-born, female)

> It would make a start because at least then you would have people within the system, so hopefully, you'd think it would be more difficult for them to conspire against other [Black] people... but that means a lot of police, a lot of ethnic minorities in there to be able to start doing that. One or two here or there, that's not really going to make much of a difference. (Marcus, 44, Black, British-born, male)

> I think an influx of Black police officers could only have a positive impact. I'm not sure, I think you might struggle to get a lot of the Black community to move into a role like that but just the fact that I'm even saying that all the police I've dealt with have been White obviously suggests that it bears some significance... It would just help reverse the racism. I don't think it would solve all the problems but it would help. (Lee, 23, Black mixed-race, British-born, male)

This echoes a narrative which emerged from the *Scarman Report* recommendations and was repeated in the *Stephen Lawrence Inquiry Report* recommendations. As Lee suggests, there are challenges which need to be addressed in terms of presenting the police service as an attractive career option to communities who see their relationship with the police in dichotomous terms as Us and Them. Andrew reflects upon the police as a less than desirable option for his children;

> it wouldn't be a career choice that I would want. And obviously I want the best for my kids, and my kids are well educated, but that wouldn't be the forefront of my choices for my kids. Because I know the institutional stuff that kind of goes on and I wouldn't want that for them. I wouldn't want that strain, that stress on a day to day basis… I just think they'll be overpowered. Overpowered by the majority and I don't think it's a transparent enough service. The police is supposed to be reflecting the needs of the wider community; I don't see officers that look like me, look like my family. And those that do it's quite interesting the roles that they get offered as well, and their limitations as far as their progression up the kind of career ladder. (Andrew, 41, Black mixed-race, British-born, male)

This reluctance to consider the police service as a career option is observed in other participant's accounts. Further, Earl reflected upon the way in which Black police officers, once they are immersed in the institution, can become part of the problem;

> Sometimes as well when Black police officers become police officers they believe in Black situations they have to be a bit OTT because they feel like the other White officers are watching them so they go in too hard. (Earl, 54, Black, British-born, male)

> Black police [officers] working on Black people- I think if they were alone they would treat you differently, but if they had their friends around they would not because they are carrying a flag. (Eric, 32, Black, African, male)

Whilst communities might want to be represented in the makeup of the police service, they also recognise the limitations of this approach in effecting meaningful change. As both Earl and David highlight, an individual's loyalty to the police service may be greater than their loyalty to the Black suspect or community (see, discussion on solidarity/isolation as key features of police culture in Reiner 2010). Further, the burden of representation which is placed on ethnic minority officers, which Andrew speaks to above, can have negative racist effects on Black officers which contribute to the issues of police retention and lack of promotion amongst Black officers (see Cashmore 2001, 2002). Notwithstanding these challenges, Black and Black mixed-race people should be able to look to the police service as a career option. However, this is demonstrably not a quick fix for the problem of institutional racism within its ranks, or the over-policing felt by Black communities.

Reducing Disproportionality

One of the enduring problems between the police and Black communities is the practice of stop and search. As discussed in Chapter 1, this is an international, rather than a UK specific phenomenon. Stop and search is one of the most significant ways in which Black communities experience routine surveillance and control. It is therefore, not surprising to note that participants, including some who had not been stopped and searched, suggested that a reduction in ethnic disproportionality in the stop and search statistics would help to improve Black people's perceptions of the police.

> They need to think about stop and search, especially for the BME community, because they seem to be doing it more often… There's got to be a valid reason rather than just for the sake of it to do with your colour. I know they [police] wouldn't say that's the reason why but a lot of people know that is the case. (Cynthia, 42, Black, British-born, female)

> I for one would like to see the stats about you the number of Black and Asian youth that are stopped and searched I would like to see more parity with White people on that. And, in general I would like to see sort of better record keeping of these things because actually I sometimes think there are a lot more people stopped and searched and just not logged, in which case it could be even worse than the stats. (Robert, 27, Black mixed-race, British-born, male)

One of the ways in which this could be achieved is through improved training. Several participants felt that training would improve police officer's knowledge and perceptions about Black communities. However, a consistent approach with regular, rather than one off-tick box approaches is thought to be more effective:

> I don't think the quality of training that they're giving them is right, the young police need some equality and diversity training… but it should be an ongoing thing. I think police officers get a bit of equality and diversity training and then because they've done that they've ticked the box and they are never going to do it again. (Earl, 54, Black, British-born, male)

Phillip thought that training did raise police officer's awareness of racially sensitive issues; however, this training is not sufficient in order overcome the effects of the historic abuse of police power;

> They are more sensitive and aware of racial issues the police, but they've got to balance that in their desire to try and either prevent crime or arrest a criminal in a community where they are not popular as a result of their, the years in which they have abused people. I think the police have suffered a culture of incompetence, they not done some things right. That's why people have died in custody… they've also lied … the old boys culture is very important in collaborating with each other and concealing the truth. (Phillip, 45, Black, African, male)

Whilst for others, personality and individual prejudices were perceived to be ingrained and not-responsive to training;

> I could be speaking to five police and I might have four that treat me fairly and I might have one that don't. Everyone's not the same, we've all got different make up, different personalities. You [police officers] get to do your training about what you should do but not everyone adheres to training, some people deviate. … So, it's just the way people are brought up or they've got their own prejudice. It could be to do with the organisation as well but also to do with their personalities, it can be a mixture. (Cynthia, 42, Black, British-born, female)

The failure of equality and diversity policies and training programmes to effect any real change is recognised in participant's accounts. Janice reflects on the failure of 'equal opportunities' agenda due to the tokenistic nature of interventions;

> We shouldn't have inequalities right about now, not with how many Acts. But it just feels like they're just chucking them in there. Oh yea, we've got an organisation, let's have an equal opportunity policy, let's have a diversity policy. Nobody reads them, nobody goes out to find what impact these policies are having. Are they working? There's no feedback. There's a meeting today in West Yorkshire that I found quite humorous for Black History Month-open floor conversation with WYP -'please submit your questions in advance as we will not take questions from the floor,'. And it is quite direct and that's not an open discussion.... it's not an open discussion so were creating a taboo. (Janice, 37, Black, British-born, female)

In the event Janice refers to, the agenda is already shaped by those in positions of power, allowing no space for uncomfortable questions which may excavate invisible racisms. This is suggestive of the ways in which the diversity agenda serves to hide racism through the erasure of the language of race within institutions (see Ahmed 2012; Tate 2016). As Janice suggests here, race and racism are 'taboo'. Racism must be made visible within spaces of White power in order for its impact to be named and challenged and its wounds healed. Training can form part of this process. However, for training to be effective it should move beyond the colour-blind approach evident in the more recent introduction of unconscious bias training, for example. This facilitates the perpetuation of racism through denial of its conscious existence. A training programme that forces police officers to reflect upon histories of race making would at least put racism on the agenda and empower individual officers to understand how their role engages in the maintenance of racism in both the institution and wider society. Such an awareness could lead to more reflexive practice.

Accountability

Significant concerns around accountability were discussed in participant's accounts. However, they suggest that having independent processes for addressing police complaints is helpful. Earl highlighted that there have been some positive changes in terms of the introduction of organisations who can hold the police to account, for example the role of the IPCC and also the new PCC roles which '*gives you another place where you can go to*'. Further, Levi pointed out the usefulness of the IPCC in addressing his complaint against the police (discussed in Chapter 4). Notwithstanding the criticisms of the IPCC specifically, centered on their lack of 'teeth', and questions around their independence (Angiolini 2017), having a third-party route does have some impact upon perceptions of accountability. Derek approached the IPCC in pursuit of his complaint against the police following the events that led to him being tasered. His experience was not a positive one and compounded his perception that there is a reluctance to pursue complaints against the police. His initial complaint was sent to the police force and he was invited to meet with the Chief Inspector. During this meeting he was offered a meeting with the officer who had tasered him; however, he was disappointed that there was a lack of willingness to accept that the use of taser was wrong and the intention of the meeting was not for him to receive an apology, but rather an attempt at reconciliation. The officers account was different to Derek's and corroborated by his colleagues, which led Derek to the conclusion that the police officers were lying. He felt that the Chief Constable knew that they were not telling the truth but solidarity within the force prevented him from pursuing it further;

> And you know what as god as my witness this man believes me and he knows what I'm saying, yeah, but he cannot, he cannot admit to that.

Sometime later Derek got a letter from the IPCC, prior to him lodging a complaint with them, to tell him that the police had no case to answer. Following his enquiries, they revealed that this was a result of their standard procedure to investigate discharge of a firearm and that if he wanted to complain he should submit a complaint to the force for investigation. Derek felt that his complaint had already been prejudiced by their conclusion that the police had no case to answer in relation the discharge of the Taser and he did not feel confident of an objective investigation. In this case he approached the local Police and Crime Commissioner (PCC) for guidance.

> I'm not leaving it right until I feel I've took it as far as I can or I've got some kind of justice in this because somebody needs to call them to answer because they cannot continue to run around the community and do all this kind of business yea for the sake of we are the gun squad yeah and we are organised gangsters. I thought you know what I'm gonna go and see the police and crime commissioner. (Derek, 46, Black, British-born, male)

At the time of the interview the issue was still unresolved, awaiting the response of the PCC; however, a sense of injustice drives his desire to pursue some kind of accountability in the absence of trust in the IPCC. One suggestion, in Earls account was the involvement of lay people, from the community, in addressing complaints made against the police. This would seemingly add a further layer of accountability and assuage concerns about the police investigating the police; a perception which damages confidence. The value of involving members of the community in the complaints process is evident to some extent through the Independent Advisory Groups that operate in some areas and involve volunteers in advising the police on issues of concern to the local community. These groups, if well established and well utilised, allow community members to build relationships with the police and provide some element of accountability for their decision-making processes to the communities that they serve. A lay panel of community volunteers could conceivably work with the police to audit the decision-making process with regards to complaints made at force level and through the independent complaints body (currently the Office for Police Conduct-OfPC).

Community Relations

For participants, it was important that the police spend time in communities rebuilding the relationships that have been damaged by over policing and under protection. Community engagement is one aspect of the Neighbourhood Policing strategy and refers to a range of activities that bring members of the community into contact with the police. This can be formal, 'structured' participation in policing e.g. Independent Advisory Groups) or informal, 'unstructured' participation (Lloyd and Foster 2009: 24). The evidence suggests that perceptions of the police are predominantly formed in relation to their informal engagement with the police, rather than through formal participation in structured activities (ibid.). Both Janice and Bianca suggested that more informal contact with police officers would improve trust and confidence in the police;

> I think you need to be more at grass roots level, on football pitches on social environments you know. Participating more, not just seen as you know you are there for help. (Janice, 37, Black, British-born, female)

> Immerse themselves is communities to rebuild that trust to rebuild that faith to rebuild that relationship that you need, the police need, that they rely on to get people to report crimes in the first place. (Bianca, 25, Black mixed-race, British-born, female)

The kind of community engagement that Janice and Bianca suggest are based on immersive involvement with the community in an informal capacity. Research finds that informal contact is more effective in building police/community relations than formal measures (Jones and Newburn 2001). However, engagement needs to be sustained and come from all sections of the police force. Overwhelmingly, police officers do not view community engagement work as real police work (Skogan et al. 1999). Further, in the context of engaging with Black communities, this role is often fulfilled by police officers from an ethnic minority background (see Cashmore 2002 on recruitment initiatives). Andrew reflected on the tendency to rely upon Black police officers to engage with communities;

> You'll see them [Black officers] doing piecemeal community type activities. I can see the times when they get compromised in them roles. Some of the Black officers for projects working with BME's, and you never see a Black officer, but you'll see one with a project that's running with some youths and his face keeps rocking up again. What's that about? That's just self-fulfilling this stuff. (Andrew, 41, Black mixed-race, British-born, male)

Further, improved community relations rely upon consistent positive behaviour from the police service as a whole, rather than one 'community relations' officer. This must be sustained in all types of police contact. As Earl suggested, *a good officer can work for ten years tirelessly building community relationships and one officer can come in and smash that* (Earl). Earl has worked in various roles within his community for several decades and is familiar with this cycle. His reflection attests to the fragility of the relationship between the police and Black communities. Even when positive steps are made, the trauma wrought by decades of over-policing and under protection is always lurking under the surface. As Earl said '*they are still police officers and we are still the Black community*' (Earl, 54, Black, British-born, male).

Future Directions

This book has highlighted the utility of Critical Race Theory in advancing criminological understanding in regards to racism within the operation of criminal justice functions. Black and Black mixed-race people's experiences of policing in the UK context are rarely analysed from their perspectives. Whilst this book has made a small inroad in this regard, there are several themes emerging from the research undertaken, that highlight the need for a race-focused research agenda. One area in which there is a complete absence of research is in regard to Black and Black mixed-race women's experiences of the police. This book has made some arguments in relation to how Black women experience policing, compared to Black men, in Chapter 6. However, the findings are based on the experiences of only five women, most of whom were professionals, over the age of thirty and did not have an offending history. It can be assumed that their experienced of the police would be different from a Black woman who was frequently brought into contact with the police as a suspect. This is illustrated in the difference between the nature of Alice's experiences, a Black mixed-race woman with a history of offending over two decades (see Chapter 6), and the other women who took part in this research. Research, which draws upon the experiences of Black women who have a history of offending would address a significant gap in criminological knowledge. This is pertinent in the context of the increasing numbers of women who are incarcerated in the UK and the over-representation of Black women in the UK prison population (Lammy 2017).

Similarly, there is a concerning over-representation of young Black men in the youth prison estate (Young 2014; Lammy 2017). Criminological explanations focus on risk factors for their offending such as poverty, living in an area of deprivation, low educational achievement and parenting style and attachment (see Youth Justice Board 2005). Notwithstanding the significance of these social factors, one area that is under-researched is the processes of racialisation which may contribute to young Black men's initial contact with the criminal justice agencies, through the police. In Chapter 4, it was shown that young Black and Black mixed-race people are treated as suspects even in childhood. The role of race and processes of racialisation in leading young people into the criminal justice system must be more clearly understood. This is particularly relevant in the context of racialised stereotypes which assume that young Black people are more at risk of offending in relation to particular crime types which carry harsher punishments, such as drug and gang related crimes. Research which considers the ways in which race and processes of racialisation intersect with other risk factors for offending is necessary in order to address the hyper-incarceration of young Black men.

The increasing militarisation of British police has a disproportionate impact on Black communities. This research has shown that Black people experience disproportionate restraint. Evidence suggests that the Taser is used disproportionately in response to Black and Black mixed-race people and the United Nations has recently raised concerns about disproportionality in ethnic minority deaths in police custody and the failure to properly investigate police involvement (Dearden 2018). In the UK context the majority of police contact related deaths are related to restraint techniques and not shooting, with some exceptions, notably Mark Duggan. The effects of police militarisation on increasing fatalities in policing contexts are plain to see. The growing trans-Atlantic *Black Lives Matter* movement illuminates the nature and extent of the loss of life at the hands of the police. In the US context this often in shooting fatalities, but also in the context of restraint, for example the case of Eric Garner (see Camp and Heatherton 2016). In the extreme, over policing leads to loss of Black lives in disproportionate numbers. Very little is understood about processes of racialisation within police use of force and restraint, in the UK context (however, see Erfani-Ghettani 2015; Pemberton 2008). A Critical Race Theory approach to understanding police use of force decisions could reveal the ways in which racialisation is implicated in the use of force and restraint and the extent and level at which it is employed.

The findings of this research illustrate the utility of employing an intersectional analysis to the operation of race at its intersection with other oppressions, in particular class, gender and nationality, for understanding how they produce different experiences of the police encounter. The analysis shows that there is not one Black experience or perception of policing, but several. These experiences are produced differently through identification and interpellation as Black on a continuum, which relies upon subordinate masculinities and femininities for the reproduction of dominant hegemonic White masculinities to uphold White power. Rather than taking a comparative approach to understanding how race, class and gender play out in police contact, i.e. the dichotomous race/class approach, the Matrix of Domination (Collins 2000) is helpful for understanding how power and inequalities are organised within society. For Collins, intersecting oppressions are organised in relation to systems of power and are structured across individual, cultural and systemic levels. The analysis of Black peoples' experiences of policing at the axes of intersecting oppressions, and in relation to the multi-level structures of power, has been particularly revealing in relation to the experiences of Black women, Black professionals and migrant participants, as shown through the counter story. This is a useful approach in understanding complex issues which impact upon Black communities, in particular crime and criminal justice responses, and has the potential to advance criminological thinking beyond the race/class dichotomy.

Concluding Comments

This book has drawn attention to the key manifestations of racialised policing from the perspectives of those who have experienced it. Their insights, and the emerging counter story that they shape, illuminate some urgent themes as discussed throughout this chapter. The findings of the research are based on the experiences of participants in a UK. However, the positioning of police racism within the structural context of 'White supremacy' gives international relevance to the central conclusion that, within a racially ordered system, the police function to control the racialised Other.

Racism, while it continues to be denied, is felt in encounters with the police. This is evident in the emerging counter-story which illuminates the operation of race and intersecting oppressions in Black and Black mixed-race peoples encounters with the police. In order for any real and significant change to occur, there would need to be a reconceptualisation of the role and function of the police within post-imperial nations, which would destabilise the system of racial ordering upon which 'White supremacy' relies. The global system of power, premised on 'White supremacy', anchors the 'permanence of racism' (Bell 1992). However, this does not mean that change cannot occur at the micro level. At an individual level, there are particular behaviours which the police can display which would improve Black and Black mixed-race peoples encounters with them, as this chapter has shown. However, as participants suggest, a sustained effort to address the manifestations of entrenched racism, such as disproportionality in stop and search and engaging with communities informally in positive ways to rebuild trust and confidence, is needed. Existing measures to improve policing in these areas have failed because they fail to engage with racism as an explanation. One of the key concerns for participants, evident in this chapter and throughout the book, is the failure of accountability. This is obvious to those who are on the receiving end of policing when their complaints of unfair treatment are not taken seriously and the processes for securing accountability fail. True accountability for racist policing must begin with acceptance of the existence of racism within the institution. Whilst this will not overturn the global system of 'White supremacy', countering the denial of racism is the starting point for meaningful change towards challenging the processes of racialisation that lead to the construction of Black people as the perpetual suspect.

References

Ahmed, S. (2012). *On Being Included: Racism and Diversity in Institutional Life*. London: Duke University Press.

Angiolini, E. (2017). *Report of the Independent Review of Deaths and Serious Incidents in Police Custody. London:* Home Office. https://www.gov.uk/government/publications/deaths-and-serious-incidents-in-police-custody. Accessed 9 March 2018.

Anthias, F. (1999). Institutional Racism, Power and Accountability. *Sociological Research Online*, 4. www.socresonline.org.uk/4/lawrence/anthias.html. Accessed 13 July 2017.

Barrett, G. A., Fletcher, S. M., & Patel, T. G. (2014). Black Minority Ethnic Communities and Levels of Satisfaction with Policing: Findings from a Study in the North of England. *Criminology and Criminal Justice, 14*, 196–215.

Bell, D. (1991). Racial Realism. *Connecticut Law Review, 24*, 363–379.

Bell, D. A. (1992). *Faces at the Bottom of the Well: The Permanence of Racism*. New York: Basic Books.

Bell, E. (2013). Normalising the Exceptional: British Colonial Policing Cultures Come Home. Cultures Coloniales et Postcoloniales et Decolonisation 9.

Bernstein, R. (2011). *Racial Innocence: Performing American Childhood from Slavery to Civil Rights*. New York: New York University Press.

Bonilla-Silva, E. (2010). *Racism Without Racists: Colour Blind Racism and the Persistence of Racial Inequality in America* (3rd ed.). Lanham, MD: Rowman and Littlefield.

Bowling, B., & Phillips, C. (2007). Disproportionate and Discriminatory: Reviewing the Evidence on Police Stop and Search. *The Modern Law Review, 70*, 936–961.

Bradford, B. (2014). Policing and Social Identity: Procedural Justice, Inclusion and Cooperation Between Police and Public. *Policing and Society, 24,* 22–43.

Bradford, B., Murphy, K., & Jackson, J. (2014). Officers as Mirrors: Policing, Procedural Justice and the (Re)Production of Social Identity. *British Journal of Criminology, 54,* 527–550.

Bridges, L. (1983). Policing the Urban Wasteland. *Race and Class, 25,* 31–47.

Britton, N. J. (2000). Examining Police/Black Relations: What's in a Story? *Ethnic and Racial Studies, 23,* 692–711.

Camp, J. T., & Heatherton, C. (2016). *Policing the Planet: Why the Policing Crisis Led to Black Lives Matter*. New York: Verso.

Carmichael, S., & Hamilton, C. V. (1967). *Black Power: The Politics of Liberation in America.* New York: Random House.

Cashmore, E. (2001). The Experiences of Ethnic Minority Police Officers in Britain: Under-Recruitment and Racial Profiling in a Performance Culture. *Ethnic and Racial Studies, 24,* 642–659.

Cashmore, E. (2002). Behind the Window Dressing: Ethnic Minority Police Perspectives on Cultural Diversity. *Journal of Ethnic and Migration Studies, 28,* 327–341.

Chan, J. (1996). Changing Police Culture: Policing in a Multicultural Society. *British Journal of Criminology, 36,* 109–134.

Cole, B. A. (1999). Postcolonial Systems. In R. I. Mawby (Ed.), *Policing Across the World: Issues for the Twenty-First Century*. Abingdon: Routledge.

Collins, P. H. (2000). *Black Feminist Thought: Knowledge, Consciousness, and the Politics of Empowerment*. New York: Routledge.

Collins, P. H. (2004). *Black Sexual Politics: African Americans, Gender, and the [H5] New Racism*. New York: Routledge.

Dearden, L. (2018, April 27). UN Issues Warning over Deaths of Disproportionate Number of Black People in Police Custody and 'Structural Racism' in UK. *The Independent.*

Eddo-Lodge, R. (2018). *Why I'm No Longer Talking to White People About Race.* London: Bloomsbury.

Equality Challenge Unit. (2013). *Unconscious Bias and Higher Education.* https://www.ecu.ac.uk/wp-content/uploads/2014/07/unconscious-bias-and-higher-education.pdf. Accessed 11 March 2018.

Erfani-Ghettani, R. (2015). The Defamation of Joy Gardner: Press, Police and Black Deaths in Custody. *Race & Class, 56,* 102–112.

Gabbidon, S. (2010). *Race, Ethnicity, Crime, and Justice: An International Dilemma*. Los Angeles, CA: Sage.

Glynn, M. (2013). *Black Men, Invisibility and Crime: Towards a Critical Race Theory of Desistance*. London: Routledge.

Goff, P. A., Jackson, M. C., Di Leone, B. A. L., Culotta, C. M., & Ditomasso, N. A. (2014). The Essence of Innocence: Consequences of Dehumanizing Black Children. *Journal of Personality and Social Psychology, 106*, 526–545.

Goldberg, D. T. (2009). *The Threat of Race: Reflections on Racial Neoliberalism*. Malden: Blackwell.

Goldberg, D. T. (2014). *Sites of Race: Conversations with Susan Searls Giroux*. Cambridge: Polity Press.

Guardian. (1999, February 25). Mets Plans to Protect and Respect. https://www.theguardian.com/uk/1999/feb/25/lawrence.ukcrime12.

Guardian. (2017, January 27). Police Officer: Black People in 'Gangster' Clothes More Likely to Be Stopped—Video. www.theguardian.com/uk-news/video/2017/jan/27/police-officer-black-people-in-gangster-clothes-more-likely-to-be-stopped-video.

Halliday. (2015, June 15). Met Chief Admits Institutional Racism Claims Have 'Some Justification'. *Guardian*. https://www.theguardian.com/uk-news/2015/jun/05/met-chief-admits-institutional-racism-claims-have-some-justification.

Jefferson, T. (1993). The Racism of Criminalization: Policing and the Reproduction of the Criminal Other. In L. Gelsthorpe (Ed.), *Minority Ethnic Groups in the Criminal Justice System*. Cambridge: University of Cambridge.

Jones, T., & Newburn, N. (2001). *Widening Access: Improving Police Relations with Hard to Reach Groups Police Research Series, Paper 138*. London: Home Office.

Lammy, D. (2017). *The Lammy Review: An Independent Review into the Treatment of, and Outcomes for Black, Asian and Minority Ethnic Individuals in the Criminal Justice System*. London: Ministry of Justice.

Lee, J. A. (1981). Some Structural Aspects of Police Deviance in Relations with Minority Groups. In C. Shearing (Ed.), *Organisational Police Deviance*. Toronto: Butterworth.

Lloyd, K., & Foster, J. (2009). Citizen Focus and Community Engagement: A Review of the Literature. London: The Police Foundation. Available from: http://www.police-foundation.org.uk/uploads/catalogerfiles/citizen-focus-and-community-engagement-a-review-of-the-literature/citizen_focus.pdf. Accessed 15 June 2017.

Loftus, B. (2010). Police Occupational Culture: Classic Themes, Altered Times. *Policing and Society, 20,* 1–20.

Loftus, B. (2009). *Police Culture in a Changing World.* Oxford: Oxford University Press.

Long, L., & Joseph-Salisbury, R. (2018). Black Mixed-Race Men's Perceptions and Experiences of the Police. *Ethnic and Racial Studies,* https://doi.org/10.1080/01419870.2017.1417618.

Macpherson of Cluny, S. W. (1999). *The Stephen Lawrence Inquiry.* London: The Stationery Office.

Mclaughlin, E. (2007). Diversity or Anarchy? The Post-Macpherson Blues. In M. Rowe (Ed.), *Policing Beyond Macpherson: Issues in Policing, Race and Society.* Willan: Cullompton.

Medina-Arisa, J. J. (2014). Police-Initiated Contacts: Young People, Ethnicity, and the 'Usual Suspects'. *Policing and Society, 24*(2), 208–223.

Mills, C. W. (1997). *The Racial Contract.* New York: Cornell University Press.

Moore, J. M. (2015). The 'New Punitiveness' in the Context of British Imperial History. *Criminal Justice Matters, 101*(1), 10–13.

Pemberton, S. (2008). Demystifying Deaths in Police Custody: Challenging State Talk. *Social & Legal Studies, 17,* 237–262.

Quinton, P., & Packham, D. (2016). *College of Policing Stop and Search Training Experiment: An Overview.* College of Policing. http://whatworks.college.police.uk/Research/Documents/SS_training_OVERVIEW_Final_report.pdf. Accessed 1 April 2018.

Reiner, R. (2010). *The Politics of the Police.* Oxford: Oxford University Press.

Sharp, D., & Atherton, S. (2007). To Serve and Protect? The Experiences of Policing in the Community of Young People from Black and other Ethnic Minority Groups. *British Journal of Criminology, 47,* 746–763.

Sinclair, G., & Williams, C. A. (2007). Home and Away: The Cross Fertilisation Between Colonial and British Policing, 1921–1985. *The Journal of Imperial and Commonwealth History, 35*(2), 221–238.

Sivanandan, A. (1982). *A Different Hunger: Writings on Black Resistance.* London: Pluto Press.

Skogan, W. G., Hartnett, S. M., DuBois, J., Comey, J. T., Kaiser, M., & Lovig, J. H. (1999). *On the Beat: Police and Community Problem Solving.* Boulder, CO: Westview Press.

Smith, D. (2017, October 31). The Backlash Against Black Lives Matter Is Just More Evidence of Injustice. *The Conversation.* https://theconversation.com/the-backlash-against-black-lives-matter-is-just-more-evidence-of-injustice-85587.

Tate, S. A. (2016). 'I Can't Quite Put My Finger on It': Racism's Touch. *Ethnicities, 16*, 68–85.

Tate, S. A., & Page, D. (2018). Whiteliness and Institutional Racism: Hiding Behind (Un)Conscious Bias. *Ethics and Education, 13*(1), 141–155. https://doi.org/10.1080/17449642.2018.1428718.

Toynbee, P. (1999, March 3). The White Backlash; MacPherson Is Now a Rallying Cry for a Vision of Nation and Race That Is Vile. *The Guardian* (London).

Tyler, T. R. (2003). Procedural Justice, Legitimacy, and the Effective Rule of Law. *Crime and Justice: A Review of Research, 30*, 283–357.

Webster, C. (2008). Marginalized White Ethnicity, Race and Crime. *Theoretical Criminology, 12*, 293–312.

Young. L. (2014). The Young Review: Improving Outcomes for Young Black and/or Muslim Men in the Criminal Justice System. London: Barrow Cadbury Trust. Available from: http://www.youngreview.org.uk/sites/default/files/clinks_young-review_report_dec2014.pdf. Accessed 26 October 2017.

Youth Justice Board. (2005). *Risk and Protective Factors*. file:///C:/Users/Home/Downloads/Risk%20and%20protective%20factors%20UK%20youth%20crime.pdf. Accessed 5 November 2017.

Index

L. J. Long, *Perpetual Suspects*, Palgrave Studies in Race, Ethnicity, Indigeneity and Criminal Justice, https://doi.org/10.1007/978-3-319-98240-3